LANCELOT HOGBEN
SCIENTIFIC HUMANIST

Lancelot Hogben
Scientific Humanist

An unauthorised autobiography
Edited by Adrian and Anne Hogben

MERLIN PRESS
1998

© Adrian Hogben 1998

First published by The Merlin Press Ltd
2 Rendlesham Mews, Rendlesham
Woodbridge, Suffolk IP12 2SZ

ISBN 085036 470 1

The right of Professor Lancelot Thomas Hogben to be identified as the author of this work has been asserted in accordance with the Copyright, Designs and Patents Act 1988 Section 77 and 78.

Printed by WSOY in Finland.

Fondly dedicated to
Clare Matthews

Contents

		page
	Editors' Note	ix
	Introduction	x
I	Salesmanship and Salvation	1
II	Stoke Newington	7
III	Schooldays	18
IV	On Going Up	27
V	Cambridge	35
VI	Marking Time	46
VII	Shades of the Prison House	56
VIII	Marriage	65
IX	Edinburgh	76
X	Montreal	85
XI	Cape Town	92
XII	Dawn of Apartheid	104
XIII	London School of Economics	119
XIV	Mathematics for the Million	131
XV	Aberdeen	142
XVI	Scandinavia	162
XVII	Madison, Wisconsin	172
XVIII	Birmingham	183

XIX	Wales	194

Epilogue	204
Postscript	209
Notes	211
Acknowledgments	225
Bibliography	226
Supplemental Bibliography	235
Index	238

EDITORS' NOTE

AFTER Lancelot Hogben's death, several unedited versions of his autobiography were discovered. He titled his projected autobiography *Look Back with Laughter*. There was also an unpublished commentary on his scientific publications, *Professional Reminiscences*.

Because of our affection and admiration, we have prepared this autobiography, *Lancelot Hogben, Scientific Humanist*. To do so, we have drastically reshaped the material in *Look Back with Laughter*, interpolating most of *Professional Reminiscences*, always respecting Lancelot's intention. Since our effort is posthumous, it is *An Unauthorised Autobiography*.

Citations Books are cited by title and year. References to Lancelot's professional papers are given by year and chronological position in that year, e.g. (LH 1924b), as designated in the bibliography of Lancelot's works.

Addendum Lancelot started writing *Look Back with Laughter* somewhat before April 1974. There is a holograph insertion dated 17 August 1975, five days before his death.

The version we edited is designated A.6–A.8 of the collection of Lancelot Hogben's papers in the Heslop Room of the University of Birmingham Library. Later this copy was identified as A.105–A.115, the last draft left by Lancelot Hogben. Copyright to all versions of *Look Back with Laughter*, including the manuscript edited by G. P. Wells, A.9–A.10 (but not his Introduction), is held by Adrian Hogben, as is the copyright to *Professional Reminiscences*.

INTRODUCTION
by Adrian Hogben

BOTH my father and my mother, Enid Charles, were forceful intellectual figures in the decade before WWII.

Society owes perhaps its greatest debt to Lancelot for being one of the earliest and most eloquent opponents of Eugenics. Today, it seems surprising how few, particularly scientists, took an insistent stand. Kevles (*In the Name of Eugenics,* 1985) has written: "The leading scientists in the anti-mainline [Eugenics] assault, those most powerful and sustained in their critique, were the British biologists J. B. S. Haldane, Julian Huxley, and Lancelot Hogben and their American colleague, Herbert S. Jennings." (Almost beyond belief, in late August 1997, the Swedish government admitted to a four-decade policy under which 60,000 people deemed genetically inferior were involuntarily sterilised.)

Lancelot's uncompromising stand on principle became evident when he protested conscription in World War I and was imprisoned. As a youngster, though I was aware of his pacifism and imprisonment, I did not appreciate the full horror of this experience until I read his autobiography *Look Back with Laughter.*

The words he chose in *Alfred Russel Wallace,* 1918, mirrored his own hopes.

> What, then, was the essential greatness of Wallace? He was great because he added to the scientific knowledge of his time; but greater, because he was inflamed with a lofty idealism that sought to place the possibilities of science at the service of mankind. He was great because he strove in the struggle with the forces of nature; but greater, because he was capable of appreciating that deeper need to subordinate science to the spirit of universal goodwill. He was great because his wonderful mentality penetrated the mists of ignorance and battled with superstition; but greater, because he took his part side by side with all good men and women who are engaged in the struggle that will never end, till there is expressed in the structure of society the right of every human be-

ing to the good things of life, and a responsible share in the control of his or her own destiny.

The year 1917 was pivotal for Lancelot. Enid Charles joined him. Enid, whom he had known at Cambridge, was an ardent socialist and feminist. Though qualified for more remunerative positions, she worked as a trade union organizer for 30 shillings a week. In September 1917, they moved into a flat, and the following year they married.

At Birkbeck and later the Imperial College, he conducted a meticulous cytological study. When eggs and sperm are formed, pairs of chromosomes divide. A prevailing view held that the chromosomes, prior to the split, lined up end-to-end (telesynapsis). Lancelot caught the fleeting event of the chromosomes pairing, side-by-side (parasynapsis). The earlier claim for telesynapsis was graciously withdrawn. The future recipients of the Nobel Prize in genetics, Thomas Hunt Morgan and H. J. Muller, made a special visit to Lancelot. The classic work of the Columbia University team exploiting the fruit fly, *Drosophila*, established the chromosome theory of inheritance, which required pairing side by side. However, the problem posed by telesynapsis had been on Morgan's mind. He wrote before the visit, "If the pairs fused end to end and the tetrad arose by two longitudinal divisions, the outcome would not be in harmony with the theory of segregation based on separation of maternal and paternal chromosomes at reduction," *The Physical basis of Heredity*, 1919, page 51. Today the potential threat of telesynapsis is quite forgotten and, thus, Lancelot's role in the chromosome theory.

Lancelot's growing reputation as a teacher led H. G. Wells to choose him to prepare his sons, Gip and Frank, for Cambridge University. Upon their return to London from Cape Town, Enid and Lancelot dined frequently with H. G. Wells. Lancelot's last letter to him was written in the year before Wells died.

On the basis of the cytologic work, Frank Crew invited Lancelot to Edinburgh, 1922. They reached a comfortable understanding that Lancelot would continue his studies in comparative endocrinology. Together they created a vibrant scientific milieu, with visits by Julian Huxley and J. B. S. Haldane, among others.

Skin pigment cells of several archaic vertebrates such as the frog and dogfish are remarkable. The pigment melanin can migrate within the cell, subject to endocrine control in response to the background. On a white background, melanin becomes concentrated at a point within the cell, rendering the frog pallid, Fig. 10C. On a black background the pigment becomes scattered and the frog dark. At Edinburgh, Lancelot, in collaboration with others, clarified the endocrine control of colour change and isolated the hormone of the posterior pituitary making the frog dark, the 'melanocyte stimulating hormone,' MSH. This was the sixth hormone to be isolated: adrenaline (epinephrine), 1894; secretin, 1902; oxytocin, 1902; thyroxin, 1919; insulin, 1922; and MSH, 1922.

In spite of the lapse of 75 years, we still do not understand the physiologic function of MSH. This is true even where colour change is so dramatic. While in the human MSH disappears at puberty, it is present in all vertebrates. But to what purpose! I am not ready to accept this persistence as an evolutionary anachronism.

In 1925, still at Edinburgh, he spent the summer at the Marine Biological Laboratory, Plymouth. With a new friend, Carl Pantin, working excitedly from 9 P.M. to 5 A.M. they devised procedures to study the coupling of oxygen and haemocyanin. The pigment haemocyanin serves to carry oxygen in many invertebrates, as does haemoglobin in man.

The following year, having moved to McGill University, he spent the summer at the Marine Biological Laboratory of Woods Hole, Massachusetts. Lancelot and Pantin continued work on haemocyanin. That visit in a congenial setting had a profound effect on our family. Our cultural horizon was expanded.

When we arrived in Cape Town, 1927, the rich biological harvest of the Cape peninsula, at the foot of Table Mountain, was a source of joy for Enid and Lancelot. But it was inevitable they would be in continual opposition to the oppression of the nonwhite people. In a dramatic episode, Enid drove over a mountain pass to rescue two men who were about to be lynched.

Lancelot carved out a small niche when he introduced the South African toad *Xenopus laevis* into biological research. An unexpected benefit is apparent today. During the years 1994 and 1995, worldwide scientific publication of work using *Xenopus* appeared every other day. Ironically, Lancelot expected that *Xenopus* would become for endocrinology what *Drosophila* was for genetics. Of 350 recent papers using this animal, I would classify only three as in the field of endocrinology. The others belong to biophysics, genetics and embryology. For U. S. scientists, *Xenopus* was initially imported from South Africa. During the embargo years, *Xenopus* having been domesticated by Lancelot's colleagues, research continued uninterrupted.

For me to add further comment on the two chapters devoted to South Africa would be, as coined in *King John*, "to paint the lily."

Lancelot returned to England to assume the first and last chair of Social Biology at the London School of Economics. The department was both productive and distinguished.

Lancelot joined the ranks of the leading human and population geneticists: along with Gunnar Dahlberg of Sweden, three from the U.K—R. A. Fischer, J. B. S. Haldane and Lionel Penrose along with Sewall Wright of the U.S. He delivered the William Withering Lectures at the University of Birmingham, published as *Genetic Principles in Medicine and Social Science*. A handsome honorarium for the Birmingham lectures underwrote the purchase of a thatched cottage in Devon, our home for the next five years; glorious ones for me. Lancelot gave me pairs of rabbits of six different breeds, which enabled me to verify Mendel's laws. But he warned me to avoid medical genetics. Genetic disorders were rare and most had been discovered.

The Royal Society of Edinburgh awarded Lancelot the Keith Gold Medal for his contribution to genetics. Based on lectures he gave at the University of Wisconsin, he unified his work in *An Introduction to Mathematical Genetics*, 1946.

Enid became attracted to the challenge of demography, reaching international renown as the author of *The Twilight of Parenthood*, 1934.

Director Sir (later Lord) William Beveridge had set aside a building that had escaped the slum clearance that made way for the campus of the London School of Economics. It became the home for experimental work. David Slome and Lancelot acquired evidence for a second colour change hormone. Localised in the anterior pituitary, it caused extreme pallor in the frog. Unable to isolate the hormone, Lancelot did not consider the evidence to be conclusive. Thirteen years after his death, the 'melanocyte aggregating hormone, MAH,' was isolated and synthesized. Landgrebe and Bellerby domesticated *Xenopus*. As a consequence, the Hogben pregnancy test was adopted exclusively by the National Health Service. Some 500,000 tests were carried out over 15 years with an extraordinary level of accuracy for a bio-assay. In that building, Enid began a study of the blood calcium level of hens during ovulation. We were much aware of this research—we had an unremitting diet of chicken for a year. The next year she worked with rabbits. Enid acquired a chinchilla rabbit coat that she cherished.

The Director of the London School of Economics, William Beveridge, established the department of Social Biology to encourage intellectual rigour in the social sciences. This could not have been expected to endear Lancelot and Enid to the faculty. With a few notable exceptions, including Harold Laski and Eileen Power, it did not. Through seven turbulent years Lancelot stood shoulder to shoulder with Beveridge. Long after the death of Enid and Lancelot, the spirit of tradition prevailed with publication of a bizarre Centennial commemorative volume.

In recent years I meet people who remember *Mathematics for the Million* with nostalgia. But for a couple of decades the great popularised work too often evoked scorn. There would be no million. This came from people who, a) had not read the book, b) were culturally disabled, or c) were professional mathematicians. But sales passed the half-million mark by 1978.

Lancelot repeatedly claimed that he wrote *Mathematics for the Million* in six weeks while hospitalised for radical (barbaric) surgery on his nasal sinuses. Of course, this was implausible. I still remember sitting by Lancelot with a shawl over his head as he inhaled balsam or some such noxious vapour. He was still working out ideas. I served as a sounding board. Much of the success of the book is due to Lancelot's imaginative drawings. He had been impressed by H. G. Wells's *Outline of History* 1922, for which Frank Horrabin skilfully redrew the illustrations. He offered a share of the royalties to Horrabin to secure his flair. Lancelot had a 'visual' as contrasted to an 'abstract' mind. Ignoring art for art's sake, he successfully exploited the ruler and compass, evident in drawings for his children (plate VII), design of furniture (plate XIII) and the Glyn Ceiriog cottage (plate XVI).

Not long after publishing *Mathematics for the Million* he produced a second 'Primer for the Age of Plenty.' For some, including myself, *Science for the Citizen* is an even more impressive tour de force. It arose out of a series of lectures delivered in the London School of Economics. However, science in all its branches began to accelerate at an ever increasing pace, and the book has gone out of print after sales of some 130,000. I am still proud that he wrote in the flyleaf of my copy "To my co-author."

I recall Lancelot and Frederick Bodmer, in the garden of the Devonshire cottage, discussing the void in the understanding of languages. *The Loom of Language* was ultimately published in 1944. Lancelot stated in the Editor's Foreword, "I have had the greatest difficulty in preventing Dr. Bodmer from refusing to publish the book without my name as co-author on the cover."

Lancelot was appointed Regius Professor of Natural History (Zoology) in 1937. The department at Aberdeen was moribund, and the skeleton staff overburdened by teaching. Lancelot reduced the teaching load to a third. With his encouragement the original staff of two gained their doctorates. Though WWII was to terminate the early promise of the department, it did flourish; some thirty papers were published over more than four years.

The senior University faculty were no more enlightened than the faculty that Enid and Lancelot had encountered in Edinburgh. But there was an important exception; Sir (later Lord) John Boyd Orr was a kindred spirit who shared and expanded Lancelot's interests.

As they had done in Cape Town, Enid and Lancelot created their own social circle by holding open house at Inverdon every Saturday. A sizeable group could be accommodated in its thirty-foot living room and adjoining greenhouse. They attracted a lively crowd of younger people, including some of my own fellow students, members of the Scottish University Labour party.

I left Aberdeen April 1939 for the University of Wisconsin. In April of 1940, Lancelot and my sister Sylvia narrowly escaped the Nazis when Oslo was invaded. For several months, along with other British nationals, they had to wait for exit visas. Leaving Sweden they reached Madison, Wisconsin. Lancelot found Madison to be as exhilarating as I did. Sylvia enrolled in the University and married my roommate, (Dr.) Wallace McCrory. Uncertain when he would be able to leave Sweden, Lancelot urged Enid to take my younger sister, Clare, and brother, David, to Canada. Their immigration was sponsored by Lionel Penrose.

When Lancelot returned to Aberdeen, most of the staff had left. He accepted the Mason Chair of Zoology at the University of Birmingham, 1942. Anxious to leave Aberdeen, he did not anticipate how difficult it would be to rebuild a science department after the war. In 1943, I visited a Birmingham physiologist. A package arrived with the following note: "Inside is your year's allocation of filter funnels." Inside was one funnel, broken.

In 1943 Frank Crew induced Lancelot to become his deputy at the War Office, directing Medical Statistics, where Lancelot's team, among other findings, reported on the emergence of bacterial resistance to sulphonamides and on the epidemiology of jaundice.

In 1946 the University of Birmingham created a new chair in Medical Statistics for Lancelot. Four years before retirement, he wrote his academic "swan song," a critical analysis of the flaws in statistical methodology, *"Statistical Theory: an examination of the contemporary crisis in statistical theory from a behaviourist viewpoint, 1957."* In what I regard as perhaps Lancelot's stellar intellectual achievement, he clarified the mysticism of "statistical significance." His illumination of this issue was reprinted as the first three chapters of *The Significance Test Controversy,* 1970. At the core, he struck down the pillars of Fisherian statistics that had become the working tools for most analyses of data in medicine and the social sciences. Even if the prose were not dense, it would have been difficult, if not impossible, to change current statistical practise. Statistics is too important to be left to statisticians.

I close with Lancelot's Creed of a Scientific Humanist (*Dangerous Thoughts,* 1939), in which he summarized his philosophy at the age of 42.

> If I had been asked to give a label to my creed, when I was starting in my profession as a scientific worker, I should have called it Socialism. That was twenty-five years ago. To-day I prefer to call it scientific humanism. Scientific humanism is the creed I profess and the profession I try to practise. This does not mean that the socialist creed of my adolescence was contrary to the scientific outlook, or that I have renounced it. I still believe that no system in which credit and industry are privately owned can take the fullest advantage of new scientific knowledge for the satisfaction of common needs.
>
> What it does mean is that when I was younger my political left hand did not bother about what my professional right hand was doing. I did not yet realize how the pursuit of science is bound up with the responsibilities of citizenship in a society which has been transformed by scientific knowledge. When I began to do so, I saw that Socialism can mean two different ways of using scientific discoveries. . . .
>
> The other Socialism, that of Robert Owen, of Charles Kingsley, of Edward Carpenter, and of William Morris, began as a protest against the dreary squalor which was effacing the common wealth of the countryside during the earlier stages of steam-power production.

It denounced the worldly wisdom which chose an ever-increasing multiplicity of gewgaws and passive distractions as the goal of co-operative endeavour. In opposition to the Liberal doctrine that prosperity is being able to choose the greatest variety of goods, it asserted the need to decide whether the dark satanic mills were making things which are good for men to choose. There was at first no clear recognition that science could create the prospect of a new heaven for uncongested traffic and a new earth for spacious living.

The Utopians—as they are usually called—anticipated scientific humanism because they saw clearly that human needs cannot be assessed in terms of "consumers' choice" and because they saw the hypertrophied metropolitanism of capitalist evolution creating psychological strains for which redistribution of spending power furnishes no sufficient remedy. . . .

While others call for change in the methods of education and rightly demand removal of restrictions to educational opportunities, scientific humanism also asserts the need for a far-reaching reformation in the content of education to endow the pursuit of knowledge with a new sense of social relevance. The scientific humanist believes that an educational reformation so conceived is an indispensable prerequisite to genuine social advance.

September, 1997
Trenton, Maine

CHAPTER I

Salesmanship and Salvation

UNLIKE many writers of memoirs, I can boast of no distinguished forebears. I came of poor but intellectually dishonest parents and was spared the experience of material poverty because they, with their offspring, lived as pensioners of my maternal grandparents, and in the same establishment, for the first eleven years of my life.[1] If my ancestors have any claim to distinction, it is because they responded to the Methodist revival in the eighteenth century and went to their graves outside the parish churchyard in the comfortable assurance: "Beloved we are of God and the whole world lieth in wickedness."

The choice of my first name had nothing to do with Alfred Lord Tennyson. My namesake was a Methodist missionary, the Reverend Lancelot Railton, prominent at that time in nonconformist circles.

With three elder sisters, I was fourth in a sibship of six survivors beyond infancy. I was what was then called a cottonwool baby, born prematurely on December 9, 1895, seven months after conception. As my mother often reminded me, this particular experience of childbirth was exceptionally painful. To ensure that I would come forth alive, she dedicated me from birth to the mission field.

On both sides my ancestors came from East Kent, where my father was born in the village of Hougham, a few miles inland between Dover and Folkestone. All authorities agree that the name Hogben is exclusively of East Kentish origin. Earlier writers have suggested its origin from *hog* and *bin* (= crib or hutch); but Reaney (*Origin of English Surnames*, 1967) has traced it through wills from its first appearance as Hogben in 1588 to Hugbone in 1549 to Huckbone in 1479. He derives *hucke* in the latter from a Teutonic root cognate with Old Norse *huka* meaning *bent*. If so, it originated as a nickname for a man with a crooked leg and joins a surname *Cruikshank* of Scotland, where the sun is even less able to combat rickets.

Short visits to the Hougham cottage of my paternal grandfather are the happiest memories of my early boyhood. He was a widower then in his nineties, tended by a housekeeper and long since retired from his vocation as hedger, ditcher and thatcher. Of the old man himself I have no recollection, except that he was edentulous as an anteater or baleen whale and subsisted largely on bread and milk.

The well-wooded and hilly countryside surrounding the cottage was scenically superb. There, and before I was nine years old, I experienced the thrill of catching and keeping newts, of first seeing a stoat, of finding bats in a barn, of collecting beetles and butterflies, of naming birds and recognising each species by its eggs. The subsoil was chalky. Accordingly, the neighbourhood had an exceptionally diverse fauna and flora, including several animal and plant species I have never subsequently encountered. In particular, I recollect a coppice matted with *Paris quadrifolia*. I wanted to be a biologist long before I was twelve.

During the first eleven years of my life, my mother's parents, William and Margaret Prescott, fulfilled a formative role in my larval existence. From insecure beginnings—I believe as a plumber, plasterer and bricklayer—my maternal grandfather made good as a building contractor. At an early age, he became the owner of a heavily mortgaged and considerable building estate around the New River Reservoir on the Middlesex fringe of the London borough of Stoke Newington. He obtained the land on a 99-year lease, the ground landlord being the Ecclesiastical Commissioners. By the time he had completed the project, he had enough money to send my mother, his only surviving offspring, to some sort of finishing school where she learnt deportment, elocution and horsemanship. More usefully, she became tolerably fluent in French.

How my father, Thomas Hogben, who left a village dame school at ten years of age, started to earn his living, I am less certain. One member of my family has alleged that he was first a bellboy in a hotel. All that is noteworthy about his early career is that he was a boy evangelist reputedly acceptable as an authentic Methodist local preacher by the age of sixteen and that he acquired a copybook calligraphy as a solicitor's clerk. He seems to have prospered in business of several sorts, including a design to import 'sirops' from France as a counterattraction to strong liquor. I assume he met my mother at this stage in his career.

Before my birth, my father's unremitting search for scriptural guidance impressed on him the prophecy (Mark 13:10) that the preaching of the Word to all peoples in all lands must precede the Second Coming of the Lord. With some business acumen, but little anticipation of the sales resistance of seamen to the Gospel message, he reached a conclusion to which his well-dowried consort submitted as to the Lord's will. He obeyed the call with what he regarded as the most economical blueprint to expedite so desirable a consummation as the Second Coming. His strategy required much less expenditure than the provision of salaries for professional missionaries and envisaged a goal more readily attainable. If someone shouldered the task of showing the way of salvation to sailors while they were temporarily on dry land, they could carry the Gospel message from port to port. In 1891, my father relinquished gainful employment and, with the financial assistance of Sarah Robinson,[2] built the *Welcome Mission* in the naval and slummier quarter of Portsmouth.

As its pastor-proprietor after 1894, he had henceforth to rely on the Lord to quicken the consciences of the faithful into making voluntary contributions to provide for his own frugal needs and ours. My arrival made him responsible for one more mouth to feed. At the time of my birth, infant mortality was exceptionally high. Stillbirths apart, my elder brother was already a neonatal fatality. If these disasters forced themselves on his attention, my father faced them with fortitude. I suspect that he accepted my intrusion with a resignation fortified by the reflection: whom the Lord loveth He chasteneth.

By then, my maternal grandfather and his wife had retired to enjoy a lackadaisical existence in Southsea, where retired officers and prosperous businessmen then lived. The house was large enough to accommodate my parents and sibs together with two underpaid domestics. From time to time, in favourable weather, my grandparents hired for the afternoon a horse-drawn open carriage to drive along a singularly unattractive seafront. On such occasions one of the younger generation accompanied them. At least one weekday evening service at the Mission and two indoor ones on Sunday, rounded off by an open-air bout, are among my earliest vivid memories of this time. Thus we had seemingly interminable excursions on foot to and fro between salubrious Southsea and the dockyard slum where the streets stank of rancid fish oil, pickled onions and stale beer.

As an adman for the Gospel, my father was in the avant-garde of the visual medium. While we lived in Portsmouth as he would say, or in Southsea which my mother preferred as the more genteel designation, one of my most picturesque memories is my father's use of visual aids at the Sunday night open-air meeting outside the Welcome Mission. For this he used a polychromatic banner about three yards wide, supported at each end by a pole held up by a convert. In the foreground was the lake of brimstone and fire. Across the middle was the edge of a cliff where stood the theatre, the brothel, the casino, the racecourse, the tavern, the *Palais de Danse* and other haunts of Satan. From the edge of the cliff the lost departed were falling in different stages of incandescence. Above the cliff was a solitary pilgrim pursuing a winding road to the rising sun; and, ironically, below it across the flames the legend: *God is Love*. As another visual aid to salvation, I recall a picture over my bed when I once visited a relative. This showed nothing but a very large eyeball with the legend: *Thou God Seest Me*. It was then a fashionable component of interior decoration. I have sometimes speculated on the possibility that it gave Orwell the idea of Big Brother Watching.

My recollections of the spoken word in the first eleven years of my life are, with one exception, vague. Spring flowers were in bloom and the Boer War was at its earliest stage. It must have been 1900, when I was four and a half. Against a background of patriotic songs. I heard a conversation between my father and a Colonel White, who was an enthusiastic supporter of the sinister alliance of Chamberlain and Rhodes. My father was what one then spoke of as a pro-Boer. More precisely, he contended that all war was contrary to the will of God. Twenty-five years later as a professor in Cape Town, I had cause to admire the good sense of those many nonconformists who refused to be deluded by propaganda that the war was a confrontation of the enlightened liberalism of the Cape Province Exeter Hall tradition,[3] and the racism of those who had trekked to the frontier when slavery was abolished under British rule. It was in fact a confrontation between a Calvinistic theocracy of half-literate farmers and a gang of cosmopolitan adventurers determined to get control of the gold seams around Johannesburg and diamonds elsewhere. Those who naïvely identified the forces of light and darkness, respectively, as British and Afrikaner were factually wrong. The truth is that leaders of the Cape Dutch—the Schreiners and the Hofmeyrs—were most articulate in pressing for safeguards for native civil rights in the conferences leading up to the British South Africa Act of 1909. Had there been no war, and had not Britain been the first to set up concentration camps, there is good reason to believe that the more prosperous and enlightened Cape Dutch would have eventually dominated the outlook of the more backward, bigoted Afrikaners of the Transvaal and the Orange Free State.

A familiar sight of my early childhood was the Italian organ grinder. Perched on top of the organ sat a small monkey wearing a red fez without a tassel. Another was the Breton onion seller, whose beret made him unmistakable even after he had sold his crop. He carried the onions, tied together by their plaited stems, in strings suspended from each end of a pole balanced on his shoulder. After 1914 I did not see one again till ten or so years ago in the Welsh valley of my retirement. I offered him the price of his entire crop if he would join me and my companion, whose French was better than mine, in a pub crawl by car round all the nearest inns where only Welsh was spoken. He and my Welsh neighbours conversed in Welsh, Breton, French and, occasionally English. This did not surprise me since Welsh, Breton and the virtually extinct Cornish language are all representatives of the same branch of the Celtic family.

My mother's unwavering concern for my spiritual welfare limited any friendships I might otherwise have formed while we still lived in Southsea. She discouraged me from accepting any invitation from any household which did not conform to her evangelical standards, and I can recall only one friend of my own age before we left Southsea.

Till my grandfather died, he and my grandmother had their own quarters and took their meals apart. Like myself, my brothers and sisters saw little of them except at family prayers in the morning, when the two domestics they employed were conscripted participants. They did not put in an appearance at the evening, often more protracted, performance.

My grandfather treated his son-in-law with benevolent tolerance, though ostensibly with less confidence in the unaided assistance of Him who feeds the ravens and counts every down feather of a sparrow as it falls to the ground. He believed that God helps those who help themselves, and his will left all his property to my mother, with legal safeguards lest my father should sink the capital in spreading the light of the Gospel.

Presumably this is why we left Southsea for London shortly after his death to make a new home in one of what were now my mother's houses, backing on the New River Reservoir of Stoke Newington. I was eleven at the time, and what happened to the Welcome Mission, and to the banner with the way of salvation in glorious technicolor, I never learned.

CHAPTER II
Stoke Newington

It seemed that my father had prepared his spiritual back door. Installed in our new home, he continued, till his death in my middle twenties, to expedite the Second Coming by recourse to a plan which cannot have been highly remunerative. Since, however, he was able to employ two whole-time secretaries, one of them my eldest sister, Margaret, it would seem that my mother, from the interest on her capital, did what she regarded as the right thing by him. The new design for salvation, a sort of chain-prayer league called the *One by One Band*,[1] was interdenominational, open to all who believed in the Trinity, the Atonement and the Everlasting Punishment of the unsaved. On receipt of a trifling subscription, members obtained a small pocket book. There were three columns for, respectively, the name of an as-yet-unsaved friend or neighbour, the date on which the book's recipient started to mention his or her name in daily prayers, and the date, if any, when the subject of such concern found salvation. A member could obtain a new book at the same price for further entries.

In most respects the transition from the Welcome Mission to the One by One phase of my childhood entailed a reduction of our standard of living, but not without some thrills. Our London house had from the upper rooms to the basement a hose-and-whistle telephone. It also had a real telephone for One by One use during working hours, that was surreptitiously a free-for-all when not in use by those labouring in the Lord's vineyard.

In our house there were three rooms on the top floor. In one of them were three small and very hard beds for myself and two brothers. The passage outside had a skylight, which prompted me to explore one way of seeking refuge from the Wrath to Come. I had learned to believe that the Lord would come again as a thief in the night and that true believers would be caught up in the air to meet Him (I Thessalonians 4:17). It seemed to me that this could happen at night to members of my family only if they used the roof light as an exit. If watchful, I might therefore seize the hem of the garments of my parents or my eldest sister as they levitated past the door of my bedroom. How many times I shivered in my nightdress till I fell asleep in the most favourable position at the top of the stairs, I cannot now remember. I must have soon discovered that I lacked the stamina to go through with the project.

In one important particular, the daily routine did not change when we moved to London. Family prayers preceded breakfast and followed immediately after tea. The pattern was the same for each. We started with a hymn from the Moody and Sankey collection or from the Wesleyan Hymn Book, accompanied by Margaret on a harmonium. There followed a chapter of the Bible which we read verse by verse in turn. Thereafter, except when visitors were present, my mother read a commentary on the prescribed passage from *The Christian* in the morning and *Life of Faith* in the evening. When an itinerant revivalist visited, he or my father, or both, addressed the audience extemporaneously. Otherwise there followed a prayer by my father, and last of all the Lord's Prayer in which we all joined.

After we came to London, I became more acutely aware that we had, as a family, little in common with our neighbours. I dreaded to go into a public conveyance with my father, who had always in one pocket a bundle of religious tracts, the message of which was: *Prepare to meet thy God.* These he distributed to the other passengers without embarrassment to anyone but myself.

I recall most clearly my father's uncompromising condemnation of any deviation from the doctrine that the fate of the unsaved in hellfire is everlasting. His conviction was that any mitigation of their lot such as promulgated by Dean Farrar in his collected sermons entitled *Eternal Hope,* 1878, deprived mankind of the only effective incentive to morality.

Needless to say, any flirtation with Darwinism by the Nonconformist ministry provoked uncompromising condemnation. My parents subscribed to Lightfoot's chronology according to which the Trinity created man on Sunday, October 23, 4004 B.C., at 9 A.M.[2] Commenting on doubts expressed by a preacher tainted with a liberal theology about whether a whale had swallowed Jonah, my father averred that he would have been confident that Jonah swallowed a whale had the Word of God said so.

The occasion for the high-water mark of the Sunday mealtime witch-hunt was the publication of *The New Theology*, 1907, by R. J. Campbell, a Congregationalist minister who attracted large audiences to desecrate the Sabbath by using public conveyances, converging on the London City Temple. I had no access to this publication, being at the time about twelve years of age. It is memorable to me because the denunciations it evoked, not merely at home but from many Methodist pulpits, first familiarised me with the terms *Lower* and *Higher Criticism*. They whetted my appetite to learn more about which was which. The Lower was concerned with the quest for the earliest and least corrupt texts and the Higher with their historical credibility.

My father used to say that the Lower Criticism leads to the Higher Criticism and the Higher Criticism to Atheism. This happened, I am happy to record, to be a correct forecast of my own spiritual pilgrimage. Well before I was fifteen, I had a foretaste of the Lower Criticism by the discovery of a discrepancy between the Authorised (King James) Version of the Bible (A.D. 1611) and the Revised Version sanctioned by Parliament and completed for publication ten years before my birth. This discrepancy disclosed my father's hostility to the R.V. and preference for the A.V. It occurs in I John 5. Therein the seventh verse in the A.V. reads: "For there are three that bear record in heaven, the Father, the Word and the Holy Ghost: and these three are one." It was eliminated in the R.V. as an indisputably late intrusion and contains the only explicit reference to the Athanasian Triune deity in either version.

There were two ways in which I could earn pocket money as a child. The earliest and least remunerative was to memorise thirteen verses of holy Writ per penny. I recall the figure because I received threepence for memorising the eighth chapter of the Epistle to the Romans. After sufficient Scotch, I can still repeat much of it. The second opportunity developed when the family moved to a London suburb among neighbours who were enthusiastic gardeners. Before I left school for Cambridge, motorcars were an unfamiliar sight. Goods were transported by horse-drawn carts so that there was a continuous renewal of excrement on the roads during the daytime. Twice a day in our suburb, the London County Council sent round vehicles equipped with ten-foot-wide rotating cylindrical brushes to collect what the horses had left in their wake. Between whiles, one could slip out of doors with a shovel to fill a bucket with manure, knowing that a neighbour would pay twopence for it. With hindsight, it is easy to understand how the infant death rate from fly-borne diseases such as infantile diarrhoea continued to fall steeply after World War I. The Gallipoli campaign had made the medical profession fly-conscious, and a national campaign to "swat that fly" was launched at the Mansion House shortly after the war. It was a case of locking the stable doors after the horses had made off. Throughout the war, Ford lorries had been displacing horse-drawn transport. At the end of it, city and suburban streets were comparatively free of horse manure.

I was released from the Sunday afternoon Bible class in exchange for membership in the Wesleyan Methodist Church. In those days, this entailed attending a session once a week of Bible reading, exposition and prayer by the officiating minister. As I recall, it made me a member of the "Society of People Called Methodists." I surmise this was a relic from before the final separation of the followers of John Wesley (who in his own expiring words died a member of the Church of England) from the Clapham sect.

Upon my release from the Bible class, I was allowed to spend Sunday afternoons reading, but only books that passed parental censorship. My earliest excursions were Bunyan's *Pilgrim's Progress* and *Holy War*. Later my mother was reduced to tears when she found me reading Tennyson's *Idylls of the King*. I contrived to get hold of a copy of George Borrow's *Bible in Spain*, 1843, whose title warranted the *nihil obstat et imprimatur* of my parents. It was a welcome discovery and, in gratitude to its author, I dispute the verdict of G. K. Chesterton in his *Essays on Victorian Literature*. Chesterton wrote: "Whether George Borrow ought to go into the section devoted to philosophers or the section devoted to novelists or the section devoted to liars, nobody else has ever known, even if he did." As a devout Anglo-Catholic, later a papist, Chesterton was the last person one would expect to understand the impact of Borrow's writings.

That George Borrow first became famous as an agent of the British and Foreign Bible Society may well be because The *Bible in Spain* was then permissible Sunday reading in nonconformist homes. There is, however, another explanation for its author's popularity. He was a prodigious linguist, fluent in at least ten languages. The *Bible in Spain*, like *Romany Rye*, 1857, and *Wild Wales*, *1862*, is redolent with his lively interest in linguistic affinities.

The publication of *Romany Rye* occurred a year before Darwin and Alfred Russel Wallace delivered their joint paper before the Linnaean Society. The evolutionary controversy was at its peak when *Wild Wales* appeared in print. Nearly sixty years before the publication of the *Bible in Spain,* an Oxford scholar, Sir William Jones, then a Judge of the Calcutta Supreme Court in the Warren Hastings era, had shown that Sanskrit has a basic affinity with both Greek and Latin in respect to its flexional system and, given certain regularities of sound shift, to its vocabulary. This work, which laid the foundations of modern philology, made no impression in Britain, but German scholars, including one of the Grimm brothers of fairy tale fame, extended Jones's method to trace the affinities of other languages within the Indo-European group.

Among these, Max Müller migrated to England in 1846, becoming a Fellow of All Souls, and completed his treatise on Sanskrit literature in the year of publication of the *Origin of Species*. During 1861–3 he delivered at the Royal Institution in London lectures published with the title *The Science of Language.* He traced the affinities of different Indo-European languages to a single ancestor. It may now seem odd that this treatise became the focus of popular controversy. However, its historic context was the repeal of the Religious Test Acts[3] in force at Cambridge and Oxford, which was a challenge to ecclesiastical authority. No less than Darwinism, the new philology was a frontal attack on the teaching of the Church. Darwinism cast overboard the Genesis story of creation. The new philology disposed of the Tower of Babel myth. Borrow's books shared a theme around which controversy raged among all who felt the impact of evolutionary theory. This, at least partly, explains their popularity in his later days. The *Bible in Spain* fired my boyhood imagination when Sunday denunciations of *The New Theology* first familiarised me with the devilry of Darwinism.

It would be pleasant but false to record that I had access to Fox's *Book of Martyrs,* 1563, when I had exhausted the entertainment value of Bunyan and Borrow. I failed to find it in my father's study. For better or worse, I discovered a bulky volume entitled *The Protestant Dictionary.* Its discussion of the prime number *three* and the trinitarian controversies fascinated me. Before the age of fifteen, I had become familiar with Sabellians (my favourites) and Docetae, Arians and Nestorians, Apollinarians, Eutychians, Monophysites and Monothelites. Till I painfully discovered that God is merely a semantic misdemeanour, a large slice of my intellectual resources for scientific studies was under lock and key.

Until I learned to use the reference room of the Stoke Newington public library, my secular (weekday) reading was subject to strict censorship. No fiction which mentioned an unmarried mother, or work tainted with Darwinism, was allowed to enter the home, and the works of Mary Ann Evans (George Eliot) were prohibited because her exclusively monogamous relation with the critic G. H. Lewes was never solemnised.

Among household taboos not mentioned so far were playing cards, liquor and smoking. I once incurred severe parental displeasure by purchasing a conjuring trick, a card which could change its suit by a stroke of the hand. My mother's disapproval of alcoholic drinks made her refuse to deal with any grocer who sold Wincarnis for invalids. There was no scriptural sanction for this prejudice. Apart from the story of the wedding in Cana, St. Paul explicitly counselled Timothy: "Drink no longer water, but use a little wine for thy stomach's sake and thine often infirmities" (I Tim. 5:23).

Temperance Sunday, an annual event in the Methodist chapels when the family came to London, had been an innovation during the lifetime of my parents and, as such, rightly regarded as an unscriptural one. In Britain south of the Tweed, the first promoters of teetotalism, wrongly called temperance, were rural trade union leaders who feared what the boss could accomplish with free booze at the local for dissident employees. Religion was not in the picture, as I learned with bewilderment during my schooldays.

I recall the only visit of one of my mother's more presentable relations. An ardent Methodist and a Dover magistrate, he regaled us with the fate of the two teenage co-religionists drowned in a rowing boat during a storm in the Straits at a date he recalled from boyhood. They had been teetotallers. At their funeral, the minister delivered a sermon in which he attributed their mishap to the just intervention of the Deity, with a warning to others who might likewise ignore the clear guidance of St. Paul to Timothy and the object-lesson of the nuptials at Cana.

In our home circle the population of the planet was divisible into: (a) Christian (i.e. Protestant) civilisation; (b) Spain, Portugal, Italy and Latin America under the rule of Rome; (c) the Mission Field embracing most of the habitants of Africa, Asia and Oceania. In the last named, cannibals still extended to missionaries the offer of a martyr's crown. I often suspected that my mother's ambitions for me included this merciful deliverance.

My mother's undertaking made me an object of more relentlessly insistent spiritual solicitude than my sisters or younger brothers. She was eager to teach me to read early. My earliest recollections of birthday presents are of biographies of missionaries. Her hopes for making my calling and election sure had one salutary consequence. At the age of fourteen I had already decided to be a biologist, and a medical qualification was then the prerequisite for those without independent means. Happily, my mother regarded a medical missionary as a field officer of senior rank in the Lord's service, and encouraged my intention to become a physician.

When we first came to London, I studied French. The fluency which my mother had acquired at her finishing school allowed her to mitigate some of the hardships of homework. I recall especially, when I was less than fifteen, a set book, *Le Crime de Sylvestre Bonnard* by Anatole France. It is the story of an antiquary. Evening preparation entailed looking up in my dictionary long lists of bric-à-brac, which conveyed as little to me in English as in the original.

If my mother's grammar and pronunciation were faultless, I cannot truthfully add that her appreciation of French culture was either sympathetic or well informed. It was consistent for her to identify the Continent with the incontinent, and the unacceptable face of France with the aftermath of the fall of the Bastille. As a result of the French Revolution, she would insist, the French had no day of rest, meaning that they were spared the horrors of our Sunday at home. She cherished odd views about Tom Paine, whom she called the notorious French atheist. According to my mother, he screamed his repentance on the way to the guillotine. Apart from the circumstances that he was not French, that he was a Deist and that he died in New York in his bed, the rest is unexceptionable.

An event which excited my curiosity about reproduction had happened when I was six years old. My mother gave birth to my youngest brother. I was inevitably curious about how he came equipped with a full complement of original sin into a world in which no one was enthusiastic about his arrival. My father's story was that he had come down the chimney. Its obvious falseness rankled years later because my father was at all times fervent about my own obligation to tell the truth. He did not very often beat me. The only occasions I can remember were when I had to confess under pressure that I had told a fib. The caning alternated with bouts of prayer and Bible reading, in particular a still memorable passage in the Apocalypse (Rev. 21:8) to the effect that "all liars shall have their part in the lake which burneth with fire and brimstone."

My only heterosexual experience till more than a year after I graduated at Cambridge occurred in December 1912. When I gained a Cambridge scholarship, a contemporary pupil of my school won a scholarship to Somerville College, Oxford. Her subject was French. She had an attractive figure, pleasant features and a submissive manner which might have put me off had there not been between us a common interest in religion. Her parents were Plymouth Brethren, so I could use her as a receptacle for my doubts when we visited Epping Forest on Saturdays or during the holidays in warm weather. On such occasions we kissed demurely.

By the time I was fifteen, my biological studies had made a deep rift in my confidence in the claims of revealed religion. The youngest of my sisters and both my brothers turned out to be cheerfully and unaggressively godless while I had to extricate myself painfully from what Lucretius calls the Terror of the Gods. Any assault of doubt, I kept to myself. In conformity with St. Paul's advice to live peaceably with all men, I had early discovered that disclosure of wavering faith to my parents led only to distasteful dialectical exercises. The outcome did nothing to confirm the faith of the party of the first kind and led to despondency in the party of the second kind. Still, I was not ready to repudiate what were to me the fundamentals of Christian faith. My attitude to religion had become a love-hate relationship.

It was in this mood that I responded to my father's plea to make public my passport to an eternity of angelic singing. My father regarded christening of infants as an act of dedication whereby parents undertook to bring up a child "in the nature and admonition of the Lord." True baptism was testimony in acceptance of atonement by believers who had reached the age of theological consent. Maybe he retained his early association with Methodism because there was no nearby Baptist conventicle in Stoke Newington. His convictions about baptism underwent no change and he urged me in my last year at school to go through with the ceremony. I agreed with mixed motives. Though my father greeted my academic progress by reminding me that it profits a man little to gain treasure on earth, he had celebrated my scholarship success by raising my pocket money to sixpence a week. I wanted to please him and still hoped uneasily that baptism would help me flee from the Wrath to Come.

The ceremony took place midweek in a fashionable West End chapel. The officiating minister, the Reverend F. B. Meyer, a prominent Free Churchman, was a friend of my father. Till recently, in the Welsh mountain valley of my retirement such ceremonies took place in the river and the candidates, who wore their daily clothes, went home soaking to dry them before an open fire. I was more fortunate. The tank in front of the pulpit contained warm water, which reached up to my shoulders and above the waist of the minister. Before immersion, my instructions were to put on a plain watertight blue serge costume with heavy boots to resist any tendency to float. This part of the programme took place in a well-heated vestry where I retreated to change back into my own outer garments.

Where I now live in North Wales, the Baptists have congregations larger than any other denomination. The hill farms specialise in sheep rearing and, till recently, the annual dipping of the flock was legally obligatory, being carried out with the local constable in attendance. I have no familiarity with other parts of Britain where sheep farming is predominant, but in England the Baptist denomination has little or no foothold in rural communities where sheep-rearing is of minor importance. It may be merely a coincidence that sheep-dipping and believer's baptism go hand in hand in my Welsh valley. Dipping may be all very well for removing maggots where the sheep scab is endemic, but baptism solved none of my own spiritual problems. I still had a crying need to conform, but a still more compelling need to rebel. I had two worlds which met as little as Kipling's East and West.

Before my last year at school, I can remember only one exposure to a frontal attack on the credentials of Christianity. This happened when there was some trouble with our water supply at home. I vividly recall conversations with the plumber, a disciple of H. M. Hyndman and a member of his Social Democratic Federation or its offspring, the British Socialist Party. The weather was fine and he ate his midday snack in the garden where we could converse unheard from the house. This was my first introduction to Karl Marx, whose teachings made little impression on me at that time. What did sink in was the disclosure that an unfrocked Anglican clergyman had lately published a book or pamphlet called *The Christ Myth* challenging the historical accuracy of the entire gospel story.

Many years passed before I could regard with equanimity so radical an assault on the faith of my father or, for that matter, the teaching of scripture at school.

What helped me to steer a comfortable course between the Scylla of apostasy and the Charybdis of credulity during my adolescent years were intermittent visits of the son of one of my mother's cousins, a Wesleyan minister. When he first began to call on us, he was teaching and studying for the preliminary examination leading to the London University external degree of B.D. He had the good sense to refrain from arguing with my father, but in walks we had together he introduced me to liberal theology.

During the summer vacation of 1913, I spent a month alone with him in a Lancashire manse. Each of us studied throughout the morning and late evening. We spent the afternoons and early evenings walking on the Lancashire moors. I remember how one excursion brought us near to Preston, where we came upon a large patch, at least half an acre, of horse-tails (*Equisetum*) looking in miniature like a forest of the carboniferous epoch. It must have been during this visit that walking became a favourite hobby for me. It was well suited to my build, not over 115 pounds. Until my arches fell in my fifties, a thirty-mile walk was effortless.

For this visit to the Lancashire manse, I had brought with me the two volumes of the *British Flora* by Bentham and Hooker to identify any new species I might find on our afternoon excursions. Most of the mornings I spent reading my cousin's textbooks on biblical criticism. I learned that the Book of Isaiah was the work of three authors. That the Book of Genesis is a synthesis of two narratives, the *E* and the *J*, did not come as a surprise. I had already discovered that Chapters 2 and 6 are inconsistent. When this holiday ended, I had finally freed myself from the bondage of fundamentalism. Knowing as yet nothing about the role of the English puritans and their fellow Calvinists in Holland as the parents and promoters of the slave trade between the Gold Coast and the colonies of the New World, I postponed indefinitely a final break with my family by means of the comforting reflection that Christianity had brought into the world brotherly love. The horrors of the Inquisition and persecution of the Albigenses did not damp my confidence in the reassuring compromise. I had never become accustomed to think of papists as a brigade of the Church Militant on earth. Our family was as ecumenical as an Ulster Orange Lodge.

I was more sensitive than most adolescents to the implications of increasing international tension. The chauvinistic hysteria of the Boer War was among my earliest memories and, during much of the first eleven years of my life, preparation for war was an ever-present preoccupation.

The first world war came at the end of my first year at Cambridge. During that year, war and the Christian ethic were uppermost in my thoughts when I was not immersed in academic study. When I arrived at Cambridge, the fact that several of my undergraduate contemporaries were both Wesleyans and members of the Officers' Training Corps was one of the circumstances which estranged me from my Methodist past. Long before the fateful August of 1914, I was committed to becoming a conscientious objector. To that extent my father and I could meet on common ground. We could at least agree that war is contrary to what we each identified as the Christian ethic.

CHAPTER III

Schooldays

BEFORE I reached the age of eleven, the contrast between Southsea and the commercial part of Portsmouth, where the Welcome Mission stood, had made me very sensitive to what Disraeli called the Two Nations. When the family came to London, my schooldays reinforced my awareness of class distinction.

True to her finishing school tradition, my mother never fully felt that free grace was an adequate substitute for respectability. She vigilantly obstructed any contact with most boys of my own age in the Mission milieu. If my father had had his way, I should probably have attended an elementary, so-called Board, school in Portsmouth. This would have been an affront to the social status of my grandparents. I assume that my grandfather paid the fees of a small private school, advertised as for the sons of gentlemen and kept by a Dr. Cody, ostensibly having a German degree. He had a single assistant who rarely lasted more than a year. None had any apparent qualifications higher than the Licentiate of the College of Preceptors. Under one of these, I started Latin and Euclid at about the age of eight. Though I became fascinated by philology in my middle age, I never outgrew a repugnance for Roman literature, morals and language.

We came to London in 1907 and, as noted earlier, I was sent to a coeducational Middlesex County Secondary School, which had recently been opened in Tottenham in response to the provisions of the 1902 Education Act. The fees were nominal, 30 shillings a term, and pupils other than myself had free places with or without maintenance grants for travel and apparel. When I passed the entrance test, I had what was initially a thrill but soon became a bore—a mile-and-a-half tram ride from and to the end of the road where we lived. This offered the opportunity for walking and diverting to other purposes the daily fare of a penny or two.[1]

Though our standard of life was now more frugal than that of most of my schoolmates in Tottenham, I was very much alert to the social gap between them and myself. My home was in an ostensibly prosperous district. I was the only boy whose parents paid a fee, such as it was. All the other pupils had previously attended Board schools, though the 1902 Education Act had by then liquidated the local School Boards. That I had not attended one was an educational handicap. When I entered, I had a confused smattering of Latin and Euclid, neither of which was part of the primary school curriculum. I had also a detestation of arithmetic as I had been taught it, the methods instilled at my private school being out of step with those then prescribed by the Board of Education.

I can confidently pinpoint when I began to pick up in the pedagogic rat race. Shortly after my fourteenth birthday, I had scarlet fever and missed a school term. In quarantine, I occupied a room formerly allocated to my cousin Rowland Hogben and still the repository of textbooks prescribed at his training college. One of these dealt with the teaching of arithmetic and made clear to me for the first time the rationale of the algorithms. I had been near the bottom of my class till then. On returning I was at the top. I had made the momentous discovery of how to teach myself.

School made little impact on my intellectual life and less still on my emotional life, but it was a neutral environment in which I could sort myself out with no interference, with no reminder of guilt to impede my recovery from brain washing at home and with no censorship of reading matter with which to explore a wider world.

It must have been about this time when I began to spend as much of my leisure as possible in the Stoke Newington Public Library. There I made the acquaintance of the dozen or so volumes of the *Cambridge Natural History* and of a textbook based on the syllabus for zoology of the external London Intermediate B.Sc. examination, originally written by H. G. Wells when employed as a coach by a University correspondence college. The title of *Cambridge Natural History* is misleading. Though it does give particulars of habit and habitat, it is essentially a compendium of comparative anatomy covering all groups of the animal kingdom. At this stage I was able to buy a few dissecting instruments and to procure carcasses for dissection from butchers, fishmongers and others. I was comparatively adept at dissection by the time I reached the age of specialisation.

Biology did not restrict my secular reading. Since most novels and all plays were taboo at home, they had the flavour of forbidden fruit. Before I was sixteen I had sampled Richardson, Fielding, Fanny Burney, Sterne, Walter Scott, all the works of the Brontës, most of Jane Austen, Bulwer Lytton, Thackeray, Dickens, George Eliot, Charles and Henry Kingsley, Wilkie Collins, Meredith and Thomas Hardy. Denunciation of Hardy's works from Methodist and Baptist pulpits conferred on them a fascination out of all proportion to their intrinsic merits. The local library had a few of Shaw's plays and a surreptitious suggestion by my chemistry teacher introduced me to *Candida*, which I still regard as the least plausible of Shaw's works.

In my excursions, I mercifully sidestepped Trollope. I say mercifully because when I finally made the acquaintance of Barchester Towers I was mature enough to appreciate the saga. Needless to say, I struggled through half a dozen novels of Meredith as an act of entirely unrewarding self-discipline. Did not Oscar Wilde properly declare "Meredith is a prose Browning. So is Browning"?

Masochistic pursuit of art for art's sake forced me to read to the bitter end both *Sartor Resartus,* 1833, and *Heroes and Hero-Worship,* 1841. That Carlyle was a stupendous bore, whose Teutonic grandiloquence plays havoc with the English language, calls for no comment. The prestige he enjoyed among contemporaries of enlightened views never ceased to be incomprehensible to me. Carlyle was to Hitler what John the Baptist was to the Hero of the Gospel story.

Like *Heroes and Hero-Worship,* all his other writings are saturated with the *Führer Prinzip.* If little remembered today, his paranoid racism, so anticipatory of the filth excreted by Julius Streicher during the Third Reich, was well known to the generation in which he loudly supported the slave owners of the Southern states during the American Civil War and the infamy of Governor Eyre's repressive regime in Jamaica. He invariably referred to African ex-slaves of British colonies as 'niggers' or *Quashee.* Only 'beneficent whips,' his own phrase, would compel a Negro to perform a day's work.[2]

In my visits to Stoke Newington Library, I renewed acquaintance with authors from whom the selections for the school curriculum might otherwise have estranged me permanently. As I recall the study of English literature in my schooldays, every specimen was one of the least attractive examples of its author's work. Of Keats we sampled *Ode to a Grecian Urn* when we might have read *La*

Belle Dame Sans Merci. Of Shelley we were offered the twittering *To a Skylark* instead of *Adonais,* of Matthew Arnold *Sohrab and Rustum* instead of *The Forsaken Merman,* of Macaulay the *Essay on Clive* instead of that on Frederick the Great and Voltaire.

Our playing fields at Tottenham adjoined what is now the home ground of the Tottenham Hotspur soccer team. They were then in open country, where I could collect plants during summer to identify by use of a borrowed copy of Bentham and Hooker. In winter if I could escape the obligation to join in soccer, I could be well content left alone to construct a galvanometer or a microphone with odds and ends of wire, old tins, boxes and scrap metal. In my last year at school, I played cricket without much enthusiasm and boxed once a week with a teenage laboratory attendant I met at Birkbeck College. I went to the baths next door to school without reluctance though my swimming was inept.

During the year after the scarlet fever episode, I was studying for the London University School Matriculation with determination to go to college by means as yet not clearly envisaged. I discovered that a pass in Latin was obligatory for medical registration. Because of my defective aptitude for Latin, I entered on my own initiative for the Oxford Senior Local Examination as an insurance policy. In this a pass was fortunately attainable if one knew the set books, in my year two of *De Bello Gallico.* For the London University matriculation, I offered successfully English, French, Mathematics, Physics, Chemistry and History.

I surmounted these hurdles when I was fifteen and qualified for the Upper Sixth form in which pupils worked for either the London Intermediate B.Sc. or B.A. Four subjects were then required for the former. I chose Chemistry, Physics, Botany and Zoology. There was no provision for teaching the last at school, but I had permission to study it in the evenings at the London County Council's Hackney Polytechnic. It turned out I was the only applicant so there were to be no lectures in Zoology that year. Luckily for me, the Head of the Biology Department, a botanist, saw to it that I had bench space, use of a microscope and the prescribed specimens for dissection that I could not obtain elsewhere. While dissecting, I had one ear open for a course of lectures on the origin of flowering plants for candidates preparing to take the London University external honours degree in botany. On Saturdays I spent many hours in the Natural History Museum in South Kensington.

The gap in my schedule from choice of Zoology as one subject gave me ample periods for private study, which I elected to take in the room where the Arts candidates were having lessons in economic history. Their teacher was almost the only one from whom I learned much, though without benefit for my examinations. Indeed, what scholastic success I had was almost entirely due to my inclination to teach myself.

In the summer of 1912, I passed the London Intermediate B.Sc. in all four subjects with little difficulty. I was now ready to explore what scholarships would take me through a University without any need of assistance from my parents. The only member of the teaching staff of Tottenham County School with a degree from one of the two older Universities was my Chemistry master, an Oxford graduate. He helped me get relevant information. I picked on Cambridge because Trinity College offered the highest emoluments, then £80 per annum for a Major Entrance Scholarship, with the possibility of a Senior Scholarship at £100 at the end of one's first or second year.

Luckily for me, our home was on the London side of the London—Middlesex County boundary though only by a matter of yards. A few years earlier the Webbs and Graham Wallas had permeated the so-called Progressive Party, then in control of the London County Council, with forward-looking Fabians who had introduced much higher maintenance grants than elsewhere for school-leavers who gained the highly competitive Cambridge or Oxford open scholarships.

My recollections of the long vacation before the scholarship examination, which I sat a few days before my seventeenth birthday, are hazy. I studied obsessively and otherwise spent time in botanical field work in Epping Forest, within an hour and a half bicycle ride from home. The bicycle was purchased from the proceeds of a favourable harvest of horse dung. The forest had at that time a richly varied flora and fauna. There I first made the acquaintance of the scorpion fly *Panorpa communis* and the delightful Snake's head *Fritillaria meleagris*, neither of which have I met elsewhere in Britain. My favourite pets were the limbless lizard *Anguis fragilis*, commonly called the slow worm, and adders which I made innocuous by snipping off the fangs at their base.

I continued to have pangs of religious doubt. I had already digested both Paley's *View of the Evidences of Christianity*, 1794, and its Oxford twin, Bishop Butler's *Analogy of Religion Natural and*

Revealed, 1736. It would be difficult to find two treatises less likely to confirm the faith of an intelligent adolescent in theism of any sort, still less in the credentials of Christianity. Since adolescents in search of otherworldly satisfactions today rarely read Paley or Bishop Butler, I digress to summarise the brief for the prosecution.

Paley's argument proceeds from the assumption that the doubter is lost, though not as yet necessarily without hope of salvation, on a moor where he or she finds a watch. She or he concludes that the watch could not be there unless there had been a watchmaker to make the watch. When we casually come across a universe in one of our off moments, we must therefore reach the conclusion that there must have been a Universe Maker. Needless to say, there is no moor on which to pick up a universe—the meaning of the word 'universe' is all-inclusive, and what is all-inclusive would be its own creator if the word means anything intelligible.

If Bishop Butler also played on a sticky wicket, his brief was no less translucently idiotic, and more specious in his own social context. After the Revocation of the Edict of Nantes, the famous mathematician De Moivre, then a Huguenot refugee, had made a livelihood as an actuary in the emerging business of life insurance. Less than thirty years after publication of the *Analogy*, the Equitable was destined to make good under the gratuitous counsel of a once famous preacher, Dr. Price. As it happened, success was less a triumph of mathematics than the consequence of a gross error in the Northampton Life Table. In an intellectual climate favourable to its bogus claims, Butler advanced the case for faith as if it were an endowment policy for the Life to Come. We cannot be sure that hellfire exists, but a prudent person would prefer to take no chances about a prospect which so many of one's neighbours entertain as a likely risk. Eager as I then was to catch at any straw to salvage some of my family's indigestible propositions, *Analogy* failed to fortify my faith. One cannot take out an effective afterlife endowment or fire risk policy simultaneously with the Mosque, the Cathedral and the Mission Hall.

One issue that disturbed my confidence in revelation before I was fifteen was how to square the omnipotence, omniscience and omnipresence of God with His omnibenevolence. Long ago, Omar Khayyam, in FitzGerald's translation, states the issue thus:

> Oh Thou, who Man of baser Earth didst make,

> And who, with Eden didst devise the
>   Snake;
> For all the Sin wherewith the Face
>   of Man
> Is blacken'd, Man's Forgiveness give—
>   and take!

In the fall of 1912, I entered for the final B.Sc. course in Zoology as an evening student at Birkbeck College, then foremost among the night schools of London University. Meanwhile I continued to attend Tottenham County School with special coaching in chemistry and botany. During this term, a remote cousin of my mother heard that I was working for a Trinity scholarship. Then Second Master of Christ's Hospital, the renowned Bluecoat School near Horsham, he was a bachelor and a Cambridge mathematician of sorts. Whether prompted by compassion or idle curiosity—I know not which—he invited me down at half term for a short weekend. It was my first encounter with contemporaries in a 'public' school and my first plunge into a milieu which was unaggressively godless. I spent part of the Sunday reading *The Invisible Man* by H. G. Wells while Palmer, my host, played records of song hits from *The Merry Widow*.

My Birkbeck studies constituted all the formal teaching in zoology I received up to the time when I sat for my scholarship examination in Cambridge. In those days, college authorities allocated scholarship candidates to rooms within its precincts and they dined in Hall. One of the others in the Trinity group was a Bluecoat boy whom my host at Christ's Hospital had coached. I was by far the youngest candidate and the only one from a county secondary school. It was agreeable to have at least one, if distant, acquaintance with whom to exchange a few words. My liveliest recollection of the examination week is a large and beautiful assortment of botanical and zoological preparations which one had to identify. Before then I had seen them only as black and white diagrams in books, and it was more than a mild thrill to meet them, so to say, in the flesh. One was the radula of the garden snail. I believe that all my identifications were correct. One of my examiners was Leonard Doncaster, the first geneticist to recognise sex-linked inheritance. Few men influenced my professional career more than he did during the next six years.

I heard the results on the day I was due to return to London. I had become a Major Scholar of Trinity with the right, otherwise restricted to Fellows, of walking across the grass lawn in Great Court and the obligation of reading lessons in chapel one week during the academic year.

At my school Empire Day, the 24th of May, had lately become an occasion for a short lecture on the benefits of the Colonial System, followed by Kipling's *Recessional* and *Land of Hope and Glory*. In my last term, I had already become a pacifist and I refused to stand when the rest of the school rose to sing the second of these. Actually, it took little courage to do so. My examination record had made me a mascot, and I knew that I had acquired immunity to punishment.

Word of my success in the Scholarship examination had come from the then Master of Trinity, Montagu Butler. He is memorable only for a slim volume of sermons to College servants and for having, in his former capacity as headmaster at Harrow, flogged Stanley Baldwin for harbouring a pornographic book. His letter of commendation mentioned his particular approval of the essay on general topics obligatory for candidates in all subjects. The title was 'The Organisation of Lasting Peace.' I had lately passed through a Tolstoyan phase in my general reading and it was the first time I had been asked to write an essay on a topic which interested me. I once scored 0 out of 50 when the assigned theme was 'A day at the seaside.'

The only hurdle left to surmount before I came into residence in October, 1913, was Little-go. I was entitled to exemption in all subjects which were compulsory other than Greek. The syllabus prescribed two set books, one of which was St. Matthew's Gospel, the other *Plutus* of Aristophanes. The former offered me few difficulties. I already knew the crib almost by heart, and the Welsh schoolmaster who had propelled me through *De Bello Gallico* coached me successfully through the play. I found Greek much less repugnant than Latin. This may have been partly because literary Greek is far closer to the spoken word than literary Latin and partly because, by means of it, I was getting a foretaste of Biblical criticism. Besides, I now had an extensive scientific vocabulary based on Greek roots and thus agreeable and lively associations.

As my schooldays came to an end in the summer of 1913, political controversy mounted to a climax, to be seen in retrospect as the end of an era. Among other themes with which the headlines reverberated were many which portended social change or war on a hitherto unprecedented scale: the introduction of Old Age Pensions, of National Health Insurance and high taxation of land values, the hunger strikes of the Suffragettes, soup kitchen queues of unemployed dockers on the Thames embankment, rumblings of armed revolt in Ulster, high-powered salesmanship of the Navy League for bigger and better battleships, the Entente Cordiale and a mounting fear of the might of the German military machine.

CHAPTER IV

On Going Up

When I became a Cambridge undergraduate, I had more affection for my mother than the account of my schooldays may lead the reader to infer. On a dismal and foggy Saturday afternoon two days before term began in early October 1913, I boarded a train almost exclusively occupied by other undergraduates. My mother came with me to Liverpool Street station. Many of the undergraduates travelled first-class, and the platform was a hat parade, Ascot-style, for their aunts, sisters and sundry who had come to see them off. While waiting for the whistle, I was acutely aware that my mother's black outfit and bonnet were conspicuously dowdy. Inwardly I blamed myself for feeling half-ashamed, and blamed my father for producing so large a family that he could have provided for it well only had he remained a respectable business man. Forty years elapsed before I learned to think more kindly of his singleness of purpose and to respect my mother less for her respectability.

I had few misgivings about my financial prospects. If I lived frugally, my London County Council maintenance grant of £70, with £80 as a Major Scholar of Trinity, would suffice to keep me at College and make henceforth a contribution to the family to cover my vacations. Luckily, the L.C.C. grant was supplemented by an initial allowance of £25 for books, stationery, clothes and gown. I had no need to beg or borrow from my father.

My previous visits to Cambridge for the scholarship examinations had given me a few indications of what to expect when I arrived at the licensed lodgings allocated to me a few yards from the gate of Whewell's Court on the side of the road opposite to Sidney Sussex. These were the cheapest available, but I was fortunate to have as fellow lodgers two other Trinity men several years older than myself. Though scholarships at Trinity were then open only to candidates aged nineteen or younger, older graduates of other universities could compete for exhibitions.

John Marshall was a St. Andrews Master of Arts, a mathematical exhibitioner and the son of a miner. Being four years older than myself and a Scotsman reared in a long tradition which endowed learning with as much claim to respect as prudent choice of one's parents or school, he was able to anaesthetise my initiation into a social routine for which I had been prepared neither by my school nor by my home background. He regarded all *commoners* (students whose parents were wealthy enough to pay their fees and who had not gained scholarships) with the tolerant amusement one extends to God's intellectually underprivileged children. At the time, his attitude was largely justifiable. If the colleges then applied any test of eligibility other than the entrance examination, Little-go, to applicants whose parents could pay the fees, I never found out what it was.

My second neighbour was P. W. Burbidge, a New Zealand physicist who had come to undertake post-graduate research in the Cavendish laboratory under J. J. Thomson. Like John Marshall and myself, socially he was a fish out of water and, like the former, he was too grown up to let it trouble him. It was a great shock to me at the end of my first year when pulmonary tuberculosis forced him to return to his own country and an open-air life on a farm. Happily, he recovered and later became Professor of Physics in one of the New Zealand universities.

Those who know only the Cambridge of more recent years will have little conception of what it was like to be a scholar of Trinity in 1913, still less to be a scholar from a county secondary school. The terms *grammar* and *secondary* as officially applied to schools had very different meanings in 1915 and 1950. In the earlier period, local authorities were free to discharge their responsibility for secondary education in either of two ways. In London, the L.C.C. wholly or partly took over most of the schools founded by the Livery Companies: the Grocers', Haberdashers', Brewers' and Skinners'. In recently urbanised districts, such as those parts of Middlesex and Essex drawn into the London conurbation during the last decades of the nineteenth century, County authorities could fulfil their statutory responsibility for secondary education only by creating new schools with nominal tuition fees, if any. Such were the county secondary schools of my boyhood.

In my time, most of the secondary schools were coeducational. The Livery schools in London were not. The Skinners' school for girls, attended by my youngest sister, was in the borough of Stoke Newington within easy walking distance from our house, but the nearest boy's school of the same sort was the Grocers' in the neighbouring borough of Hackney. Transport was a difficulty here.

The Middlesex County Secondary School in neighbouring Tottenham, however, was on a tram route within a five-minute walk from where we lived, so this is where I went. At the time, there was also in Tottenham a so-called grammar school. It recruited its pupils exclusively from private preparatory schools and was neither owned nor run by the county or borough. A county secondary school recruited its pupils almost exclusively from publicly funded elementary schools.

When I gained my scholarship, what were later called state scholarships did not exist, and only the more progressive local authorities gave sufficiently generous maintenance allowances for adolescents who won open University scholarships. In Cambridge, scholars from county secondary schools were then a novelty, and in Trinity I was the first of the species. In contrast to the commoners, who were the overwhelming majority of the undergraduate population, scholars and exhibitioners formed an intellectual élite. When not entertaining one another with conspicuous expenditure, commoners, most of them from wealthy homes, were preoccupied with sport, including primitive methods of aquatic transport and hunting the hare with beagles. Very few of them prepared for the tripos (honours degree) examinations, or participated in the cultural life of the university. Whether all the colleges insisted on at least nominal preparation for the pass degree, I do not recall.

Happily, in those days students fed together in college only at dinner. Four days a week, dinner in Hall was compulsory. Large as were its buildings, Trinity could not accommodate the whole undergraduate body, so it was usual for an undergraduate to reside during three of his nine terms in licensed lodgings within a five- or ten-minute walk from the college. When resident in college, the more affluent students had breakfast, lunch and tea brought to their rooms by waiters from the Buttery (the college kitchen). One rarely fed alone. Breakfast, perhaps even more than lunch, was a social event. If brought from the Buttery, the first course was porridge with thick cream, followed by grilled kidneys. A fashionable main dish was a fish pie made of cod steaks in a rich sauce. Such luxury came my way only when asked to a meal with a don. In summer term, lunch menu at a don's invitation included cold salmon served with freshly made mayonnaise, cucumber and new potatoes, followed by strawberries and cream or melon.

The domestic routine of college life at that time entailed the employment of an immense retinue. Aside from the chef and his staff, there were three sorts. The bedmakers, who were women of advanced years, came in the early morning to put the porridge on the boil and, in the colder part of the year, to light one's fire. What charms their hard years had left them could no longer excite the jealousy of celibate dons in the Hellenic tradition. Waiters and porters were male and distinguishable by the fact that the latter wore top hats. The precise duties of the porters during most of the day were a mystery except for delivering messages and keeping an eye on who came and went. Women could intrude into college precincts or licensed lodgings only with permission of a tutor, and then only if accompanied by an elderly chaperone of good repute. We had to be in college or lodgings by 10 P.M. The porters and landladies had the responsibility of checking that we were. The Head Porter made himself responsible for telling newcomers what they could or could not do.

At that time several colleges of both the older universities had no hot bath facilities. In one of its courts—I forget which—Trinity had a small segment which housed a few. They were not greatly in demand. As I recall, there were no queues, and there was a latent sentiment that the use of hot water was not quite manly. In all rooms, there was a foot-bath and a bulky, ornately corrugated porcelain jug, filled daily by a bedmaker with cold water, in readiness for pouring over one's shoulders before taking breakfast. There was no central heating. Washing in winter was character-building.

As an educational institution, Trinity was ideally fitted to foster my intellectual development. Perhaps because of an overdose of family prayers, I had acquired a lifelong resistance to information transmitted by the spoken word, especially to monologues. There was very little pressure on a scholar of Trinity to attend lectures or, if present, to attend to what a lecturer was saying. Few of the lectures on biological topics were inspiring, but the organisation of laboratory work and the equipment provided could not have been much better.

The College itself made no provision for lectures in the natural sciences. It was a highly expensive residence with a minimum of

On Going Up

tutorial supervision. In Trinity the tutors, three in my time, were responsible for approval of one's courses and for domestic discipline. They also offered counsel on lectures of cultural interest but of no benefit for examinations. One's tutor had no tutorial responsibilities in the usual sense of the term. *De jure* he was *in loco parentis*, but one did not have to see him more than once or twice in the term. *De facto*, the Head Porter discharged his parental responsibilities.

When I went up in the autumn of 1913, my tutor was E. W. Barnes, a mathematician already a Fellow of the Royal Society and ordained as an Anglican priest, subsequently Bishop of Birmingham. He was exceptionally kind to me, but I was too much overawed by him at the time to appreciate his benevolence. At my first interview, he drew my attention to three courses open to all members of the University, two weekly ones on philosophical themes delivered by Fellows of the College and one on English literature by Quiller-Couch in the University auditorium. One of the Trinity lecturers was a Hegelian named John McTaggart, who gave us a Reader's Digest of Western philosophy from Heraclitus to Hegel.

As a theologian Barnes was ultra-modern, even by Cambridge standards. In his occasional pulpit appearances, his rejection of the miraculous extended to the Virgin Birth, the Resurrection and the Ascension. Needless to say, his evangelical critics denounced his views as inconsistent with his clerical vows. His firm conviction was that the only hope of preserving the ethical teaching of the gospel was to jettison those ingredients no reputable historian could accept as factual. Though I did not realise it at first encounter, he was a sincere Christian pacifist and a socialist.

In Trinity, each of us had a Director of Studies whom we met for a tutorial once a week. In any one term, there was therefore no supervision of one's work in two out of three subjects taken for the tripos examination. I myself had in succession three directors. Two of them were physiologists, Keith Lucas and his most distinguished pupil E. D. Adrian, afterwards Lord Adrian, who became in turn President of the Royal Society and Master of the College in succession to G. M. Trevelyan. The weekly sessions with Keith Lucas and with Adrian were merely occasions for stimulating conversation. Both had been Scholars of the College and both took the view that a Trinity Scholar should already be able to read books. My third mentor was Clive Foster Cooper, a palaeontologist who was a very skilful draughtsman. He became Director of the British Museum of Natural History.

Foster Cooper took a more exacting view of his duties than did his colleagues. Each week he gave me an essay topic and was a helpfully candid critic of what I wrote. He remarked that my first exploit was less an essay than a nonconformist afflatus. By introducing me to Faraday, Hume and Huxley, he showed me that the models for essay writing then, and still, prescribed by school teachers of English have little relevance to lucidity in the domain of exact thought. He also quickened my interest in writing as such. I learned to keep notes illustrated, wherever possible, by visual aids in colour, and to test my understanding of a scientific problem by recourse to an appropriate visual aid of my own. Although I gravitated early towards experimental biology, I retained as a result of his influence a lifelong interest in palaeontology. During my professional career, it has been my good fortune to be on the spot in three continents when discoveries of important fossils have been made.

Like many other admirable features of the Oxbridge system, individual attention of the sort I had from Foster Cooper was a luxury which the welfare state of today cannot afford.

He made me aware for the first time of the criteria for effectively conveying sustained reasoning about observable phenomena through the written word. Education below the university level should have made such attention unnecessary. It had not. As it affects the pupil destined to specialise in the natural sciences and their applications, the teaching of English in most schools is no better today. In several ways it is worse, especially if the teacher's qualification is a degree in English with no recognition of linguistic scholarship. Needless to say, we cannot expect teachers whose standards of good prose are set by pundits with a distaste for science to be able to grasp the semantic requirements of scientific discourse.

One of the great advantages of Cambridge was that the laboratories, colleges and licensed lodgings were all within a few minutes' walk of one another. The same is true of most of the universities which came into being after World War II, but I doubt whether many of their policy makers fully recognise another advantage of Cambridge as I knew it. I have mentioned that one took meals other than Hall dinner in one's own rooms. This gave one unique opportunities for serious discussion with friends and the cultivation of conversation as an art.

On Going Up

When I went up, few scholars who specialised in the natural sciences belonged to the Union where the more prosperous dined when not in Hall. Having sampled one of its debates as the guest of a member, I did not regret that the fees were far beyond my means. I still regard the Union Debating Society of Cambridge (even more that of Oxford) as a potting shed for the cultivation of mentally retarded politicians. The most lively discussions at an intellectually high level were those which took place at the *Moral Sciences,* colloquially *Moral Stinks, Club,* where Bertrand Russell and Gilbert Moore minced words with their philosophical competitors, in the Fabian Society and its study circles, and in the *Heretics* founded by C. K. Ogden of Basic English fame. The last two held weekly meetings with guest speakers, and were open to women students chaperoned by a lady don. When the topic was sex, the experience could be more educative for the latter.

Within a few weeks of the beginning of my first term, I became a Fabian. Not having to work to support myself, I could well afford to spend time in study which had no connection with a syllabus before retiring around 1:30 A.M. I read avidly the works of Sidney and Beatrice Webb, starting with their *History of Trade Unionism,* 1894. I even skimmed through their several volumes of *English Local Government,* 1906–1929. It must have been about this time that I read G. D. H. Cole's *World of Labour* and John A. Hobson's *Imperialism, a Study,* 1902.

Student activities of my first year included weekly sessions of the Trinity Scholars' Club. After dinner in Hall, we met in the rooms of a member to read a play. Ibsen and Oscar Wilde were favourites. Why the former, I cannot say. It was fashionable to talk about art for art's sake. Therefore Shaw was no artist, though, oddly enough, regarded as a thinker, and our programmes included none of his plays nor those of Galsworthy.

During one of these otherwise enjoyable sessions, I made a *faux pas.* I was one of the cast for *Lady Windermere's Fan* and my lines included the first reference to a Lady Jedburgh. I pronounced Jedburgh as a two-syllable word and did not understand the reason for a titter till another participant pronounced the second half as *borough.*

The most memorable meeting of the University Fabian Society in my first year was one addressed by Sidney Webb. Most of his contemporaries and his obituarists have regarded him as a desiccated efficiency addict who would shun any appeal to kindness. My own first impression, reinforced at a much later date when I used to stay at Passfield Corner, was otherwise. Indeed, I could count on the fingers of a hand the number of equally or more moving addresses. So long after the event, I cannot do it justice. It was delivered in a monotone without the aid of gesture and on that account was more compelling to a cynical audience which had come from dinner in Hall or at the Union. It began with a quotation from Kropotkin. Men had to toil and face danger daily in the mines to provide us with the good things in life and with what opportunities we enjoyed in our student days. Such privileges put us in debt to society, a debt we could repay only by the resolve to join others in building a new social order. We owed to society the use of our leisure to gain knowledge relevant to this task. More than others of his audience, I had good reason to realise that I had become a member of a highly privileged enclave.

CHAPTER V
Cambridge

THE Cambridge of my time conferred on a few students with the brains to benefit a rich opportunity for mental growth. It is no less true that it perpetuated a pattern of living inconsistent with the health and happiness of a large proportion of their fellow citizens and far beyond the means of a nation geared to mobilise its manpower for technological advance.

The Tudor oak panelling, the retinue of waiters with white ties and the massive array of solid silver implements gave Hall dinner in my day a flavour of baronial pageantry appropriate to its gastronomic profusion. The Fellows' table was on a dais and that reserved for scholars and exhibitioners immediately below it. We were separated by a conspicuous gap from the commoners. At the head of the Fellows' table sat the Master, the Vice-Master and the Dean. All of us stood while the first two recited alternate verses of a long Latin grace, the Master mellifluously using what one then called the new pronunciation, the Vice-Master belligerently the old.

The menu of six courses, with a choice of at least three items for each, was the equivalent of more than a week's civilian food ration during World War II. First came the soup, thick or clear laced with wine. An entrée such as sweetbreads or woodcock legs on toast either preceded or followed the fish, served with anchovy sauce, tartare or freshly made mayonnaise to taste. Then came several sorts of meat, hot and cold. The options included fowl or duck and game in season: venison, pheasant or jugged hare. Of the vegetables, I recall only the novelty of a dozen unsuspected ways of making potatoes enjoyably edible. The fifth course offered one a choice of ice cream, crème caramel, fruit jellies with fresh cream. Then followed a savoury such as hard or soft fish roes on toast. If I did justice to such a meal, I found that I could get by with very little else to eat. While in lodgings, each week I had three execrably home-cooked meals—meat, two veg, pudding—in addition to the obligatory four in Hall. Later when living in College, I stuck to porridge for breakfast, bread and cheese for lunch and self-prepared odds and ends for the three nights when I need not incur the expense of a Lucullan orgy. Perhaps this is why I found it difficult in later life to eat more than one cooked meal a day.

Hall was the site of one of many blunders in the first few weeks. For the fifth course, I had chosen apple pie and cream. The pie itself was tart enough to invite the addition of sugar. In front of my place was a tall container of solid silver with perforations at the top. I had previously seen nothing like it except an electroplated facsimile holding brown sugar. On shaking it, I managed to cover my apple pie with red pepper and immediately became aware that the other scholars were looking on with restrained amusement. Happily, I had already begun to realise that the moral strength of the governing class lies in conveying to lesser breeds their unshakeable belief in their sheer inability to do the wrong thing. Determined not to let down my side in Tottenham County versus Eton, Harrow and Rugby, I looked around the table with an assumed assurance intended to convey that red pepper with apple pie was the newest manifestation of gastronomic good taste. When I got back to my lodgings, I vomited copiously.

Unfamiliarity with the drinking no less than the feeding habits of the higher Mammalia could also exact its penalty from the unwary and uninstructed. Coffee after Hall was one of the functions to which dons invited undergraduates. When I received in my first week the intimation from the Head Porter that Dr. Barnes expected me next day to coffee at 8 o'clock, I flattered myself with good reason that I knew what coffee was.

Coffee as the French made it was an ingredient of gracious living in the Hogben household. As one could then do, my mother bought white beans and roasted them twice weekly. She or my eldest sister ground an appropriate number immediately before breakfast in a wooden-cased grinding machine, then prescribed by Mrs. Beeton for the well-appointed kitchen. We drank the suspension within a quarter of an hour of grinding with addition of a little chicory.

Occasionally, my mother also bought cracked cocoa beans from which she prepared chocolate as the club houses of the seventeenth century learned to do from Spaniards in the manner of Montezuma's court.

Where I went wrong was that so far breakfast had circumscribed my social experience of coffee consumption. Having set my alarm for 7:15 A.M., I presented myself at my tutor's rooms at 7:55 to be on the safe side. The inner green baize door of a study lounge of dimensions fitting for a major Trinity don was ajar. Since I elicited no verbal response to a gentle tap, I entered but found no one present. Not knowing how many rooms constituted a tutor's suite, I crossed the room to knock at a second door and heard what I took to be a murmur of assent. On opening it, I saw Dr. Barnes half rising from his bed in his nightwear to greet me with imprecations whose meaning defied recognition owing to the speed of my withdrawal.

I had still much to learn about clothes. On previous visits I had observed that most undergraduates during the day and in Hall wore, as did younger dons, a beltless Norfolk jacket with gray flannel trousers. Cap and gown apart, such was my external wardrobe. Second-hand gowns prescribed for use in lectures, in Hall, in thoroughfares and on official visits to one's tutor, to the Dean or to one's Director of Studies were conspicuously on display when I came up for Little-go so I had purchased one in advance. The inadequacy of my outfit became apparent when the Head Porter announced that I must attend chapel for the ceremony for admission of scholars and exhibitioners "with bands, sir." Being an exhibitioner, John Marshall had also to attend, and I learned in good time from him that bands are the two, happily inexpensive, flaps of white linen worn by barristers below the chin and by John Wesley in the Wedgwood medallion. The ceremony went off with no mishap after a lucid briefing from the Head Porter. The Master sat in the pulpit of the College Chapel. In turn we ascended and knelt before him with palms pressed together between his, like those of little Samuel at prayer. He then repeated the formula: *admitto te auctoritate mihi commissa in discipulum hujus collegii.*

My next meeting with the Master was far more memorable. This occasion was dinner at the Lodge for new scholars only. The hostess was his second wife, who allegedly had tied for top honours in the Classics Tripos. I had not the slightest idea what the Head Porter meant when he coupled the summons to appear with the words "white tie, sir." When my friend John Marshall explained, I sustained a shock. I did not possess, nor had I previously worn, anything like this. Even if the cash had been at hand, three days would not have been enough for a tailor to custom-fit a suit with tails. Marshall brushed aside my alarm. Near our lodgings, a pawnbroker's shop announced gents' evening dress for hire on state occasions such as Freemason dinners and weddings. Since I was short and slim, a good fit was too much to hope for. I must have looked a little like Charlie Chaplin when I presented myself at the Master's Lodge in baggy trousers and with spare room in my waistcoat for a football.

I was not yet eighteen and much younger than any of the other scholars, all from one or another of the major 'public' schools and impeccably tailored. Maybe this is why Montagu Butler, majestically white-haired and white-bearded like one's picture of a major prophet, took me by the arm at the head of a procession along the first-floor picture gallery. There we paused beneath portraits of past members of the College. The ones that stick in my memory are Byron, Macaulay and Edward VII. We gazed reverently at each in turn to the refrain "and he too was a Trinity man." Each time he said this, the Master pinched my arm with paternal affection. Perhaps because I was the baby of the party and to put me at ease, my place at table was next to the Master's wife who did her best with such socially unpromising material to work on. With the kindest intention she went into action by asking which school I came from.

When I went to Tottenham County School in 1907, it had not as yet its own building. It shared with the local night school premises which had been in the mid-nineteenth century a highly reputable educational foundation known as Grove House under Quaker management. Lister of surgical fame attended it before he entered the 'Godless College of Gower Street'—University College of London. The name Grove House was still visible on a foundation stone during my own schooldays. I can see that it would not have occurred to my hostess that a scholar of Trinity had attended a County Secondary School, even if she knew what a County Secondary School was. Nor was she any the wiser when I told her that I had been at Grove House. That this was a half truth did not console me when I lay in bed later, recalling every Biblical reference to the fate of liars in the hereafter. What made this lapse most shameful was that sheer cowardice was the motivation. Of no other action in my life have I ever felt more guilty. Even half a century later, its recollection is still painful.

Among incidents which I recall without shame or reluctance is my short-lived ministration in College Chapel, which had an early morning and early evening service in accordance with the ritual of the Established Church. A fellow read the lessons on Sunday, on weekdays a Scholar. Each of the latter officiated in that capacity for a week in the course of the academic year. In my second year, I enjoyed the unique privilege of exemption. On my first appearance in a surplice provided free by the College, I read the wrong passage and received a well-earned rebuke from the Dean, a rubicund and genial Friar Tuck with meagre aspirations to scholarly fame or theological subtlety. Before my next appearance, I rehearsed what I deemed to be the prescribed segment of Holy Writ. When I reached the Chapel door, the Head Porter was there to tell me that the Dean had left the lectern Bible open at the appropriate place with a note to indicate the first and last verses of the lesson. I mounted the pulpit and what confronted me was not the slice I had rehearsed. Rashly self-confident, I turned over the pages till I reached what I deemed to be the appropriate passage. It was in the Apocalypse. Halfway through it, I came to the words "woe, woe, woe to the inhabitants of the earth." As my eye caught them, I suddenly realised that I was a month out in my consultation of the Church calendar. In my alarm I uttered the words "woe, woe, woe" in quick succession more like a cab driver than a lay reader. The Dean took the view that I was a hopeless case, and I never had to read the prescribed lesson again.

Attendance at Chapel did not make me a convert to the Anglican faith, and it took me little time to off-load my membership in the Wesleyan Methodist Communion. What catalysed the decision merits a few words of local colour. For the prosperous mill owners of the Methodist northern counties, there was then a boarding school aspiring to, or already registered as, of 'public' school status. The *Leys* was comparatively near the College centre. Its obese and singularly repulsive headmaster, a minister exempt from the triennial itinerary of a Methodist circuit, was *ex officio* father-in-god to undergraduates who clung to the faith of their Wesleyan fathers. At my mother's request, our local Methodist minister gave me a letter of introduction. He received me in the manner of headmasters about to administer chastisement and asked me what had been my school. This time I told the truth. He then pressed me for details of my financial support. When told that the London County Council had given me a maintenance grant to supplement my scholarship, his comment was "Ah, the London County Council are very generous to the poor these days."

Thenceforth, I ceased to attend a Methodist church, but did not abandon Sunday attendance at a place of worship. A New Zealand friend introduced me to a quaint Quaker survival called an Adult School, superintended by Leonard Doncaster. I already knew of the Quakers as a denomination which had taken part in the emancipation of the slaves, that they regarded military service as contrary to the profession of a Christian and that they proclaimed no dogma to which a modernist could not subscribe. This was how I came to attend the Meeting House of the Society of Friends. Among its local members were the physiologist Joseph Barcroft and the astronomer Arthur Eddington. By the end of my first year I had decided to become a member. As Voltaire conceded, it is the least pernicious variety of the Christian religion to profess if one feels the need for it.

Despite all the minor injuries sustained by my *amour propre* adjusting to a milieu so alien to my boyhood, life at Cambridge had abundant compensations. Membership in the Fabian Society was one. Laboratory work was pre-eminently so. Plant ecology was then asserting its claims in the Cambridge School of Botany, and there was enjoyable scope for field work on free afternoons in late Spring as well as Summer Term. I could roam the countryside with a friend as far afield as the fringe of the Fen country in search of unfamiliar species. Otherwise in warm weather two or three of us, for less than a shilling apiece, could take out a punt from a landing place where the river flowed through the Backs between the grounds of Trinity and those of Clare. On such occasions my notebook accompanied me. I did not waste time in transcendental meditation.

Undoubtedly the site of the happiest recollections of my freshman year was Plymouth, with which I retained an agreeable association off and on for forty years. Flanked by the citadel and by the stone pillar commemorating the legend of Drake and his bowls on the Hoe stands the Marine Biological Laboratory with front windows facing what will always be for me the most picturesque bay in Britain. The wooded headland on one side is Cornish, that of the other, Devon. In the middle lies Drake Island. The Hoe is well above the level of the town so that on a clear day one can see Dartmoor in the distance. The coast below the site had an exceptionally rich rock pool fauna. The laboratory had a trawler which dredged daily for marine specimens beyond the sound. Its public aquarium was a minor tourist attraction.

Even before the first world war, the staff laid on an intensive Easter vacation course in marine zoology for undergraduates from

English universities. This gave one opportunities for studying embryonic development with which an inland university could not hope to compete. The fee for the course was nominal and my keep cost me nothing. The parents of a medical student with whom I had made friends before I left school lived in Plymouth where his father, a Plymouth Brother, had a medical practice. His wife had once been a camp follower of my father in his capacity as pastor-proprietor of the Welcome Mission. She now decided to be a second mother to me, and remained so until her death in the thirties. Their family lived within easy walking distance of the Hoe. The doctor had a former R.A.M.C. orderly who acted both as his driver and dispenser. His clientele extended well into the moor on the Ivybridge side, and for late night visits far afield he welcomed my company.

I returned by invitation during the first fortnight of the summer vacation of 1914. This visit was chiefly memorable because I had my first taste of early Bronze Age remains, the hut circles and the row of tall Menhirs at Drizzlecombe on the side of Dartmoor nearest Plymouth. To reach it, my friend and I followed a route through the deep glen of the Plym below Sheep's Tor. There is a place where the river tumbles steeply over the mouth of a cave concealed by a sheet of foam. At times in later life when I revisited Plymouth in warm weather, I used to take a dip in the pool below and climb into the cave mouth behind its water window. It was well worth the thirty miles on foot.

On the same visit, I went by car with the family for a few days to Dawlish on the south coast of Devon. It was my first introduction to ragtime by way of a Pierrot concert on the beach. The singer evoked barrel organ memories of the Boer War when she came shrilly to the lines from "Alexander's Ragtime Band":

> They can play a bugle call
> Like you never heard before
> So natural that you want to go to war.

There was something sinister in the way the crowd joined in the repeat. Prospect of war with Germany was already threatening. At Cambridge in undergraduate circles that year, and doubtless elsewhere, there had been much argument about a book by Norman Angell, *The Great Illusion,* 1910. He advanced two propositions. One was that none of the great powers could materially benefit from a conflict involving any pair of them as opponents. The other was that no responsible British or German statesman would therefore be party to declaration of a war from which neither country could hope to profit. Gullible liberals proclaimed the book a masterpiece. Tories attacked it as a trick to justify lack of preparedness for a war which many believed to be both inevitable and imminent. I shared their misgivings about its imminence.

My early boyhood in Britain's premier port and dockyard of Portsmouth had left me with no illusions about the nation's imperial status or pacific intentions when her colonial possessions were at stake. In no small measure, socialism initially enlisted my allegiance because its advocates asserted hopefully that the unity of the international working class movement was a bulwark against militarism. Contact with Indian students at Cambridge had intensified my hostility to colonialism. To that extent, I was more at ease with my Quaker contemporaries than with the Fabian set who were, with few exceptions, indifferent to international affairs. The disclosure by E. D. Morel of the power politics behind the Moroccan crisis of 1911 and the exposure by H. N. Brailsford of political intrigue to gain concessions in undeveloped territories, *War of Steel and Gold*, 1914, did not ruffle the complacency of the Webbs. They seemed to regard the first world war, like the Boer War before it, as a tiresome intrusion of amateurs into the domain of politics.

An event in my first year puts the spotlight on the parochialism which so long kept H. N. Brailsford aloof from middle-class socialism. In the Summer Term of 1914, a posse of white South African labour leaders from the Rand visited Cambridge as the guests of the Fabian Society to tout for their strike fund. One meeting ended in community singing of the Red Flag. No one cared enough for the causes or consequences of the Boer War to ask about the *casus belli*. The aim of the strikers was in fact to exclude Bantus from the right to do skilled work. When I resided years later in South Africa, white labour was still in the vanguard of the movement for apartheid.

My summer fortnight in Plymouth and Dawlish ended a few days before the Archduke Francis Ferdinand met his death in Serbia. Less than six weeks were to elapse before Britain declared war on Germany at midnight on August the fourth. That so few people in Britain realised during the first week of July how close was the ensuing conflagration is explicable only if one recalls what the Liberal government then had on its hands. The tactics of the movement for women's suffrage, W.S.P.U., would alone have sufficed to keep Central Europe off the front page, but Asquith had also to face the greater menace of armed insurrection in Ulster. In the spring of the same year, the Curragh mutiny had led to the resignation of the Secretary for War. Such was the gravity of the threat that the Prime Minister himself had taken over the portfolio for War. At the end of April, Carson's volunteers were armed with 50,000 rifles dispatched from a German port. In a last attempt to find a formula for peace after the Lords had mutilated a Bill for Irish Home Rule, a conference summoned by the Crown met at Buckingham Palace in mid-July. It was inconclusive and disbanded by July 24th. Troops in readiness to embark for Ireland were instead dispatched a fortnight later to Flanders.

A few weeks after my return from Devon, Germany and Russia were at war. I was in France at the time. Somehow or other, my father had decided to make a trip to friends of his business days in Calais. For reasons incomprehensible to me, he took with him my brother Hamilton and myself. We bedded in a dingy, shuttered apartment with an odour of confined cats, and fed at what one would now call a transport café. There we could get vegetable soup, an omelette *aux fines herbes,* rolls and butter with aromatic black coffee for a franc, ten pence, apiece. On the third day of our visit, there was a general mobilisation and an exodus of foreigners. We made our way to the docks in streets thronged with men responding to the call-up. When we arrived in London just before midnight of August 4th, traffic converging on the Houses of Parliament from the Embankment, from the Mall, from Trafalgar Square and from Victoria, the terminus of our boat train, was at a standstill. Thousands of cheering dervishes, waiting for public announcement that Britain was at war, executed a dance of death.

Within the next few weeks, hysteria swept the country. Crowds wrecked the premises of shopkeepers who had German names, not a few of them Jewish refugees from the ghettoes of the Austrian empire. Few outside the corridors of power could have previously known about Britain's commitment to Belgium or would have cared much about its implications if they had. People without the haziest notion of where its frontiers lay worked themselves into a frenzy of indignation about the martyrdom of Britain's gallant little protégée. Nonconformist pulpits, no less than those of the Established Church, thundered with imprecations to enlist youth in a crusade which was to prove the most senseless slaughter in the history of Europe. *Deutschland über Alles* was cited as German intention to world domination by people who had a few weeks earlier on Empire Day been singing lustily *Land of Hope and Glory* with the plea "wider still and wider may thy bounds be set."

The first world war was even more senseless, if less horrific, than the Thirty Years War, in which issues of principle did indeed divide the participants. No issue of principle was at stake here. Those who kept up the pretence that so sordid a sequel to imperialist rivalries was a crusade against Prussian militarism would not have indulged in such a fantasy if they had been able to foresee that the so-called war to end war was the prelude to the end of capitalism in Eastern Europe and to the collapse of social democracy in Germany. It is more than a mere tautology to say that there could have been no World War II without World War I.

One of the manifestations of the war psychosis reinforced my disposition to discard the miraculous in the gospel record. Rumour of entirely fictitious signs and wonders spread throughout the country with great rapidity. For weeks after the retreat from Mons, there was a story that Russian troops had landed in Britain en route for the Western Front. In the length and breadth of the land, there can have been few families without someone willing to attest their transport, and a formidable crowd of witnesses, including my mother's solicitor, claimed to have seen the snow on their boots.

Though John Morley and the cloth-cap cabinet minister John Burns resigned their posts in silent protest shortly after the war began and before the introduction of conscription in 1916, scarcely half a dozen persons in public life dared to raise a voice against the grim folly of it all. Marxists who had most loudly proclaimed that the international solidarity of the working class could defeat the machinations of the warmongers were among the rowdiest in their profession of patriotism, and the London headquarters of the Fabian Society came to a standstill. Women who had walked in procession, picketed Parliament and chained themselves to its railings to demand the vote two months earlier were distributing white feathers to civilian males and lining up for the more or less menial forms of service deemed suitable for the alternative sex. What had seemed till lately a united front of socialists, feminists and pacifists with an assumed common denominator of human values proved itself to have had no internal unity other than that afforded by an ephemeral antagonism to the establishment.

Looking back half a century later, I realise how slowly I sorted out the intellectual consequences of any disillusionment to which my private assortment of ethical principles and modernist theology succumbed. Till the year before the next war, when I addressed an International Congress of Free Thought on the contemporary challenge, I had often been puzzled by the number of inconsistent views which men such as H. G. Wells and, of my own age group, Julian Huxley could accommodate without mental discomfort. By that time, and probably because of the somersaults which brought intellectuals with widely different political philosophies into the same camp in opposition to Nazism, I had begun to realise why nineteenth-century Rationalism could shelter under the same umbrella so odd an assemblage of unrelated or inconsistent propositions. When possible, those who profess minority creeds unite forces against traditional authority. It then seems to be a psychotherapeutic necessity for those who do so to delude themselves that they share a unique substratum of positive aspirations.

At the time World War I began, the membership of the Fabian Society in London and the provinces afforded a comic illustration of this thesis. Ostensibly for the promotion of socialism by peaceful persuasion, it attracted anti-vaccinationists, vegetarians, anti-vivisectionists, dress reform and Morris dancing enthusiasts, advocates of cremation and of the abolition of corporal punishment in the schools.

In the universities, what Henry Nevinson once referred to as 'the stage army of the good' was less in evidence, but Cambridge had a hard core of vegetarians seemingly for no better reason than that Bernard Shaw had set the fashion. During the eight weeks after the outbreak of war, I had little time for such reflections as the foregoing, and if time had been available I was far too immature to entertain them.

At the end of my first year, I had decided to sit as an external candidate in the coming October for the B.Sc. of London University. This decision turned out later to have been shrewd. The Ph.D. degree did not come into the picture till well after the end of the war, and the lower degree made me eligible to proceed directly to the D.Sc. when conditions were favourable. I buried myself in my books during August and September. That I was not yet nineteen years of age when I became a London graduate was good for my morale when my hopes for a scientific career were waning.

CHAPTER VI

Marking Time

THE main difference between Cambridge in October 1914 and Cambridge in October 1913 was the rush to join the Officers' Training Corps. Members were exempt, if in khaki, from use of cap and gown in public, at lectures and in Hall. The O.T.C. commandeered football fields and cricket pitches of the colleges for military drill. Man-sized sacks of soil suspended from improvised scaffolding gave undergraduates opportunity to gain skill in driving a bayonet into the human abdomen. At the beginning of term, the only conspicuous absentees were O.T.C. personnel of the previous term. There was no premonition of food shortage.

During my second year, I had rooms successively in the Billiard Table and in the Spittoon as we then called two of the three enclosures of Whewell's Court. Even though I worked successfully to become a Senior Scholar at the March examination, I took a very active part in the Fabian Society. I read during the first term a paper on a socialist medical policy based on the Webbs' book *The State and Medicine*. I also participated in a study circle of eight or nine undergraduates led by a liberal Trinity theologian with a London science degree. Its topic was the Existence of God.

At each session we examined one of the stock arguments for the defence—ontological, teleological and so forth. The outcome of the exercise did less to strengthen our faith in the deity than in the broad-mindedness of divinity dons. Our instructor was at pains to emphasise candidly that no single argument is conclusive. In the manner of a judge instructing a jury concerning the credibility of circumstantial evidence, he left us to derive what comfort we could from the possibility that six merely plausible independent propositions might collectively sustain a semantically obscure assertion. At the time, I was willing to suspend judgment. By joining the Society of Friends I had renounced any intention of becoming a Methodist missionary. I therefore regarded metaphysical issues as of less topical interest than ethical ones, especially while there was a war on.

For the first time in my life, I was happy in the enjoyment of friendship with contemporaries who shared my own outlook. Two newcomers in Trinity, both exhibitioners reading modern history, were from county secondary schools and both were Fabians. The father of one was a co-founder with Keir Hardie of the Independent Labour Party, the only influential body other than the Society of Friends opposed to the war from the start. Few guest speakers were available, and we held many meetings of the University Fabian Society in our two-room suites in College. Though members of Newnham and Girton could still come only if accompanied by chaperone, there was more fraternisation between male and female students than the year before.

My academic work did not suffer. While preparing during summer vacation for the London degree examination, I had happily bettered my technique of self-education and had freed myself of a bad habit which might have crippled my academic career. In those days, the larger colleges had chess clubs. It was possible for one to gain a quarter blue if selected to play chess for the University. In Trinity, nearly all members of the club were mathematical scholars or exhibitioners. While I and others were at work in the laboratory, they had ample time free for matches among themselves or book work on chess problems. All that I can now recall of the activities of the club is that Trinity men favoured the Muzzio gambit, then alleged to guarantee a win to white if one performed the first twelve or so moves correctly. Some club members spent several hours a day working out every possible variant. I have been told that experts have since shown that white is actually bound to lose. By that time I had long since lost interest. When I sat the May examination, a Freshman tryout for the Tripos which would come at the end of the following year, I obtained a good first, but not a first which the College authorities regarded as good enough for a Trinity Scholar. Their view was that I should have been first or second on the list in at least two subjects. Probably I would have been if I had not gone to sleep most nights with a chessboard at the bedside.

The results of the Tripos in 1915 fulfilled their expectations. There were two University prizes for first places in biology: the Frank Smart Prizes for Botany and for Zoology. I had hoped to get the former but came second on the list. Happily, I gained the Frank Smart

Prize for Zoology. I received the news from one of the College porters on the day I was due to go down. Since it was customary to reward the bringer of good tidings with a coin, I parted with the only one in my pocket. In the excitement of the moment, I assumed that it was a sixpence. It was not. At that date gold coins were still in circulation and I had given a half-sovereign. After disposing of unpaid bills, I had only a few pence for the journey to London so I walked fifty miles with my few possessions in a grip on a sunny June day.

I had already decided on my next course of action. In those days Part I of the Natural Science Tripos sufficed for graduation, the second part being comparable to the M.Sc. degree of a provincial university. Since the University treated war work in any capacity as grounds for exemption from residence, I had little to lose if I threw in my lot with one or other of the two Quaker organisations for noncombatant service in France or Belgium. One of these, the War Victims contingent, worked under the wing of the *Service de Santé Militaire,* the French equivalent of the R.A.M.C. in the battle-scarred villages of the Marne. Its job was to build wooden bungalows for families left homeless after the retreat of the Germans from their most advanced alignment in the fall of the previous year. The other organisation, which worked under the R.A.M.C. itself, was the Friends' Ambulance Unit. Its members manned a train which brought in wounded from Poperinghe on the Belgian front to a hospital in Dunkirk. The leader of the War Vics was T. E. Harvey, a scholarly Liberal M.P., that of the F.A.U. Philip Noel Baker, who became prominent in the Labour Party during the years between the two wars.

Recruiting mania intensified as the prospect of an early end to hostilities receded. It was evident that there would be only a skeleton staff and a few male students in Cambridge in the academic year of 1915–16. With no prevision of conscription at a later date, I had volunteered for service on the Marne at the end of my second Summer Term. Little more than a month elapsed before I had my kit, uniform and instructions to proceed to the War Victims Relief Headquarters in the Marne sector. In the interval, I took a job as a teacher in an East End elementary school.

Based on what remained of Epernay, Chalons, Bar le Duc and Vitry le François, each of the local units of the War Vics then consisted of fewer than a dozen members, including a lorry driver and a leader with some knowledge of the requisite skills. Otherwise none of us was a specialist. We worked putting together the framework of the housing, laying the floor with boards we ourselves had to plane and to groove, inserting window frames, fitting the glass and placing the tiles on the roof. I have always derived satisfaction from the acquisition of constructive manual skills, for which biological research offered plenty of scope in later years. Work in the summer and early fall was therefore congenial, and the one day of rest set apart for Quaker Meeting also offered opportunities for walks among the nearby vineyards or in the Forêt de Trois Fontaines. Our mealtime menu was simple but edible: for lunch fresh Camembert cheese, rolls and a glass of *vin rouge* which then cost twopence.

A small allowance of pocket money, five shillings a week if my memory does not deceive me, was adequate for my few needs. I had not started to smoke and an occasional glass of local *vin blanc* for less than sixpence was my only extravagance other than paperback novels by George Sand, Balzac, Victor Hugo, de Maupassant and Anatole France to while away the evenings in our home-made hut. My companions were not intellectually stimulating, and my sole profitable mental acquisition was a copious reading vocabulary of French. Working in another unit in the same sector were David Garnett and his friend Francis Birrell, son of a Liberal Cabinet Minister. Garnett was somewhat older than myself. He had graduated as a botanist at the Imperial College of Science, and I suspect that the author of *Lady into Fox,* 1922, and *A Man in the Zoo,* 1924, had not as yet relinquished an aspiration to biological research. As the son of the Heinemann translators of Russian novelists, he was at home in literary circles and was by far the most sophisticated member of the whole outfit.

Had I been in the same local team, I might well have remained in the Marne. I have no clear recollection of why I decided to transfer to the Friends' Ambulance Unit in the late autumn of 1915. Nominally, I was a registered medical student, though with little prospect of financial backing to complete the course. I may have hoped to gain some experience of the inside of a hospital with a view to clinical studies if opportunity later came my way. As a medical orderly in the Dunkirk military hospital, my most absorbing activity was emptying and cleaning bedpans, but I sometimes stood in as an anaesthetist. In that capacity, I had the good fortune to be a spectator at a brain operation, then somewhat of a novelty.

Modern anaesthesia may be a soothing experience with no need to fear unpleasant effects on awakening. In my Dunkirk days, the procedure was almost as barbarous as the production of local numbness by a ligature when the ship's surgeon amputated Nelson's arm. Four beefy corporals held down the writhing victim while the anaesthetist clamped a mask with cotton wool over his face and poured ether on it till he relinquished an unequal struggle.

Before Christmas I was on night duty for a month and had to make myself competent in the craft of synthesizing fish rissoles from potatoes and tinned salmon for the midnight meal of the nursing staff. Otherwise I had more time for reading French fiction and composing excruciatingly bad verse to the accompaniment of sirens from the monitors inside the three-mile limit. Only the administration and medical orderlies were then members of the Society of Friends. The nursing staff, two or three surgeons and a dentist were paid by the army authorities or by the British Red Cross. During the first year of the war there were no army psychiatrists, but a mounting toll of shell shock was beginning to create in medical circles curiosity about the views of continental writers on mental disorder.

Most people in Britain assumed that the voluntary system of recruitment to the armed forces was an inviolable principle of our own brand of democracy. By the autumn, the press disclosed hints of pressure on the British government from the French High Command for a greater contribution of available man power than the recruiting drive could ensure. Before the year 1916 began, it was a foregone conclusion that parliament would capitulate to French demands for what was then called equality of sacrifice. Those of us enrolled in the noncombatant service in France and Belgium were not vulnerable. Nevertheless letters from home made us aware of a growing, if still numerically small, movement to demand an end to the carnage, to curtail restrictions on political discussion under the Defence of the Realm Act and to resist conscription by all peaceful means.

As noncombatants in opposition to the war, several of us at Dunkirk were acutely unhappy at the prospect of whatever penalties our friends might incur as objectors. Among the hospital orderlies, I had two friends to whom, as to me, the need for decision on a course of action became more and more compelling. Of these, one was the son of George Gissing, the author of *New Grub Street*, 1891, *The Odd Women*, 1893, and *The Private Papers of Henry*

Ryecroft, 1903. He had possibly joined the F.A.U. less from strong convictions than because Gissing père had attended a Quaker boarding school. The name of the other was Priestley. His sentiments, like my own, favoured an immediate negotiated peace, and all three of us felt that one should now either enlist in the army or engage actively in opposition to the continuance of the war. Before the first week of 1916, each of us had made up his own mind: Gissing to apply for a commission, Priestley and I to rejoin our pacifist friends in Britain who were liable to call-up.

Still a Scholar of Trinity, I went again into residence in the Spring Term of 1916 and registered for the second M.B. in human anatomy. Being exempt from further examination in Physiology by virtue of my tripos, I had many free periods at my disposal in the daytime. I was therefore glad when Joseph Barcroft, at that time working on gas poisoning with a view to remedial treatment, enlisted me as his research assistant. At the end of the Summer Term of 1915, the University Fabian Society had elected me one of its Secretaries, an assignment I now resumed with enthusiasm and a newly acquired self-confidence.

Disagreement about the war had driven a deep wedge of disillusion into the Fabian Society as a national movement. In Oxford, G. D. H. Cole led his own schism, guild socialism. This was a cross-breed of syndicalism and collectivism, anathema to the Webbs and in opposition to the official line of the Independent Labour Party as laid down by Ramsay MacDonald and Philip Snowden. Soon after my return from Dunkirk I met Cole, whom we had invited to address the Cambridge branch of the Fabian Society. Shortly after, and at my instigation, it changed its name to the University Socialist Society. Cole's visit forged a close link between us and our Oxford counterpart. Together we met at Oxford, then at Cambridge during the Lent and Summer Terms of 1916.

Among our Oxford contemporaries, I recall Gordon Childe, who was to be a lifelong friend and academically eminent as Professor of Archeology at Edinburgh; R. P. Dutt, who later became editor of the Communist *Labour Monthly;* and Raymond Postgate, who much later changed course and promoted a *Good Food Guide*. Among my friends in the Cambridge Society were three women: Enid Charles, whom I later married; the Fabian Co-Secretary Helen Wedgwood, a direct descendant of the great Master Potter; and Dorothy Edwards, who later married Lord Archibald, the Labour peer.

Clements, the only brother of R. P. Dutt, had a brilliant record at Cambridge as a biologist. He was a year my senior and we were intimate friends. Their only sister, older than both, had a creditable record as a Cambridge graduate and was a lady of great charm. After the war she joined the staff of the League of Nations International Labour Office. They were a remarkable family. The mother was a Swede who attended the meetings of the University Fabian Society and its successor. The father, an Indian, practised medicine in Cambridge. When I first met R. P. Dutt, he seemed to me to be somewhat isolated, doubtless because he alone was alert to the evils of colonialism and its relevance to the struggle between the imperialist powers. If his impact on British political life has been negligible, no one of my vintage has exerted a comparable influence on the leaders of now independent ex-colonial territories. He would have been more at home in Cambridge. Oxford socialists of his entourage were intensely conventional about everything other than a belief in peaceful revolution by the general strike, a delusion to be rudely shattered in 1926.

If the socialism of G. D. H. Cole, who towered above the rest of us as a don and as a writer, embraced territories other than England's green and pleasant land, it was a paradise for white males only, in which the status of women and the claims of 'coloured folk' were irrelevant distractions. I retain for Cole, and for his wife, Margaret, the respect due to those who cherish the opportunity to enlighten men's minds more dearly than the power to dictate their actions. Cole himself deserved a better epitaph than the contribution of his teaching to the composition of subsequent Labour Cabinets. These disciples were a dreamy circus, smugly self-seeking complacent careerists such as Hugh Gaitskell, devoid of Cole's unaffected idealism and of his integrity.

Among my Cambridge intimates, none of us had any aspirations to political celebrity. We were unashamedly eclectic. We regarded socialism as merely one facet of a wider programme of human betterment. We could at least face the possibility that the majority of folk could enjoy a standard of life comparable with our own only if technology could guarantee a level of productivity much higher and a rate of population growth much less than that of our own generation. Insofar as we denounced the war, we denounced it as the offspring of imperialist intrigues for the exploitation of colonial territories. Most of us were agnostics even if, as was true myself, we had not as yet relinquished all connection with a religious denomination. To all of us the movement for women's rights and the spread of contraceptive practice were relevant to our socialist creed.

That several of us fraternised with the University Indian society (Majlis) was symptomatic of our conviction that the movement for colonial freedom was as important as any issue on the home front. It was at one of its meetings that I first met Lowes "Goldie" Dickinson, who delivered an address on the differences between Western and Eastern ways of thinking. Its title was "The Religion of Time and the Religion of Eternity." I can understand the affection he inspired in undergraduates, but he failed to impress me as an expert in the Western way. He lived in a dream world of kindly sentiments unruffled by the impact of scientific discovery on a disintegrating society and unable to assess its relevance to the possibility of planning for plenty on a global scale. To be sure, his sceptical attitude to the credentials of Christian dogma may have stimulated freshmen fearful of estrangement from a pietistic family setup, but he had nothing new to offer the Fabian nursery of my own set.

No personality in Cambridge dominated the political scene as did Cole in Oxford. At my invitation, Bertrand Russell delivered as lectures to the Socialist Society several of the essays later published in *Principles of Social Reconstruction,* 1916. He exerted an influence over its members more because of his outspoken hostility to the war than because he had any close affiliation with the Labour movement of the time. Greater than that of Russell was the influence exerted on us by C. K. Ogden, then a don of Magdalene, editor of the *Cambridge Magazine* and founder of the University society known as the *Heretics.* To the undergraduate, the latter offered a package deal of sex reform, rationalism and pacifism.

Ogden was passionately internationalist and made an impact on public opinion far beyond the University. Early in the war, the *Cambridge Magazine* started a regular feature of comments on the hostilities from the European press. It was salutary because the British press had cast the Kaiser in the role of Attila and neutral powers as spectators of a gladiatorial show, loudly cheering the plucky Christians facing a phalanx of famished lions. As exhibited in the *Cambridge Magazine,* the approval of Swedes, Danes and Dutchmen was less enthusiastic. This project, which won him international prestige, was not Ogden's sole contribution. His *Cambridge Magazine*

Bookshop was one of the few vehicles for distribution of the writings of E. D. Morel and others on the secret military entanglements which followed the Agadir incident in Morocco in 1911.

Under the pseudonym Adelyne Moore, add-a-line-more, as from the Bookshop on King's Parade, Ogden himself published two pamphlets with the titles respectively of *Feminism and Militarism* and *Fecundity and Civilisation*. The aim of the first was to show that the glorification of soldiery is inconsistent with equality of opportunity for women, a conclusion not wholly sustained by the active role which women were beginning to perform in the conduct of the war. The main contention of the second had more substance and was more novel. The writer claimed that militarism rather than religious superstition is the main obstacle to contraceptive practice. Possibly he got away with this line of talk because prevailing opinion identified militarism with the Kaiser and patriotism with Lord Kitchener.

The Heretics, which met weekly on Sunday evenings, was not merely a forum for modern doubt or for a sceptical appraisal of the ethical credentials of the Anglo-French War Lords. It also provided a platform for the discussion of the need for birth control, a theme hitherto shunned in university circles. More boldly still, the Society invited a new look at prohibited variants of sexual experience. That the University authorities did not interfere when one member read a paper making a plea for the regularisation of the legal status of adult consenting homosexuals is not of itself remarkable. More than a few celibate dons had good reason to sympathise with a view which some of them may well have had in mind when rhapsodising about the Greek way of life. A contingent of Newnham and Girton Students present on the same occasion, with attendant lady dons to chaperone them, continued to attend subsequent meetings with their academic duennas.

Among the Heretics I formed several friendships, warm but not erotic. One was with Frank Winton who collaborated with me in scientific research during the early twenties. He was then in the Freudian avant-garde. Later he became Professor of Pharmacology at University College, London, and Dean of its Medical Faculty. Through the Heretics, I also became friendly with E. J. Dingwall, then assistant librarian in the University library, and subsequently the author of two slim monographs—one on the mediaeval chastity girdle, the other on the practice of male infibulation among preliterate people. Dingwall was then planning an encyclopaedic work on prostitution in Europe. Whether he ever finished it I do not know. His contribution to my sophistication was to introduce me to the writings of Havelock Ellis, Kraft-Ebbing, Ivan Block and Forel on the varieties of human sexual enjoyment.

Despite my primly puritan upbringing and strong disapproval of males who abdicate parental responsibility, my introduction to such writers evoked no distaste. I still regard reproduction as an undertaking with imperative ethical obligations but have never regarded reciprocally satisfying sterile physical relations between consenting adults as a proper topic for moral censure.

By the time World War I ended, Freud's polymorph perverse thesis had reinstated original sin with headquarters in Bloomsbury. The revelations of a new messiah had invested with Christo-Judaic guilt any recipe for sexual gratification not sanctioned by the cultural group from which he drew his patients. Harley Street quacks with a minimal qualification, or without one, could guarantee the penitent full assurance of salvation after a two-year course of weekly sessions at five guineas a time. Meanwhile, the poorest Irish peasant could get absolution from the Catholic confessional.

CHAPTER VII

Shades of the Prison House

WHEN a war is in progress, one lives from day to day in a miasma of uncertainty. My award of the Frank Smart prize had momentarily reinforced my hope of becoming a biologist, but the introduction of compulsory military service early in 1916 extinguished it. A rational prospect of completing the course in human anatomy was inconsistent with my reason for returning to Britain. I found it increasingly irksome to concentrate on preparation for an examination I could sit only if I abandoned my resolve. When the summer term began, conscription was a *fait accompli,* and the execution of the leaders of the Irish rebellion of Easter Week had stiffened the determination of the minority opposed to the war.

The Act which introduced for the first time in Britain compulsory military service created a category of exemption on grounds of conscience with *ad hoc* tribunals to validate the credentials of conscientious objectors. There was no comparable provision in military service legislation of European countries.

The insertion of the conscience clause in the Conscription Act of 1916 may have been influenced by events which occurred early in the first decade of the century. There had been a hard core of nonconformist opposition to the South African War. Lloyd George was in the forefront when he had to escape disguised as a policeman from a howling mob in the Birmingham Town Hall. This incident in 1900 immediately preceded a mass nonconformist movement of civil disobedience prompted by tax provision for state subsidies to church schools in the Education Act of 1902. Not a few of these so-called passive resisters, who risked a prison sentence and had their goods attached, were men of substance who contributed in more ways than one to the Liberal landslide of 1906. Rhetorically, though not actively, Lloyd George himself had been in sympathy with them.

Such was the background to a situation in which a Liberal parliamentary majority, dependent on nonconformist goodwill, introduced a measure which would have been anathema to a Liberal administration in the days of John Bright and of Campbell Bannerman. Doubtless, the conscience clause softened Liberal opposition to conscription, but the introduction of compulsory military service also encouraged more vocal opposition to the war. The Independent Labour Party was not the only focus of opposition. Also with their support, but more oblique in its tactics, the Union of Democratic Control mobilised the sympathy of Liberals who favoured peace by negotiation. Their campaign against secret diplomacy basked in the editorial approval of the *Manchester Guardian* and of a now defunct Liberal weekly, *The Nation*.

The introduction of the bill to make military service obligatory brought into being the No-Conscription Fellowship, N.C.F., under the leadership of Clifford Allen, former Cambridge Fabian, and Fenner Brockway who became a socialist Life Peer in 1964. Though a member for no better reason than that all my friends were, I disliked the designation. To me, the conscription issue was quite secondary. What was important was an end to so futile a slaughter of people who had no intelligible reason for hating or even fearing their opponents. However, I did not disapprove of the decision of the N.C.F. leaders to urge its members to appear before the tribunals to state their case. It gave them a pulpit for anti-war propaganda which censorship did not exclude from the daily press.

In providing the tribunals, the government seemed to have assumed that only an insignificant number of religious cranks would refuse to serve and that those denied exemption would fall into line when the call-up came. Seemingly, it was not anticipated what penalties would have to be imposed if objectors remained recalcitrant. France, like Germany, treated their objectors as deserters, and deserters automatically faced the firing squad. Such indeed was the sentence of the court martial on the first few conscientious objectors arrested after failure to respond to their induction notices. Priestley was among those sentenced, a possibility both of us had envisaged when we returned from Dunkirk. The announcement of their sentences in the press evoked a sensational response from leading ministers of the Free Churches, so much so that the government, with an eye on the nonconformist vote, overruled the implementation of their sentences. Henceforth, the initial charge was failure to obey a military order. For this the penalty was three months hard labour, followed by a two-year sentence for repetition of the offence. Faced with the prospect of insufficient prison accommodation, the authorities offered each prisoner work as a navvy, housed in roadside camps for the duration of the war.

When the local tribunal in Cambridge settled down to their task in the Summer Term of 1916, my legal position was that I was automatically exempt as a registered medical student or as a member of the Society of Friends if I pleaded as one or the other. Furthermore, Barcroft was anxious to secure for me exemption as his research assistant, and he could easily have done so. Had I taken advantage of any one of these possibilities, my course of action would have been inconsistent with the decision that Priestley and I had made. Propinquity had now given me an additional motive for standing by my friends who had no back door. The Cambridge and Oxford tribunals turned down every application from students not willing to undertake some form of noncombatant service for the war effort, including my own.

My call-up did not come till the end of the summer. Thus I had completed the statutory period of residence and graduated in June 1916. When I went down, T. Edmund Harvey, whom I had got to know in the Marne, had resumed his duties as a Liberal member of parliament. He offered me a temporary job as his private secretary, a post in those days reserved for men only. The use of typewriters to answer letters of complaint from constituents was not then *de rigueur*, and my handwriting was equal to the task.

This episode is memorable to myself because I frequently spent question time in the privileged position below the strangers' gallery, for private secretaries and personal friends of members. Tail coats and top hats were still fashionable on the floor of the House. First prize for fox-hunting fancy dress was deserved by Walter Long, who inspired Chesterton's *Lines to a Statesman:* " . . . then silence fell, and Mr. Long was born."

I also recall the polished prolixity of Asquith, still at that date prime minister. His performances from the Front Bench were a model for the chairman of an open-air gathering entrusted with the task of collecting a crowd without unduly anticipating the rhetoric of the principal speaker. As such, they were easy to parody: "We are facing as a great nation *(pause)* and a great empire *(pause)* a formidable challenge *(pause)* not merely to the security of these islands *(pause)*, not merely to that of the continent of Europe *(pause)*, but also to the security of Western civilisation *(pause)*, a challenge indeed to men and women of good will on all five continents of our world *(longer pause)* and gentlemen *(pause)* faced with such a challenge, *(pause)* a challenge which I repeat *(pause)* is a menace not merely to our own survival *(pause)* but to . . . *(here repeat the previous lines of the libretto)*."

It is difficult for me to write about my recollections of the summer and fall of 1916 light-heartedly. Of a period when so many of my contemporaries in rat-infested and rain-drenched dugouts were undergoing ear-splitting bombardment hourly for days on end, it would be indecent to record my own experience with self-pity. I was indeed far more fortunate than some of my friends who were called up before me. Fifty years after, the *Observer* published an article citing the relevant data. According to this source 5,739 men were court-martialled, of whom 71 died "either while undergoing punishment or immediately after hastily contrived release on medical grounds." My guess is that many more—as was true of two of my closest friends—died subsequently from tuberculosis contracted while in confinement. Among leaders of the opposition to conscription, not himself liable to call-up, Bertrand Russell served a jail sentence.[1]

Writing of objectors reprieved after sentence of death, the *Observer* stated:

> The Army devised its own means of bringing the rebels to heel. Legally the objectors were soldiers of the King. Soldiers could be posted overseas. Disobedience at the front was punishable by death at the hands of a firing-squad. So the War Office reached for its ultimate deterrent, and in its determination to make the deterrent credible clashed dramatically with the civil authorities. . . . In April, 1916, a squad of hard-core objectors were confined in irons at Landguard Fort, Harwich, built by French prisoners in the Napoleonic wars. They were kept in total darkness on bread and water after refusing all military orders. In the early hours of May 7th, while it was still dark, 17 men were released from their irons and packed into a Southampton-bound train with 300 men of the Eastern Non-Combatant Corps.

Informed by the parents of one of the seventeen, Gilbert Murray called on the Secretary for War, Lord Derby, who upheld the authority of the military command, and on Asquith who promised to write immediately "forbidding the executions without the knowledge of the Cabinet." On May 15, Sir Phillip Morrell, a Liberal M.P., raised the issue in the House of Commons. Again from the *Observer:*

> Barely three weeks after the dispatch of the Harwich men the Army felt free to bring out its ultimate deterrent again. On May 28th, 16 objectors at Richmond, Yorkshire, were attached to a unit leaving for France. On May 29 eight men at Kinmel Park, Abergale, were sent to France via Southampton. And on May 30 a group of nine military prisoners at Seaford, Sussex, at least some of whom were conscientious objectors, were dispatched by the same route in handcuffs.... The first 17, those from Landguard Fort, arrived at Le Havre on May 8 and were immediately separated from the non-combatant soldiers with whom they had travelled. On arrival at camp they were told they were no longer prisoners but ordinary soldiers.... On the Afternoon of May 10 they paraded with their regiment. The order was given: "Right turn: Quick March!" The Company briskly marched off—but dotted on the parade ground were 17 objectors, standing rigidly in their original positions.

When news of this reached London early in June, Hubert Peet, a Quaker and a friend whom I remember with affection, and F. B. Meyer, the minister who had baptised me while I was at school, set out for France to investigate. A week later, according to the *Observer:*

> The first four were singled out for sentencing. They were marched to the parade ground, where several hundred men were assembled on three sides of the square. A chaplain intoned prayers. Then the adjutant read out the sentences: 'For disobedience while undergoing field punishment, sentenced to death by shooting.' A pause. 'Confirmed by General Sir Douglas Haig.' A longer, more deliberate pause. 'And commuted to 10 years' penal servitude.' Each of the men in turn, 34 altogether, received the same sentence, delivered in an identical manner.

Commutation of the death sentence did not immediately lead to the leniency which was the lot of those of us, like myself, called up much later in the same summer. The publicity which Field Punishment No. 1 received from its use to intimidate objectors led to its abolition from the penal code. One individual, cited by the *Observer,* describes his experience of it as follows:

> Each of us was placed with our backs to the framework, consisting of uprights at intervals of four or five yards, and cross-beams at a

height of about five feet from the ground. Our ankles were tied together and our arms then tied tightly at the wrists to the crossbeams; and we prepared to remain in this position for the next two hours.

The following evening we were placed with our faces to the barbed wire of the inner fence. As the ropes with which we were tied fastened round the barbed wire instead of the rural thick wooden post, it was possible to tie them much more tightly and I found myself drawn so closely to the fence that when I wished to turn my head I had to do so very cautiously to avoid my face being torn by the barbs.

Subsequently, I have sometimes been tempted to speculate about my own attitude had I faced, like Priestley, the immediate prospect of a firing squad. In reality, second thoughts would have been as fruitless as the recantation of Archbishop Cranmer. Having refused to obey the first military order after the call-up, one had no options. Events took their course regardless of any doubts about the usefulness of one's earlier decision.

In comparison with that of my associates called up before me, my own fate was a bed of roses. If I relate what I can remember of late August and September 1916, it is of some historic interest to students of penology because my experience of prison life was representative of that of any other convict. Neither the warders nor the chaplain displayed the slightest interest in why we happened to be their clients. My call-up followed the usual routine. The local police handed one over to a military escort after a brief interrogation by an army officer. The one who interrogated me was impeccably courteous, indeed charming. On arriving at a camp on Salisbury Plain, I joined three others in the guard room awaiting court-martial. One was an actor, one an official of Hyndman's British Socialist Party which, like the Fabian Society, was deeply split on the war issue. What unpleasant experiences of these few days I now recall were the common lot of every uncommissioned recruit, a crew-cut hairdo and the difficulty of getting any sleep when lying on the hard floor with only a blanket for bed clothes and a kitbag for pillow.

The court-martial was necessarily perfunctory, the sentence being read at a parade called for the purpose. On the way to Wormwood Scrubs we waited for about half an hour on the platform of Clapham Junction, crew-cut and manacled, to confront the curiosity of the crowd. At prison we parted with our normal wardrobe to put on the coarse serge costume of the convict. Apart from communal work in the laundry one morning a week and about twenty minutes' walk around the yard in single file for morning exercise in fine weather, we were almost continuously in solitary confinement with a daily allotted task of sewing pre-cut strips of canvas to make mail bags. When otherwise at large, one had nominally to observe a silence rule as rigorous as that for a novice in a Trappist monastery. Actually, we could communicate by whispers when the warder in charge was not looking towards us.

Prison hygiene, like that in the Army, had progressed little beyond what was prevalent in the Crimea of Florence Nightingale. For excretory use, each prisoner had a dual-purpose tin receptacle equipped with a lid which did little to curtail the stench incident to an almost exclusively carbohydrate diet. It remained in the cell till, at twenty-four-hour intervals, a warder lined us up each at the door of his cell to proceed to the wash house before we got down to the day's assignment of mail bag manufacture. Like our food utensils, a tin platter and tin mug, we had to keep this receptacle clean and bright by scouring it with a ration of brick dust.

One outcome of World War I, especially in Germany as a result of the naval blockade, was widespread malnutrition. Neither the Army nor the prison authorities were as yet cognisant of what food requirements are essential to the maintenance of human health. At about 6:30 A.M. we started our day by collecting a platter of coarse oatmeal gruel and a mug of water. At midday, we had a plate of potatoes boiled in their skins and a mug of soup in which there might be a few shreds of boiled mutton. At the end of the day's work, our reward was a hunk of bread to chew and a large mug of unsweetened cocoa without milk. The calories were at least adequate for a sedentary worker of my own weight. Seemingly the skin of the potatoes protected enough of the green layer immediately below it to supply sufficient ascorbic acid to prevent scurvy. Otherwise, as was true of many civilians, our victuals were grossly deficient in vitamins A, B and D.

For my part, the greatest privation was lack of books or writing materials other than a slate of the type then still used in primary schools and a broken slate pencil for which I had to wait a week. When my daily task was complete, I amused myself by testing my recollections of Euclidean geometry. On the one occasion when the prison chaplain called, the only response elicited by my request for something to read was a children's book in the Victorian ethical tradition, something like *Little Women*. I do not think that Oscar Wilde exaggerated the inanity of the prison chaplain then representative of his kind.

I did not remain in Wormwood Scrubs till completion of the initial sentence of three months. The No-Conscription Fellowship was at this time divided between those willing to work on the road gang and *absolutists* who refused the offer. Personally, I could see no greater moral obligation to make mail bags in a warm building than to use a pick and shovel in somewhat colder surroundings. When T. Edmund Harvey, who had devotedly attended my court-martial, learned that my health was at a low ebb, he used his parliamentary influence to have me brought before an army medical board which discharged me. For convalescence, I welcomed an invitation to stay with my friends at Plymouth for a few weeks. Apart from night drives to the moors with the doctor, I spent much of my time in the public library reading treatises on criminology, penology and related subjects.

Thereafter my most pressing problem was to secure a means of livelihood. I could see little prospect of fulfilling my ambition to devote myself to biological research, and my short spell as a teacher in an L.C.C. primary school had made life as a schoolmaster unthinkably repulsive. Through Ruth Fry, a gracious lady of great charm associated with T. E. Harvey in wartime activities of the Society of Friends, I obtained a temporary job assisting the production of the journal of the Peace Society, largely a Quaker organisation whose secretary was then Herbert Dunnico, a congregational minister. He later became a Labour M.P. and party whip.

In this capacity, I spent part of my time in the Reading Room of the British Museum collecting materials for a series of articles about early writers on the organisation of world peace—Erasmus and Emeric Cruce (or de la Croix) in the sixteenth century, Abbé St. Pierre and William Penn in the seventeenth. Making contact with Erasmus through his *Complaint of Peace everywhere despised among men* was a rewarding experience. I was reading it when the first aeroplane attack on London took place in broad daylight about midday. Zeppelin attacks were already a familiar feature of the night sky in London. The surface they offered to anti-aircraft installations, then in their infancy, had by then begun to make them a liability.

My stipend while working with the Peace Society was thirty shillings a week. Out of this I was able to rent a room in Highbury.

There I bought and cooked my rations. Butter was unobtainable and the margarine used as a substitute would have done better service for greasing cartwheels. No estrangement from my parents dictated my decision to live away from home. They did not disapprove of my attitude to the war. I simply craved privacy and wanted to be nearer the centre of London.

The job with Herbert Dunnico was for the duration of the war at best. In the first half of 1917, journalism seemed to be the only likely way of earning a living sufficient to support my frugal needs. I had a few articles and reviews published in George Lansbury's *Herald* and in a stuffy literary periodical called *The Athenaeum*. When the opportunity of acting as subeditor of the *Kentish Times* came my way, I left the Peace Society and thought myself lucky to be able to accept it. The *Kentish Times* was a syndicate which issued weekly parish pump news and advertising space with coverage for Chislehurst, the Crays, Sidcup and Eltham. My most noteworthy exploit during this episode happened when a local archdeacon, meriting a complete column, had the bad taste to die half an hour before we went to press. My improvised obituary was warmly received by his widow, who was convinced by it that I had known her husband intimately.

I continued to work in a subeditorial capacity for some months after I had accepted a lectureship in the Zoology Department of Birkbeck College. The only son of the Head of the Department was one of my contemporaries at Cambridge and also a conscientious objector. I took on the job with little promise of opportunities for research or a living wage. The salary was £120 a year. Before implementation of a report by a Royal Commission in 1919, few British academic posts other than professorships would keep the wolf from the door.

CHAPTER VIII

Marriage

OTHER than microscopes, my appointment as a lecturer in Birkbeck College did not carry with it any facilities for research. Initially I had no opportunities for getting materials had I formulated a workable programme. As the prospect of peace became less remote, I could foresee little likelihood of a career in biological research and even less of completing a medical degree. Meanwhile, I continued to dabble in politics when I was not engaged in teaching. Somehow, for reasons I have forgotten, I became involved in a free-for-all left wing organisation called the Stepney Herald League, formed initially to promote the sale of George Lansbury's journal, which emerged after the war as the *Daily Herald*.

In the summer of 1917 occurred an event which was to change my vacillating and aimless attitude to life. Enid Charles had come to London. At Cambridge she had done creditably both in the maths tripos Part I and economics Part II. She also had spent a year in a Liverpool settlement to gain its university diploma of social science and could therefore have had a well-paid civil service job for the asking. Being an ardent socialist and feminist, she preferred to take a thirty-shilling-a-week job as an organiser for the women's wing of the trade union movement, led by Mary MacArthur and Margaret Bondfield, who was later to become the first woman Minister of State in the first Labour government. Like so many other young women in or on the fringe of the Suffrage Movement, she then disapproved of the institution of marriage. Among my contemporaries, other women students I knew came from more privileged surroundings than myself. Enid's father, on the other hand, was a Welsh-speaking Congregational minister who had never earned as much as £200 a year. She was his only daughter by a second marriage, and his sole worldly ambition was that she should have a university education. Being a descendant of Thomas Charles, both founder of the British and Foreign Bible Society and author of the first Concordance of the Bible in Welsh, she had an ancestry of good repute in Wales. Tourists still pause to look at his statue in Bala.

Politics apart, we shared an interest in the same poetry—at that stage Yeats, de la Mare, James Elroy Flecker, Shelley and Swinburne. Enid read verse with the peculiarly seductive charm of a Celt and was at her best when declaiming dreamily the choric odes in Gilbert Murray's translations of Euripides. In the autumn of 1917, we secured a barely furnished flat in Gray's Inn Road at a weekly rent greatly reduced by the nightly visits of the zeppelins. Relevant information about the reliability of contraceptive devices on sale was still difficult to get. When our first child was on the way, Enid reluctantly relinquished her objections to wedlock. Without other concessions to convention, we regularised our relation in a registry office during the lunch interval of a working day.

By this time, we had moved into Stepney, where we had equipped with second-hand and home-made furniture three rooms in a house near the home and office of Sylvia Pankhurst, with whom we were both friendly. The chief reason for this move is that I was now the representative of the Stepney Herald League on the Stepney Trades Council. This drew its strength partly from unions in the mainly Jewish trades of small-scale tailoring and furniture manufacture, many of the members being exiles nurtured in Marxism. It had also the support of the dockers of a district embracing three parliamentary constituencies, Aldgate, Stepney and Limehouse. In preparation for an election following the promulgation of a new constitution of the parliamentary Labour Party, I undertook the unpaid task of mobilising a campaign as the Council's official political secretary.

Labour had not hitherto contested any one of the three constituencies. The search for suitable candidates for an election to follow within weeks of the armistice was one of my main preoccupations. I was able to bring two assets to this undertaking. I had personal access to many speakers who were active in the several socialist groups of Greater London. I could also mobilise London University students for addressing envelopes and door-to-door canvassing. Their adolescent enthusiasm was a financial bonus for the constituency machine. At the election of December 1918, none of the Labour candidates for the three Stepney constituencies topped the poll, but they laid the groundwork for the 1922 election when Clement Attlee was successful in Limehouse.

In the few weeks before proclamation of the 'Hang the Kaiser' election, I cemented a lasting friendship with George Lansbury, then Labour candidate for the Bow Constituency adjacent to Stepney. I had met him already when he addressed the Cambridge Fabian Society as an outspoken opponent of the war. He became First Commissioner of Works in the second Labour government and Leader of the Opposition from 1931 to 1935. Unlike any other politician I have met, he was transparently sincere and loveable.

The political climate of Britain during the months immediately preceding the armistice was tense. By the beginning of 1916, Trade Unionism was already assuming a new guise. With mounting pressure for production of munitions, the provisions of the Defence of the Realm Act had prohibited official strikes. Bargaining about wages or conditions of work could thus take place only at the level of the shop floor. Unofficial strikes, beginning especially on the Clyde, acquainted the British middle class for the first time with the spectre of the shop steward. Before hostilities ended, a national organisation of shop stewards had become a credible threat to parliamentary authority.

That a new constitution could override the deep cleavage between the Independent Labour Party (I.L.P.) wing led by Ramsay MacDonald and the residue of what had earlier been the Labour Representation Council under Arthur Henderson might have seemed unlikely a year before the final offensive which ended in the total defeat of Germany and Austria. For one reason or other, they buried the hatchet without recriminations. Within the working class movement, disillusion had grown apace as casualties became more and more colossal with less and less to show for it other than a shortage of fresh food.

In 1917, I had attended a meeting convened to celebrate the first phase of the Russian Revolution. Arthur Henderson, then lately and ignominiously dismissed by Lloyd George from office in the coalition government, received a tumultuous welcome from the left-wing rank and file. From then onwards there was readiness to let bygones be bygones. Labour emerged as a united party with a fifty percent increase of its parliamentary representation in the election following the armistice. Lloyd George had attempted to rally support for a disintegrating coalition with the slogans: *Homes fit for Heroes* and *Hang the Kaiser,* by then out of harm's way in Holland. The old Celtic rhetoric had however lost its magic. On the home front Lloyd George's final achievement was to wreck beyond repair the Liberal Party machine. For the first time, in the 1918 election Labour aspired to govern.

During this period, I had to grapple with the need to supplement a salary which was insufficient for the Spartan needs of Enid, who was now housebound, and for our daughter, named after Sylvia Pankhurst. Her birth occurred on my own birthday, December 9th, 1918. Fortunately there were then no fewer than three weeklies which circulated among poultry farmers. By writing a series on recent advances in the fields of poultry genetics and poultry diseases, I turned my zoological training to good account, but this was not enough to fulfil my obligations. I had the offer of a safe seat on the London County Council in the tide which brought Herbert Morrison, himself a conscientious objector, to the forefront in the political arena, but I preferred to take a chance on fulfilling my ambition to become a biologist. Under the pretence that Germany nearly won the war because science in British universities was moribund, parliament voted a substantial increase in university salaries, with a retrospective payment. I abandoned with relief my aspiration to a political career, for which I lacked the essential aptitude for compromise and the gift of suffering fools gladly.

Happily, neither Charlie (Enid) nor I had as yet expensive tastes. I first entered a pub when speaking for the I.L.P. at a Lancashire by-election in the Rossendale Valley. A tot of port, an execrable beverage but one of which I knew the name, cost sixpence. After Enid came to London, I went to a theatre for the first time in my life. At the Old Vic Shakespeare Repertory we saw Sybil Thorndike in *Romeo and Juliet*. Our tickets cost ninepence apiece. We had by then painlessly attained immunisation against nostalgia for a theism we shed with little discomfort. For each of us, socialism now filled the religious vacuum that human nature abhors.

A reader who has suffered me so far will have realised how much of my mental energy had been hitherto absorbed in a fruitless search for an intellectually compelling rationale to rescue some fragments from the wreckage of my family faith. The mood of liberation I experienced when I finally discarded the last remnant of theism was no less exhilarating than that of Bunyan's Pilgrim when the burden of sin fell from his back. I was at last free to mobilise all my intellectual resources to pursue a career of scientific research with steadfastness of purpose and with almost demoniacal energy. In retrospect, the final steps seem as sudden as they were painless. I can call vividly to mind a morning in late summer or early autumn of 1918. The location of Birkbeck College was then in a street off Fetter Lane and I was on foot in the neighbourhood of the Inns of Court. The sky was of a Mediterranean blue and cloudless. As I looked upward, I realised that the sole prospect was limitless expanse of unthreatening and impersonal emptiness—but for unapproachable galaxies—of a universe without purpose of punishment or reward for a lately arrived animal species, free to make or mar its own destiny without help or hindrance from above.

Suddenly I was aware of an onlooker staring. I had been reciting audibly the final lines of Swinburne's *Hymn to Man*, written to celebrate the Vatican Ecumenical Council of 1869–70:

> By the name that in hellfire was written,
>   and burned at the point of thy sword,
> Thou art smitten, thou God, thou art smitten;
>   thy death is upon thee, O Lord.
> And the love-song of earth as thou diest,
>   resounds through the wind of her wings—
> Glory to Man in the highest!
>   for Man is the master of things.

Having made the decision to withdraw from active participation in politics after the December election of 1918, I set about exploring the possibility of undertaking the only type of research for which I had the means at my disposal. There were then no facilities for experimental work at Birkbeck. In 1919 I accepted the offer of a junior lectureship at the Imperial College of Science.

At the suggestion of my old teacher Leonard Doncaster, I concentrated during the next three years on cytological enquiries. The three main ones, entitled *Studies on Synapsis* (LH 1920c,d; 1921a), published in the Proceedings of the Royal Society, attracted the attention in America of T. H. Morgan, first Nobel Prizeman in Genetics, and of F. A. E. Crew, thereby initiating a lifelong friendship with the latter and many congenial exchanges with the former. At this time, the linear alignment of genes was still a novel concept disputed because of a widely held belief in the end-to-end pairing of chromosomes. The first of this series dealt with parthenogenetic Hymenoptera. It satisfied Doncaster, who entertained some doubts of his own work on the same species and had urged me to look into the issue to clarify it. Nonetheless, after my *expertise* became more mature I never felt that my interpretation of the events (in contrariety to his) was wholly convincing.

The second paper which caught the eye and won the approval of T. H. Morgan dealt with synapsis in the cockroach. My interpretation was at variance with a then classical memoir by Farmer and Moore. Those who opposed the belief that the chromosomes do indeed pair side by side in meiosis based their case very largely on the latter. Everything depended on whether the authors had missed a stage which is indeed very short-lived, so much so that I did not find it until I had sectioned nearly a thousand testes. At that time, Farmer was also a professor in the Imperial College, and had been initially somewhat scornful to my own professor about my scepticism concerning his findings. It is to his great credit that he frankly admitted what is now the accepted view of the situation when I invited him to see my preparations. I recall that his charm did not compensate for my chagrin when he assured me that he felt no need to see two dozen or more other preparations after looking at the first. Morgan visited me especially to see these.[1] This cytological work during the period 1919–22 gained me the London D.Sc.

Early in 1919, concentration on scientific research and teaching unavoidably involved withdrawal from the circle of friends I had formed in the war years. A succession of promotions inaugurated a new domestic routine. Six months after I started at Imperial College, I succeeded the senior lecturer in a somewhat more lucrative post. Enid and I decided to make a home in a rural setting on the Chilterns. It was within easy walking distance from Amersham station where I could take a train to Marylebone on the Leicester line. In fine weather I could walk from the terminus to the College through Hyde Park. Since the train journey was nonstop, I was able to settle down to systematic work in transit.

Both in the field of genetics and in applications of physical chemistry to physiological problems, I had long felt the inadequacy of my mathematical background. I could now supplement homework, while commuting, with attendance at lectures by Hyman Levy, then Assistant Professor in the Department of Mathematics, one floor below my own office. Till my seventy-fifth year, I made it my practice to keep one day a week free to acquire familiarity with a new intellectual technique or branch of knowledge and to switch over to a new one every five years.

One outstanding incident of my term of service at the Imperial College of Science was the arrival of G.P. and Frank Wells as students. Their father, H.G., had decided that they should study for a year in what had been the department of Thomas Henry Huxley, prior to taking up residence in Cambridge. Their attendance was a challenge to my teaching expertise. G.P. had already won an entrance exhibition at Trinity. I made up my mind that he should become a Senior Scholar in his first year of residence, and he did. How far I contributed to his success, I have no means of knowing, but H.G. took a generous view of my teaching capabilities. Mrs. Wells invited Enid and myself to a weekend in their Essex country residence on the estate of the Countess of Warwick. It proved to be the first of several visits.

We faced the prospect with some misgivings because our wardrobe was then minimal. All I had to wear externally was a Norfolk jacket and grey flannel trousers. On the platform at Liverpool Street we saw G.D.H. and Margaret Cole board a first-class compartment with other guests whom we did not as yet recognise as such. Needless to say, we ourselves travelled third, arriving about an hour before the first dinner gong. The Wells household then had an Edwardian roll call of domestic personnel, who behaved as befitted the social prestige of a highly successful author. In particular, one of their duties was to pounce on the baggage of the guests as soon as they vacated their bedrooms, empty the contents and transfer them to drawers, wardrobe and washstand. Our own social experience did not as yet encompass nor anticipate such a calamity. The sole contents of our small grip were toothbrushes, combs, pyjamas, handkerchiefs and change of underwear.

Happily, Catherine Wells always gave the guest rooms a final once-over. It says much for both herself and her husband that they did everything possible to minimise the misgivings of two otherwise so conspicuous misfits. When the guests assembled, men with dinner jackets and black ties, women in evening dress, H.G. and Catherine took the two end seats of the table in the sort of clothes one reserves for weeding a wet garden. Among the guests were Frank Horrabin and his wife, whom we already knew well when we were still immersed in left-wing politics. He was contributing his genre of map making to the *Outline of History*, 1920, which Wells was then writing.

Watching Wells at work taught me two things one does not learn at school about the art of writing. To get down what he wanted to say, he wrote his first draft at great speed for typing and edited it at leisure into a second, more polished piece. Sometimes he would require a third draft. During all the period I knew him best, until the beginning of World War II, he had more than one private secretary. If only two drafts were necessary, he had one type the first draft and another the second to minimise word blindness through boredom.

During the summer weekends I spent at Easton Glebe, he wrote a first draft for an hour before a leisurely breakfast and alternated short spells of writing with editing throughout the day. Often he edited while carrying on a conversation with guests in a corner of the garden with Scotch and soda at hand. Wells and his wife were endearing hosts in more than one way. After dinner, Wells himself sidestepped the tedium of the usual card party by introducing his guests to ingenious games of his own designs. In one, the winner was the one who could cheat most successfully. I have forgotten how we computed the score. While we played, Wells often had a pencil and a pad on which he doodled. He would say that this was to bring home to us our faces.[2]

Until 1930, my most satisfying friendships were almost exclusively with other scientific workers. My only link with the socialist movement was through the 1917 Club.[3] Not all the members were political activists. There were among them a few representatives of the stage—notably Miles Malleson and Elsa Lanchester. In the same milieu, I first met Lytton Strachey with whom I later lunched at his club. He had recently published *Eminent Victorians,* 1918, and talked brilliantly, but without affectation, about Queen Victoria, on whose life he was then at work. First and foremost among my new friends I should mention Julian Huxley, who had an influence on the rising generation out of all proportion to the originality of his research record. This was partly because he had been teaching in the United States during the vintage years of 1913–16, when American biology was making spectacular advances on several fronts—genetics, endocrinology, cytology, sex determination and experimental embryology.

Only after the end of World War I did Britain recognise the biological research going on in the U.S.A. From 1919 onwards, Huxley lectured by invitation not only in Oxford but in London, Edinburgh and elsewhere with infectious and unaffected enthusiasm about discoveries which had as yet made no impact on the British scene during the years of stagnation. Thus it happened that I abandoned cytological research in 1921 to take up work on the comparative physiology of the ductless glands, which became my major preoccupation for the next twenty years.

While I was a lecturer in the Imperial College of Science, I became interested, as did Julian Huxley at the same time, in recent discoveries on the relation of the thyroid and pituitary to metamorphosis. Though we worked quite independently, we agreed to publish together. The joint publication (LH 1922a) added little that was new, but confirmed recent investigations of other workers on several issues. In retrospect, it would scarcely be worthy of mention if it were not for the fact that it drew our attention to pigmentary changes associated with administration of pituitary extracts.

When Julian was in London, he took me out several times to lunch with Aldous. I enjoyed his hospitality and that of his wife, Juliette, more than once in Oxford where I once entered, more puzzled than reverential, the charmed circle of Lady Ottoline Morrell. On the occasion when I was one of the party at this hothouse of dilapidated liberalism, the beauty of the garden around her Oxfordshire manor house at Garsington impressed me far more than the profundity of the verbal fare.

Only one incident marred the serenity of the period when I was on the staff of the Imperial College. I would hesitate to record it had it not been mentioned in the autobiography of Ivor Montagu, youngest son of Lord Swaythling and at that time one of my students.[4] In the previous year I had been responsible for a class, all of whose members were recently discharged officers, each on informally good terms with me. They aspired for employment in the Colonial Service as pest control officers or other appointments for which a degree in applied biology was prerequisite. Accordingly they enrolled in the Department of Entomology housed on the floor above mine. Perhaps because I made no secret of my own role during the war to some of my students of the succeeding year, the ex-army officers had lately learned about it. On the notice board of my own department, under my own name they had pinned in the shape of a Victoria Cross a flattened piece of lead piping with "Awarded for Funk" in large letters below it. Though I was by no means confident about the risk to security in my job, I went next day to their own professor, asking for a letter of apology. He backed me up and I received one in due course.

My *amour propre* prevented me from mentioning the incident to Enid, who was expecting the birth of Adrian that week. I was moody and too preoccupied to give her the consideration and kindness which was her due in such circumstances. Our marriage lasted thirty-nine years, but as we drifted apart in the pursuit of our several professional careers, I learned too late that she had never ceased to cherish a grievance for what was in the circumstances my callous behaviour. All might have been forgiven and soon forgotten had not my personal pride dictated my determination to make unpleasant decisions without invoking sympathy. The incident is not one I look back on with pride.

Imperial College, embracing the Royal Colleges of Science, Mining and Engineering, then occupied the greater part of Imperial Institute Road, South Kensington. On the periphery of this enclave was the town residence of the Swaythling clan. It was but a few minutes' walk from my department. Ivor was an ardent naturalist with no aspirations to high finance, and an equally ardent socialist. Soon after he entered my department, his mother mysteriously invited me to lunch. She regarded it as part of my responsibilities to make Ivor a good little conservative or liberal. I could do no better than assure her that boys will be boys. Later she invited me to dine. Somehow, Ivor made her see that dressing for dinner would be incompatible with my research work.

While I was at Imperial College, the head of my department was Professor E. W. MacBride. He had long since passed from the dynamic to the prostatic phase of the life cycle of a professional man. Till the beginning of World War I, he had carried out research on the embryonic development of sea urchins, starfishes and other marine forms. In the course of the war, he had relapsed into mental hibernation during the colder part of the year and aestivation during the warmer half. By birth he was an Ulsterman, and in a precocious dotage, he had exchanged the Calvinism of his forefathers for eugenics and had become a pillar of the Eugenics Society. This was a circus of snobs and racist cranks.

In my first term at Imperial College, MacBride invited me to attend a lecture he gave on behalf of the Society. To improve the race, he urged on his audience the desirability of legislation to make sterilisation by vasectomy obligatory for males earning less than £400 a year. At that date my own modest salary was £350 and I had already committed paternity—and quite legitimately. On the whole though we got on well together. My output of published work from his department was prolific. It gave him something new to talk about at lunch in the Athenaeum Club, one of the geriatric wards of the Establishment.

My father's death occurred before we left London for Edinburgh. Since the end of my second year at Cambridge, I had seen little of my parents. My father had acknowledged the news that I had won the Frank Smart Prize with a lengthy letter on the theme: what shall it profit a man if he shall gain the whole world and lose his own soul? Not unnaturally, I resented his failure to register any trace of parental satisfaction with my academic success. Shortly before his death in 1921, he expressed the wish to visit our cottage in the Chiltern country, there to see his first grandchild. He spent with us a warm July afternoon and early evening without any reference to the deity. By then he was over seventy. After we parted at the Amersham railway station, it seemed to me that he had all too late come to value secular human satisfactions more than the opportunity to proselytise. At the time, I could not bring myself to explore a new relationship of friendship without strings.

CHAPTER IX

Edinburgh

THE sojourn in the Buckinghamshire Chiltern Hills came to an abrupt, unexpected and professionally propitious end. One day F. A. E. Crew turned up unannounced in my laboratory at Imperial College, tall, handsome, charming and endowed with a pleasing voice. Frank was an Edinburgh University alumnus with a medical degree. During the 1914–18 war, he had served first as a combatant with the rank of major, having been in the Territorials as an undergraduate. Later he served in the Royal Army Medical Corps with the same rank.

Before the outbreak of war, he had undertaken experimental work in genetics at his own expense. After demobilisation he abandoned medical practice to teach in the zoological department of his alma mater. There, his seductive dramatic gifts as a lucid expositor of the newly hatched theory of the gene enlisted the attention of Sir Edward Sharpey-Schafer (Schäfer, E. S.). The veteran endocrinologist was at that time promoting the inauguration within the University of an Animal Breeding Research Department. Frank became its first Director in 1921. There were then few cytologists in Britain, and Crew was understandably anxious to enlist one as his deputy. Recognising my experience in this field, he approached me.

By that time I had already turned my back on cytology and had published two papers on the role of the pituitary gland in the control of colour change in cold-blooded vertebrates. However, Frank Crew was quite content for me to continue my work in the endocrine field if I were willing to train some of the post-graduate students in cytological techniques. On his invitation I joined him in 1922 as Deputy Director of the Edinburgh University Animal Breeding Research Department with the stipulation that the post carry with it, at a peppercorn salary, a lectureship in Comparative Physiology. The combined salary was little more than I had been getting in London, but the Royal Society awarded me at the same time its Mackinnon Studentship with a stipend of £300 a year. On coming to Scotland, we could therefore afford a housekeeper, who lived with us as part of the family. This set free some of Enid's time to take up biological studies. Shortly before, Cambridge had sanctioned degrees for women, so she obtained her M.A. on payment of the fee.

When I joined Frank Crew as his deputy in Edinburgh, I had delved a little more deeply into the relation of the pituitary to metamorphosis. In one publication (LH 1923c) I reported that injection of anterior lobe extracts would induce metamorphosis of thyroidectomised as well as normal axolotls. Two American workers contested both propositions, but at my suggestion a colleague followed up a clue with reference to different methods used for preparation of extracts, and confirmed my claim with respect to the response of the normal animal.

My work on the chromatic function remained a major preoccupation for many years, with several interruptions, until my Croonian lecture (LH 1942a). F. R. Winton, who had been a very dear friend of my Cambridge days, joined with me while completing his medical course, and we put together Nos. 1–3 (LH 1922b,c; 1923b) out of the ten of the series called the *Pigmentary Effector System*. The most important of these three dealt with the effects of hypophysectomy on the frog. I myself successfully performed the initial operation which Krogh had however done about the same time without my knowledge in connexion with his studies on capillary control.

Owing to financial difficulties which faced the new institute in its first years, my partnership with Frank lasted only till Sharpey-Schafer offered me a year later a senior lectureship in the Physiology Department of the Edinburgh Medical School. It seems that he entertained a flattering view of my earliest work in endocrinology, a field of which he had been a pioneer in the year of my birth.

By that time, I was interested in the identity or otherwise of the hormone or hormones in posterior lobe extracts responsible for the melanophore reaction and other previously known responses, in particular the pressor, discovered by Schäfer in the year of my birth. In the Physiology Department at Edinburgh, this initiated a series designated *Studies on the Pituitary*. One of these (LH 1924e) is notable because it prescribed what for the next fifteen years was the only reliable method for standardisation of pressor activity, and thus enabled us to confirm Dale's, in contradistinction to Abel's, view of the separate identity of the pressor and uterine stimulants. It is delightful to record that two of my protégés, Landgrebe and Waring, later devised a better test procedure.

About that time, I attacked the same general issue from a different angle with the collaboration of Gavin de Beer (LH 1925b) by extending on a wider front Herring's earlier attempt to answer the question: do extracts made from members of different vertebrate classes all evoke the same responses?

Before coming to Edinburgh, I had opportunities to acquire surgical skill only on frogs, toads and salamanders. My duties in the Physiology Department greatly extended my range, most of the prescribed demonstration material being mammalian. The change gave me more scope for endocrinological research and did not greatly interrupt my friendship with Frank, which lasted till his death in 1973. I owe to no one so much as to him the realisation of my ambition to become a man of science.

At Birkbeck College I had for the first (and last) time to lecture to a syllabus, and a very stupid one, over which I had no control. There I had announced to my class that I would devote two-thirds of the time to talking about important things not included in the syllabus, and the last third to the somewhat different task of drilling them in the skill of getting through an examination of London University. An appreciation of this episode by Richard Church in the British Council's wartime (*circa* 1943) publication entitled *British Authors*, written twenty-five years after the event, was neither unflattering nor apocryphal.[1]

With Schäfer in Edinburgh, my task was a rewarding challenge which influenced my more mature teaching policy in two ways. Sir Edward gave the lectures; and my job was to give the lecture-bench demonstrations, which had to be faultless. These were mammalian non-survival experiments before postwar (1922) classes of 200, including many ex-officers. As at Birkbeck, where they were teachers or civil servants qualifying by evening classes, most of my students were much older than myself. Thereafter, when I had a department under my direction, I consistently adopted the Scottish plan that the professor gives the lectures to the large first-year classes. I also introduced lecture bench experimental demonstrations, then (and still) new in zoology departments, as a feature of practical work. My association with Schäfer had brought home to me that laboratory work as commonly prescribed in the natural sciences confuses two issues: (a) the need to give students a non-authoritarian confidence in bookwork by demonstration of what only an expert can bring off; (b) the need to train students in techniques which will not achieve the same result until he or she has acquired sufficient expertise.

When I came to Edinburgh, the Animal Breeding Research Department had as its temporary premises, acquired by Frank's inspired opportunism, a dilapidated and abandoned infirmary in High School Yards, a back street of Old Edinburgh. This provided ample laboratory space. The acquisition of several acres, on the periphery of the city, made poultry breeding possible. Actively engaged in work on the physiology of reproduction in general and the mechanism of sex determination in particular, Frank was determined that the policy of what was to become the University Institute of Animal Genetics should shun the splendid isolation of Cambridge genetics. To promote a hothouse atmosphere, he made opportunities for research workers to visit us during vacations. Among these were Julian Huxley and J. B. S. Haldane, who were already our friends. Both F. R. Winton, later Dean of Pharmacology at University College, London, and Gavin de Beer, later Director of the British Museum of Natural History, collaborated with me.

On one such visit, Crew, Huxley, Haldane and myself became the founding fathers of the now flourishing *Society for Experimental Biology*. The initial intention was not to found a society. Our common concern was the lack of any British medium of publication other than the *Transactions* and *Proceedings* of the Royal Society, for research of the sort which interested us (LH 1974c).

Shortly before I left for Edinburgh, I had brought up the paucity of British research publications with H. G. Wells. He was helpfully informative about costs and, to my immense gratification, offered to underwrite the initial outlay for starting a biological journal for the publication of experimental work. With such encouragement, I had myself tentatively explored the publicity requirements and expenses of launching such a journal before discussing the project with Frank Crew. When I mentioned the offer of H. G. Wells, Frank weighed in with the handsome declaration that he had in hand enough cash to finance the initial venture from his war service gratuity, and that he would be delighted to put it at our joint disposal. There were sufficient reasons why the editorial office should initially be in Edinburgh. Crew had the ear of an Edinburgh publisher of good standing in academic circles, and I alone of the four of us was willing to handle, with student help, the circularisation of libraries, university departments and institutes. Huxley, Haldane and I persuaded Frank Crew to be the first managing editor.

At that time there was no allocation of public money for an enterprise of this sort. A journal devoted to scientific research relied heavily on its sponsoring society since membership required subscription and thus embraced most of its would-be contributors. It seemed to Frank and myself that only a supporting society comparable to the Physiological and Biochemical Societies, the Royal Microscopical Society, the Linnaean Society and others of the sort could ensure the viability of the Journal. Haldane, Huxley and Ruggles Gates, a plant geneticist who had joined the editorial board, agreed. Accordingly we called for an inaugural conference at Birkbeck College in the Christmas vacation of 1923. The invitations went to university departments of botany, zoology and physiology and to selected research institutes. Attendance exceeded the most extravagant hopes of the promoters. Botanists turned up in strength. More than we dared expect, Joseph Barcroft, with associates from the Cambridge Department of Physiology, gave the meeting the full weight of his influential standing.

Among those present was Dr. G. P. Bidder, a Cambridge zoologist with substantial private means and business interests. He placed his experience at the disposal of the Society and founded a Company of Biologists as a secure financial base for the Journal. Otherwise it was essentially a youth movement with the good fortune to attract among its youngest founding members C. F. A. Pantin, who succeeded me as zoological secretary. From the atmosphere of the first session, it was evident that there was a well-nigh unanimous acceptance of the need for an organisation which could bring together experimental biologists from a wide range of specialities. The Society decided at its inaugural meeting to have two secretaries, one a plant and the other an animal physiologist. It elected Gates and myself.

Apart from conferring greater opportunities for research and new opportunities for scientific companionship, the Edinburgh milieu was not congenial. The grey buildings and the bleak winds of the city harmonise with its Sabbatarian gloom and Calvinistic creed. As seat of the Scottish Law Lords and Scottish Ministries, it had a highly inbred élite which preserved in the early twenties a social tradition of pervasive Victorian propriety and Victorian pomposity appropriate to its bogus Acropolis within sight of Waverley Station. Social intercourse within the University was rigidly hierarchical. A yawning gap between the salaries of the best-paid lecturers and those of a professor reinforced the social barriers which local etiquette prescribed. When the University created in 1928 a chair in genetics for Crew, he made academic history by taking his staff on Saturday nights to a *Palais de Danse* whose saxophones flagrantly defied the prevailing civic preference for psalmody.

Fifty years later, it may seem surprising that I was the only member of the Labour Party on the academic staff of the University. One of the few forms of relaxation in which Enid and I indulged was an open house on Saturday evenings for the students' Socialist Society. Discussion was lively and topically unconfined. One of the regulars was Jennie Lee, who became the second wife of Aneurin Bevan. When he was Minister of Health in the 1945 Labour Government, he told me that Jennie learned the facts of life from me, verbally that is to say.

Scottish medical students were, in those days, even less inhibited than those of the London teaching hospitals. Classes were large— 150 or more—because there was still a backlog of ex-service men. In the Department of Physiology they used to pelt one of the lecturers, a man much older than myself, with soot, flour and fireworks. Personally I was able to hold my own with little difficulty. Tub thumping in the London socialist movement during the last year of the war had taught me the hard way how to handle an audience. The local scene exposed me to few temptations which might have curtailed an eighteen-hour working day. I gained early experience of organising teamwork in research from collaboration with younger colleagues without the distracting responsibility for securing financial support. Sharpey-Schafer, then over seventy and otherwise no longer active, had ready access to funds.

During the last two years of my stay in Scotland, I had the good fortune to secure the means for a busman's holiday by successfully applying for the Ray Lankester Investigatorship of the Marine Biological Association. The emolument from this made it possible for me to spend my vacations at the Plymouth Laboratory in projects which considerably widened my stock in trade as a research worker in comparative physiology and initiated a gratifying companionship with Carl Pantin, recently recruited to the staff and later Professor of Zoology at Cambridge. On my visits to Plymouth, I usually had the company of a student co-worker. Once it was my good fortune to have with me Maurice Richardson, then an Oxford undergraduate, later known as an *Observer* critic and novelist. He has related one incident of this vacation with little embellishment. While helping me, he slipped into a tank the water level of which was neck-high. It housed an octopus and several formidable lobsters. According to Maurice, I sat on the edge greeting his *cri de coeur* for help with assurance that I was pondering on the best course of action. Eventually I remembered that the tank had a plug and let out half the sea water.

One night the two of us decided to take out a boat to row across the Sound. Halfway across, a gale started. Clouds covered the moon and we drifted for what seemed like six hours under a starless sky. Meanwhile, we joined in prayers to Darwin, Marx and Bernard Shaw. Our invocations were eventually successful. We felt the keel of our boat hit something solid, and I let myself cautiously into the water to discover that we were on a shelf of rock. We then disembarked and climbed a cliff at the top of which a light was visible. It came from a coastguard station. The coastguards disclaimed any responsibilities for intruders who were not *bona fide* mariners, but grudgingly gave us a box of matches. On the beach below we made a fire with corks and driftwood to dry our clothes and waited there till daybreak.

My visits to Plymouth included two Easter and two summer vacations. In the summer ones, Enid and our children accompanied me. My first investigation was into the effect of adrenaline and one of the pituitary hormones on the heartbeat of several invertebrate species: lobsters, crabs, scallops and snails. This led me to explore the relative amounts of potassium, calcium and magnesium in a perfusion fluid able to maintain the activity of the isolated heart. Incidentally, I studied the effect of varying their proportions on the electrocardiogram of the lobster. Among other things, I later embarked (LH 1925c) on a comprehensive study of the role of the several ionic constituents of the blood of crustacea, mollusca and annelids. This work gave me much satisfaction, in particular what was somewhat a *tour de force* of technique—the isolated preparation of the heart of the common snail. Thereby I was able to correct (as he cordially and generously acknowledged) an erroneous conclusion about the role of potassium previously put on record by Lovatt Evans.

The red pigment of our own blood, haemoglobin, combines loosely with oxygen, acting as a carrier of the gas to the tissues. It is of a bright scarlet colour when fully oxygenated, as seen when an artery bleeds, and dull purple when fully reduced, as seen when a vein bleeds. The haemoglobins of vertebrates and many worms are proteins whose molecules contain iron. The haemocyanins, which do the same job in the blood of the larger crustacea, snails, cuttlefish and other invertebrates, are proteins whose molecules contain copper. They are blue when combined with oxygen and colourless when fully reduced.

During my last summer at the Marine Biological Laboratory in Plymouth, my friend C. F. A. Pantin was about to give there a vacation course on Comparative Physiology. One night when we were rounding off a long day's work with a few glasses of sherry at about 9 P.M., I suggested it should be possible to demonstrate the reduction of oxyhaemocyanin by connecting a test-tube with a filter pump. Carl expressed scepticism about the possibility of getting a sufficiently low pressure in this way. To settle a small bet, we went back to the Laboratory, bled a large spider-crab *(Maia squinado)* and attached a test tube containing the blood to a filter pump, with the result I had anticipated. However, reduced crab or lobster blood is not colourless. Owing to the presence of a lipochrome, it is orange. Happily, a single trial showed that shaking thoroughly with chloroform removes the lipochrome very quickly.

It was Carl himself who was then first to suggest that we might make colour standards to assess the percentage of reduced haemocyanin by simply diluting blood so treated with water. The prospect was so enthralling that we proceeded (11 P.M.) to make a set of standard dilutions in 5-percent stages in tubes of roughly the same bore as the specimen for reduction. We inserted a home-made manometer and connected thereto the tube joining the pump to that containing the specimen from which to read off the pressure. The result yielded a dissociation curve of the familiar haemoglobin type. By this time, we had lost interest in going to bed, and when we stopped at about 5 A.M., we had satisfied ourselves that the facts of hydrogen ion variation, temperature and salt concentration also follow the familiar haemoglobin pattern.

This simple technique opened up a new field of physical chemistry which was to keep me busy throughout my subsequent stay in Canada. Colourimetric methods of estimation are an invitation to self-deception if one has grounds for expecting a particular result. I was able to sidestep this from the start by enlisting another to do the matching, someone who had no knowledge of what to expect. In that summer of 1925 at Plymouth, I invited my mother, then a widow, to stay with me for a fortnight and kept her busy with the matching process. While I was in Canada and later in Cape Town, her letters warning me of the prospect of a Christless eternity, as she put it, became unbearably wearisome and I had no urge to visit her when I returned to Britain.

In the same summer, the tenure of the Mackinnon Studentship of the Royal Society was due to terminate, and we had by then a baby daughter, Clare, the third addition to the family. It was therefore a relief when Sharpey-Schafer secured for me the offer of an appointment in Montreal as Assistant Professor of Medical Zoology at McGill University. We packed up at the end of the summer term, and the family came with me to a little fishing village off Plymouth Sound. I continued my work in the Laboratory on the Hoe till the end of September, when we embarked third class on a Canadian liner from Southampton for Quebec.

CHAPTER X

Montreal

On arrival at Montreal, we learned that the Agricultural Faculty of McGill University, Macdonald College, had its site twenty miles out of town beside the Lake of Two Mountains, a backwater of the St. Lawrence, and a mile or so from the French-speaking village of St. Anne de Bellevue. Its railway station on the Toronto-Montreal main line was within a few yards of the boundary of a miniature garden city estate of a large printing firm whose proprietor was a McGill graduate. For that reason, some members of the staff had cottages on the estate and, luckily, there was an empty one when we arrived.

In the nearby woods of Senneville, the maples and sumachs were at their crimson best on the October day when we moved in with an assortment of second-hand furniture which we painted in bright colours to our own taste. This was my first exercise in a hobby which I took up zestfully in later years. The railway station was within sight of our cottage. Commuting daily gave a new impetus to mathematical study, supplemented by the opportunity to attend lectures on differential equations and Fourier series. The professor, a Cambridge graduate, had taught mathematics at a naval college during the war. When not eating or helping with household chores, I kept the Sabbath wholly apart from other work to broaden my knowledge of physical chemistry from the thermodynamic approach.

My teaching assignment brought me face to face with a new problem which implanted the first seeds of an interest which intensified in later life. Having had to acquire a smattering of Greek and Latin to satisfy the entrance requirements of Cambridge before World War I, I had not found it difficult to memorise biological terms. If not able at sight to recognise the meaning of their components, I usually took the trouble to trace their source. By this time I had enough etymological knowledge to recognise at sight the difference between a Latin and Greek root. While my Scottish students had at least an elementary knowledge of Latin, at McGill I had to lecture to students nearly all of whom had no knowledge of Latin or English etymology. Not one of them knew any Greek. Henceforth, whenever I introduced a new technical term, I adopted the practice of linking its components with already familiar words of similar roots. Without knowing it at the time, I was generating the vocabulary of an international language *Interglossa*, 1943, in which every word has 'mnemotechnic' value in countries where Western medicine, modern sanitation and modern power production have prevailed.

At McGill I had no favourable material for continuing my work on the comparative physiology of the pituitary, and I went on with work on the haemocyanins, first of the snail (LH 1926c) which was obtainable locally, and then of Limulus (LH 1927c) which I collected on a visit to the Marine Biological Laboratory at Woods Hole, Massachusetts. In these two enquiries, Mrs. K. F. Pinhey, who (like my mother) had a good eye for colour and at that time knew nothing about previous work on the haemoglobins, did the matching. I greatly improved the method of calibration and published a detailed account (LH 1927b) of the improved method in the Transactions of the Royal Society of South Africa shortly after arrival in Cape Town. In the two papers with Mrs. Pinhey, there was a new feature, *viz*. the use of dissociation curves obtained at different temperatures from one and the same stock of blood to determine the molecular heat of oxidation per gram mol.

During my short period at McGill, K. F. Pinhey also assisted me in a biophysical investigation (LH 1926a) on the viscous elastic properties of muscle, provoked by an assertion made by A. V. Hill about how these change in the process of contraction. I still think that the negative results we obtained were sound.

In retrospect, I recall this somewhat trivial incident for its unintentional entertainment value. One needed a continuous photographic record of the shadow of a vibrating spring. Cambridge Scientific Instruments quoted a figure, about £50 if I recall rightly, but in excess of what my departmental allocation could stand for. With the help of a laboratory assistant then, as so often subsequently, eager to respond to the unusual challenge which mitigates monotony, we decided to make our own camera at a total cost of roughly two dollars (Canadian), i.e. ten shillings sterling. The rollers for the film were from broomstick handles. The cylindrical lens to focus the image on the revolving film was a customary piece of glass rod for stirring solutions. Unforeseen, it had not easily visible bubbles which left straight lines on the film. As it happened, this made parallel ruled lines on the latter, thus facilitating immensely, when developed, the measurement of the amplitudes involved.

The countryside around our cottage beside the Lake of Two Mountains was charming though we saw little of it during the summer when it was at its best. Having no means of recruiting baby sitters, we could not take advantage of the long winter weekends by learning to ski, and walking on an uninterrupted expanse of snow at a temperature of 10° to 20° below zero Fahrenheit was an activity one willingly undertook only to buy eatables. Thanks to the cold, the latter included oysters at a non-prohibitive price. Soon after our first short and dismal thaw was over, we explored the woods of Senneville. There we watched a posse of students tapping maple sugar and saw for the first time hummingbirds in their native haunts. When summer came, we went as a family to the Woods Hole Marine Biological Laboratory on Cape Cod in Massachusetts. There Enid had a real holiday. We fed in the canteen, and it was easy to find students willing to be baby sitters. The children bathed on the beach during the daytime while I concentrated on work started in Plymouth the year before. At night, when fireflies were on the wing, we could join a hot-dog picnic on the beach.

Though much larger and better equipped than the Plymouth Laboratory, Woods Hole was inferior in one way. Its fauna were, with one exception, a disappointment. The only noteworthy novelty was the mating season of a giant species of the king crab, *Limulus,* copulating couples of which lined the sand above the high tide mark. It was a welcome sight for more than one reason. Though called a king or horseshoe crab, it is not a crustacean. It is more closely allied to scorpions. One reason for my visit was to collect a quart or more of its serum to continue my work on the haemocyanins during the Canadian winter in Montreal. At Woods Hole the nearby countryside, where several senior professors had summer bungalows, was as English as New England should be, and social life with late-night dances as well as beach picnics was more lively than anything Britain could offer at that time. Many of the younger staff were leftist in outlook and not a few defied the 18th Amendment by making their own gin with lab alcohol and juniper juice.

With its college Daily, college yell, co-eds and campus, McGill was in most respects like a Midwestern state university. Many of the academic staff, which included more than half a dozen Fellows of the Royal Society, were however British, and the admission standard was somewhat more exacting than that of most contemporary universities in the United States.

The public sector in Montreal was surprisingly diminutive. One had to pay a private contractor to empty one's garbage can. A Community Chest, managed by a highly paid salesman, annually solicited for voluntary contributions to provide social securities for which the state has been responsible in England for centuries. Unexpected was the pressure of door-to-door salesmen offering easy hire-purchase terms for commodities of every sort.

The English-speaking part of Montreal around McGill was culturally part of Ontario though geographically part of Quebec. The staff of the University of Montreal in the French-speaking sector did not fraternise with their English-speaking neighbours. The small expatriate academic community of St. Anne de Bellevue had no dealings with the native Catholic French Canadians. Had I been as curious as I now am about the social effect of linguistic barriers, there would have been an abundance of case history material at our doorstep. Quebec was not then bilingual in the sense that rural Wales is. Predominantly it was monoglot, being English-speaking in the British sector of Montreal and French-speaking elsewhere. After leaving Canada, I regretted my failure to make the best of opportunities to become more proficient in conversational French, but there was a cultural barrier to be surmounted. Rural Quebec was priest-ridden. The local brand of Catholicism had little resemblance to the liberal Catholicism which flourishes in parts of the United States.

During my short stay in Canada, there was a very lively group of student literati, mostly left-wing and post-graduate. Their publication, the *McGill Fortnightly,* was then of a higher intellectual standard than any other student magazine which has come my way. Locally, 1925 and 1926 were vintage years as were the early thirties in Aberdeen and the mid-thirties in Birmingham. That such cultural efflorescence is transient in universities recalls the dynamic days of the Lunar Society in Birmingham, of the Edinburgh Royal Society during the last quarter of the eighteenth century and of the Manchester Philosophical Society in the first decades of the nineteenth.

Such brief episodes of intellectual activity are a phenomenon for which eugenic dogma supplies no plausible explanation.

In many ways McGill was far more congenial to both Enid and myself than Edinburgh had been. At that time, British universities had no staff residential facilities comparable with the campus Faculty Club where I could get a bed, a bath and late supper if research kept me overnight in McGill. The University Library provided a loan service of newly published books for the staff, and the Faculty Club itself had provision for indoor games including billiards, bridge and chess. The Y.M.C.A., situated near the campus, had a good swimming bath kept at a temperature which makes swimming a form of self-indulgence rather than a character-building discipline. No profession of creed was a condition of its use if one paid a trifling subscription. Sometimes I accompanied two or more colleagues in the lunch hour to swim there and to wash down a few sandwiches with a can of beer. More usually I took lunch in the Club refectory. In British universities during the twenties, staff canteens had trestle tables to accommodate forty or so individuals in a pecking order prescribed by a sacrosanct tradition. Tables of the McGill Faculty Club accommodated only four and, since the intellectual level of conversation tends to be inversely proportional to the square of the man-table ratio, talking could be agreeably relaxing if one chose one's table mates with discrimination.

On the debit side the long winter, during which only stock laboratory animals and greenhouse plants were available for physiological research, confronted one's gaze with an arctic waste of snow in all directions. Unless one was able to ski in the Laurentian Mountains during the weekends, one was housebound. Within sight of our cottage, there was an ice-hockey rink kept free of snow for Saturday afternoon use, and I occasionally put on skates. Skating on ice is, however, tedious unless one has learned at a very early age to cut figures. I had not and the dangers of frostbite to our children did not encourage us to introduce them to the art.

My prospects for promotion had improved owing to the publication in 1926 of *Comparative Physiology*. I had also edited the proofs for a second book, *The Comparative Physiology of Internal Secretion*, 1927, one of the Cambridge University Press series of monographs on comparative physiology. Though Montreal was congenial in some ways, its climate severely restricted the scope of biological research during the academic year. For this reason alone,

I was overjoyed when I received an invitation from the University of Cape Town to become professor and head of its Department of Zoology in a setting where the fauna and climate were uniquely favourable for biological investigation. I had another reason to be glad. The North American continent was at that time engaged in its pastime of witch hunting of communists, a circumstance that led me to reject the offer of an academic post in New England.

While in Montreal, I did not enter into party politics, but joined the local branch of the *Society for Cultural Relations with the Soviet Union* (S.C.R.), and attended several functions sponsored by the Soviet Trade Mission. This led to a fracas with the President of the University. Having learned that I was a member, he told the Dean of my Faculty that a man who associated with such people was not the sort of person who could safely work alone in a laboratory with a lady research assistant. He fervently believed that all Bolsheviks approved of, and practised, free love.

In the highly charged political climate of the contemporary witch hunt, none of the academic staff enjoyed such security of tenure as we now take for granted. So when my Dean mentioned in a jocular way what the President had said about my association with the S.C.R., I thought I might as well be hanged for a sheep as for a lamb. Being very angry, and in violation of protocol, I went into his room without seeking an appointment through his secretary. I had begun to exhaust my vocabulary of sophisticated abuse when, to my astonishment, he intervened with apologies. After I sent in my resignation on accepting the Cape Town chair, he wrote me a letter in praise of my research and teaching record with the offer of promotion and a substantial salary increase if I were willing to stay on.

My few visits as a member of the S.C.R. to the H.Q. of the Soviet Trade Delegation happened at a time when the U.S.S.R. had not as yet gained diplomatic recognition. Its personnel were Old Guard Bolsheviks whose loyalties were overtaxed by the uncertain outcome of the first round of the Stalin-Trotsky struggle for power during Lenin's physical decline and consequent withdrawal from administrative activity. Like Stalin himself, none of them had previously travelled outside the limits of Tsarist Russia, and one of my liveliest recollections of their outlook illustrates their comic unreadiness for bearing the red standard of revolution aloft in foreign parts. During a cocktail party at their H.Q. to bid me farewell before I left with my family for Cape Town, the leader of the Delegation expressed the view that I should find South Africa much more congenial than Canada. He believed South Africa to be more ripe for social revolution.

In North America I did not greatly enlarge my knowledge of fauna, still less of flora. Meeting alive for the first time *Limulus,* a genus of great antiquity in geological time, was a memorable experience. The St. Lawrence and its backwaters abounded in a species of crayfish (*Astacus*) very much like the British species which I have found in the wild only once in my life. More striking, and confined to North America, was the species *Necturus,* a freshwater salamander whose gills persist into adult life. The cryptofauna found by turning over a stone in the woods near our cottage did not differ greatly from what one might see in a similar situation anywhere in Britain. Otherwise, only the birds were unfamiliar, in particular the hummingbirds, a New World family.

CHAPTER XI

Cape Town

HAVING booked a passage on an Elder Dempster cargo boat from St. John's in New Brunswick, we—Enid, our three children and myself—left Montreal in January 1927, a few weeks after my thirty-first birthday. Expense dictated our choice of transport because I was not due to get a refund on travelling expenses till we docked in Cape Town. For the first and last time in my life I borrowed money, which Julian Huxley cabled in return for a cheque postdated to the time of arrival. There were three other passengers, one a missionary of the Plymouth Brethren or kindred fundamentalist schism. One was an immigrant farmer of the sort later designated by Blimps as our kith and kin in the context of Rhodesian independence. The other was a tropical wife on furlough, too plain to tempt either the missionary or the 'buck white' who enjoyed boasting of how he flogged his native employees. After our first encounter, we asked the third mate whether we could take our meals with the officers. He was a Welshman with an urge to teach the Our Father to our children in Welsh. Happily his colleagues were willing, and the opportunity of getting to know them proved to be more educational than I had foreseen.

Till then, I had never taken any interest in astronomy. Having confessed my ignorance, I found that the first and second mate were eager to enrol me as a student. After a short spell of self-tuition with the aid of a textbook of spherical trigonometry for officer trainees of the merchant navy, I spent much of the journey taking the ship's bearings by recourse to the star map. The ship's course could not have been more propitious to my initiation. I watched nightly the transit of northern constellations lower towards the horizon and eventually disappear. Nightly also, I watched southern constellations unseen in hitherto familiar latitudes appearing above the horizon. I could follow the Pole Star till it made its exit as we passed the equator. In six weeks, I was able to experience all the novelty of the changing heavens and therewith the vision of the earth's sphericity as viewed by the Phoenicians first to venture beyond the Pillars of Hercules northward to the Tin Isles or southwards beyond the equator. It would have been difficult not to recapture the reasoning of Anaxagoras, when he explained to a receptive audience at the court of Pericles what the shape of the earth is truly like.

Stargazing in the cloudless tropical zone had other compensations, aesthetic and biological. If the moon was not yet up, there was a silver ribbon in the ship's wake made by activation of luminescent jellyfishes, Siphonophora, Crustacea and pelagic Tunicates. Daytime, there were other zoological thrills for the children. We frequently sighted whales, sharks and dolphins. Often flocks of flying fish landed on the deck, where they had a hearty welcome from the cook. I celebrated the day we crossed the line by delivering the ship's cat of her gangrenous brood by Caesarian section with surgical equipment which the ship's steward kept for emergencies. The steward proved himself to be a competent anaesthetist.

Well before we reached the equator we were not far out of sight of the coast on the route which the Carthaginian Hanno followed about 500 B.C., and the ship's officers could, as in his time, gauge our propinquity by the species of visible sea birds. We had been due to off-load or take on cargo at Monrovia. However, an epidemic of some sort prevented us from docking in the Liberian port, and we continued without another halt to Table Bay. The Bay, surmounted by cloud-capped Table Mountain and fringed with densely wooded slopes, is one of the most beautiful harbours on the four continents I have visited. We had booked a flatlet at a small and pleasant hotel at the foot of the mountain and arrived in time for lunch and Cape brandy, then within our monetary resources at one and six a bottle. I shall never forget the wonder of turning over stones in the garden only a few minutes after settling in.

Perhaps because I had read before I was fifteen so much about living creatures I had not seen, I have never lost the thrill of meeting alive what I had earlier known only as a picture on the printed page. Among other animals proposed as missing links in my college days was the genus *Peripatus*, then somewhat gratuitously regarded as a halfway house between a millipede or centipede and a rag worm. Before my first lunch, I found one at the back of our hotel under the first stone I turned up. *Peripatus* and allied genera have a wide distribution in the tropics and south of the equator, but have no representative in Europe or, in America, north of the Mexican border. As I was able to discover during the first few days after arrival, the Cape peninsula had an abundant and diversified cryptofauna, i.e. animals which live under slabs of rock or logs. I had merely to turn over a sizeable stone on the side of Table Mountain to see, besides *Peripatus*, many species I had not previously met in the wild state, for instance, scorpions and specimens of the related order Solpugidae.

Later in the afternoon of the same day, the Professor of Geology, an elderly Scot with an irreverent sense of humour, picked us up in his car and took us for a ride on the coastal road which runs on each side from one end of the peninsula to the other. Built by convict labour, much of the road lies several hundred feet above the shore. It is scenic in a picture postcard way and, on first encounter, seems truly beautiful. Sooner or later, however, familiarity breeds boredom. There is no other tolerable drive for many miles—only a dreary waste of sand and wattles.

Our host on this trip had inside information from a geological survey that there were rich, then untapped, resources of copper in Northern Rhodesia. Not having the wherewithal, we could not follow up his advice by buying shares when they came on the market. One other thing I remember about my geological colleague was what might have been my professional Waterloo. He possessed an elderly tomcat which he wished to have neutered. When I offered to remove the offending parts, I had not anticipated a snag. My laboratory assistant had never before administered an anaesthetic, and I had only completed the necessary initial shaving when the cat's heart stopped beating. After injecting adrenaline, I had to open the chest and massage the heart which, happily, started beating again so that I was able to return to its owner the ambulant pet able to sin no more.

Having made the acquaintance of *Peripatus* on my first day, I was not slow to discover that the Cape peninsula is a biologist's paradise. If one stands on Constantia Nek, its narrowest point, one can see two stretches of rock-bound ocean with a temperature difference of over 10° Fahrenheit. This is because the Angullus current from the Antarctic washes its west side and the Benguela from the Indian Ocean washes its opposite face. Needless to say, the littoral fauna of the west and more rocky side is vastly different from that of the other side where the wind washes banks of Siphonophora, chiefly the so-called Portuguese man-of-war, *Physalia*, onto the beach.

The rock pools on the west are almost unbelievably rich in marine animals and luxuriantly chromatic. Hydroids and Chitons of many species abound, and sea anemones of many colours. Most picturesque, perhaps, is the giant sedentary worm *Bispira voluticornis* with its huge fan of colourful tentacles, those of some varieties white, others apple green or violet. Besides the coastal fauna, the peninsula has other abundant resources of aquatic creatures. The Cape Flats, where Table Mountain ends, has many temporary *vleis*, i.e. ponds which dry up in the hot season. They then become almost soup-like suspensions of freshwater Crustacea and Rotifera.

Apart from the abundance of native forms not found in Europe, there were many species whose explanation is of historic interest. For instance, the commonest centipede was a Javanese immigrant and the commonest gastropod in the Cape Town gardens was our own European snail. I have never read an account which does justice to this unlikely assemblage, but an explanation is not far to seek. Till the last decade of the eighteenth century, the Cape had long been used as a port of call for the Dutch East Indies Company, when the latter had a virtual monopoly of the spice trade of the Far East. Long before then—indeed, as far back as Tudor times—the Dutch led the world in the trade of ornamental plants, and the Chartered Company notoriously encouraged the search for novelties from abroad.

These included our greenhouse *Pelargoniums* (so-called geraniums) the first arrivals of which were species which grow wild on the Cape peninsula. I presume that the ships of the Company, both outward bound and sailing home, brought small quantities of soil, and therewith animal intruders, to its Cape settlement. One such anomaly is the oriental species *Bipalium kewensis*. This is one of the Turbellaria (free-living flatworms), a group of worldwide distribution. Elsewhere, I have never met a representative larger than a quarter-inch long, but in greenhouses of Cape Town I have found specimens as long as fourteen inches.

Against this opulent background, the impact of my first professional decision on my second-in-command, an Afrikaner somewhat older than myself, was traumatic. I must here explain that the sacred cow of first-year biology in those days was a whimsy of Thomas Henry Huxley known to posterity as the 'type system.' This involved the detailed anatomical study of about a dozen species chosen from different groups of the Animal Kingdom, less because they were typical of their respective phyla or classes than because it was at one time relatively easy to place orders for them with pet shop dealers in London. When I entered my department on the day after arrival, I found the shelves lined with dozens of bottles of Huxleyan types imported in formalin from the seat of the empire. On enquiry, I learned that no living creatures had ever desecrated these hallowed precincts. The same day, I therefore instructed my laboratory steward to empty all the contents of the pickle jars in the yard behind the laboratory ready for the incinerator when the sun had dried them. Henceforth, the motto was to be: only the living pass these portals. We were indeed within a mile of rock pools and the ubiquitous cryptofauna of the wooded slopes to Table Mountain, in a situation which any biological department might envy.

During my first year, I had not the equipment to take full advantage of local opportunities enthralling beyond my wildest hopes. My predecessor, whose name, not being otherwise memorable, I have forgotten, was a dedicated necrophilist. The department had not even school chemistry laboratory equipment such as burettes, pipettes or a good balance. After disposal of the formalin-preserved mummies, all I had was bottles with which, after thorough cleaning, to collect live material. For the time being, a better and brighter Birkbeck setup would have to suffice. I was not short of money. The University was very rich, but the earliest possible delivery for consignments of apparatus involved a delay of at least three months, even if ordered by cable. Fortunately some German firms, with an eye to what the University could afford to spend, had agents always within earshot.

In 1916 the University of Cape Town and in 1921 that of Witwatersrand in Johannesburg separated from the Federal University of South Africa. They became independent institutions without the incubus of the Predikants of the Dutch Reformed (Much Deformed, as we called it in our circle) Church. Cape Town University had shrewdly accumulated considerable interest on a large benefaction by successively scrapping plans for building on a new site in wooded surroundings on the slopes facing Table Bay. I arrived in time to redesign the interior of my own detached three-floor building, and I had about £10,000, at that time a tidy sum, to spend on equipment. By the beginning of my second year in Cape Town, I had moved in and had already attracted to my staff a former postgraduate student from McGill.

In such a setting, teaching was a joy. Throughout the year, spawning sea urchins were available, and I was able to start class work in the laboratory with an authentic thrill. On the first laboratory session, each student made his or her own suspension of sea urchin sperm and eggs to observe the process of fertilisation and beginning of development. Officially, the schedule for the first afternoon, including initiation into the use of the microscope, did not require observation of cleavage beyond the eight-cell stage. Actually, the majority of a class of over a hundred, mostly first-year medicos, came back after a perfunctory supper to continue watching till midnight when the hitherto inert embryo burst the fertilisation membrane as a free-swimming larva.

So they could gain familiarity with the local fauna, there was available for inspection at each class fresh living material from the rock pools and vleis. From the very first lecture, I taught comparative anatomy from a physiological viewpoint, and I always had a lecture bench demonstration of some important principle. What I showed in my first lecture for beginners was the reversible effect on the isolated heartbeat of the Cape lobster of reducing calcium and increasing potassium in the perfusion fluid. This always impresses the neophyte naïve enough to associate death exclusively with cessation of the heartbeat. Another favourite with beginners was stopping the heartbeat of the dogfish by electrical stimulation of the vagus nerve. I liked to adjust the stimulus to arrest the beat for a specified interval, say two minutes. The students kept an eye on the second hand of a wristwatch and in expectant hush awaited the exact time when the heart would begin to beat again.

Even to readers who have no familiarity with the Cape peninsula it will now be clear that it embraced within a day's drive a well-nigh bewildering range of well-defined and diversified ecological systems both animal and plant. Though the experimental viewpoint permeated my syllabus, I was anxious that my students should take full advantage of these opportunities for ecological studies. My predecessor had made no attempt to stock a departmental museum with representative specimens of the local fauna, and the task of doing so in Cape Town was much less easy than in a country where comprehensive monographs for identification of animal species and inexpensive illustrated manuals of the local flora are available. Fortunately, the national museum at Cape Town was undertaking an exhaustive survey of the Cape fauna, and I was able to attach to my own department, in a part-time capacity, one of its staff to organise field work. Being myself familiar from Birkbeck days with the drill for exhibiting specimens in museum jars to best advantage, I gave all second-year students a demonstration of the know-how and entrusted them throughout the remainder of the course with the preparation and identification of specimens duly provided with locally printed labels. When I left South Africa, my department had a handsome collection to assist recognition of material brought back from the field.

At about the time I arrived in Cape Town, the Ministry of Education had decreed that biology should henceforth be an obligatory subject of the secondary school curriculum. I got the agreement of the Senate to put on a course in the early evening for local science teachers. This was very popular, and several teachers who had not then a full graduate qualification obtained one before I left. One of these, a man more than twelve years older than myself, was Louis Herrman. After I left South Africa, I was able to get him a postgraduate scholarship in my department, where he obtained the London Ph.D. Perhaps the fact that his birthplace, like mine, was Portsmouth initially brought us close together.

Before we met, Herrman had already written a scholarly book on the history of the Jews in South Africa.[1] This divulged the role of Jewish pilots trained in Moorish astronomy, when Portuguese ships first rounded the Cape. At about the time when I first met Louis, publication of Robert Briffault's *Making of Humanity* had already whetted my appetite for more knowledge of the contributions of Moslem and Hindu culture to scientific geography, mathematics and medicine during the period when European culture was at its lowest ebb. Louis introduced me to the Jewish Encyclopedia for source material on the role of Jews as missionaries of Moorish science and promoters of medicine in the universities of mediaeval Christendom.

Nearly all my brightest students in Cape Town were Jewish, and the majority of my friends were. These included a rabbi, who was a Cambridge man and Professor of Hebrew in the University. Another, the wife of a leading lawyer whose constituency as a House of Assembly member had a large number of Cape Coloured voters, was Ruth Alexander. Before our arrival, she had the only salon which attracted the Cape Town intelligentsia. She had been a close friend of Olive Schreiner, famous in the heyday of feminist activity and sister of W. P. Schreiner, a prominent Cape statesman at the time when the British South Africa Act of 1910 conferred on the colony Dominion status. She had also been a friend of Mahatma Gandhi.

Gandhi emerged as an advocate of civil disobedience without violence, as a political technique, during his sojourn in Natal, which had a very large Indian population recruited as indentured labour from 1860 onwards. Two years after his call to the Bar in London in 1889, Gandhi came to Natal, where he soon had a lucrative practice. He gave it up to mobilise the struggle of the Indian community for political rights. With his wife, he served a prison sentence, but battled on till he returned after an absence of twenty years to India, there to lead the campaign for *Swaraj*. By then he had already won the respect even of (infamous) General Jan Christiaan Smuts.

Shortly after arrival in Cape Town I first met, in the salon of Ruth Alexander, Herbert Meyerowitz, who became one of my dearest friends. He was then Assistant Director of the University Art School and was there becoming famous for a new genre of teak murals, carved with the semblance of metallic sculpture. 'Volodja,' as his intimates called him, had lately come to South Africa to throw off incipient pulmonary tuberculosis. Before leaving Berlin, he had been an art director for the memorable Ufa trilogy: *The Cabinet of Dr. Caligari*, *The Golem*, and *Metropolis*. His political outlook was intelligently, not dogmatically, Marxist. Like all members of the circle of friends we had in Cape Town, he was anti-segregationist. Also on the side of the angels was Robert Broom, perhaps the greatest palaeontologist of all time.[2]

Till forced out by the Predikants, Broom had been professor in the Afrikaner University College at Stellenbosch. Thereafter, he supported himself in a dental practice in the Karroo. The Territory so named is amazingly rich in early land vertebrate fossils and especially Theromorpha, the group of reptiles which gave rise to the mammals. Whenever he came to Cape Town to consult with the director of the National Museum, Broom stayed with us, and at each such visit, he would produce from his pocket a skull demonstrating a new link in what, thanks to his work, is now an unbroken evolutionary chain.

The skull is the most characteristic part of the mammalian skeleton, and of pivotal importance in the transition from the reptilian to the mammalian skull is the fact that the lower jaw of the latter is a single bone. That of reptiles, like that of birds and amphibia, is compound.

In the reptilian stock leading to mammals, the loss of posterior components of the lower jaw entailed two remarkable changes. In the process of developing a new articulation, two bones of the ancestral near-mammal became detached, one from the upper, the other from the lower jaw, retaining a ligamentary connexion with the single bone which transmits vibrations of the ear drum to the inner ear of all land vertebrates other than mammals. Thus it came about that mammals have three ear ossicles.

Aside from the privilege of enjoying a preview of successive instalments of so enthralling a serial in advance of publication, the company of Robert Broom was always welcome. He was a man with wide intellectual interests, a socialist and a rationalist. When I left Cape Town, he issued to the press a very handsome tribute to what I had done for scientific research in South Africa, laying stress on the fact that my department was an innovation in South African science. In some fields, such as his own, work of the highest quality can be that of a solitary investigator. More often than not, the best work in physiology is the outcome of collaboration between two or more co-workers, each excelling in some technique and each fully conversant with that of his colleague or colleagues. During my stay in Cape Town I had recruited seven collaborators to work with me or on projects I had planned. When I left I had, as Broom testified, indeed created for the first time in South Africa a school of scientific research.

The range of our departmental research programme was versatile though with too few recruits to do justice to the many possibilities offered by such abundance of animal life in a country where there were no vivisection laws to cripple physiological investigations. I myself concentrated, though not exclusively, on work I had begun in the Imperial College and continued intermittently at Edinburgh on the role of the pituitary gland in relation to colour change in cold-blooded vertebrates. In returning to this topic, I had the good luck which an experimental biologist covets but rarely experiences.

In many fields of experimental biology, advance in the understanding of a function takes place on a wider front and at a greater tempo if one can find the animal uniquely fitted for study. For example, the expansion of genetics was spectacular when the Columbia School were able to exploit the many advantages of the fruit fly, *Drosophila*, for exploring the role of the chromosomes in hereditary transmission. For my purpose, the South African clawed toad, *Xenopus laevis*, proved to be a godsend. It opened up for me an unforeseen territory in the study of the pituitary.[3]

Having no confidence in the results obtained on animals on which one has recently operated (which are often destined soon to die of shock), I based all my final conclusions on animals which had been at least a year, mostly two years, under observation since surgical interference. In this way, I stumbled on two interesting facts which anticipated later work by others on the role of the pituitary and light in the sexual cycle of birds. In short, I found that the ovaries of *Xenopus* degenerate either after removal of the eyes or after removal of the anterior lobe of the pituitary. I published (LH 1930a) a brief note in my own name, recording that anterior lobe extracts prepared as described by Bellerby in the same year evoke ovulation, thus completing the demonstration of the dependence of ovarian function on the excretion of the *pars anterior*. A by-product of this work was the Hogben pregnancy test, used for fifteen years or more by the Edinburgh Pregnancy Diagnosis Unit.

In the course of investigations embodied in the seventh of the series *Studies on the Pituitary* (LH 1930b), I established with the collaboration of my demonstrator Cecil Gordon that what I called the melanin dispersing hormone was identical with neither the pressor nor oxytocic components of posterior lobe extract. This hormone had been the main topic of previous communications in the series.

Throughout all the work on *Xenopus* in Cape Town, I had treated colour change by recourse to the melanophore index which had been used by myself until I had had an opportunity of testing its reliability by pooling the observations of large classes of students (over a hundred). Later, when I was in London, I investigated colour response in Elasmobranch fishes during a vacation at the Plymouth Marine Biological Laboratory. This was the topic of the seventh of the series the *Pigmentary Effector System* (LH 1936a), which established that the control mechanism in the group is essentially the same as in amphibia.

My work derived much benefit from my early association with

Frank Crew, one of whose considerable merits was his lively interest in animal husbandry. I deplore a current tendency to more and more elaborate gadgeteering. Young scientific workers rely increasingly on species for which the animal husbandry is a matter of established routine, left to a technician. If one is to take advantage of particular idiosyncrasies which make some species more suitable for investigation than others, one has to be prepared to undertake extensive explorative work with a view to healthy survival in the laboratory.

Enid, who had already become interested in genetics when we came to Edinburgh, succumbed in the first weeks to the magic of the Cape rock pools. As a schoolgirl, she had been sent to a seminary for female offspring of Congregational ministers at a time when study of natural science was not widely accredited as suitable equipment for a young lady. With no other options, she exploited her aptitude for classical studies and mathematics. Had circumstances been different, she would have specialised in biology. She had an inborn aptitude for physiological enquiry and, as her opportunities for studious leisure expanded, she made up for lost time, acquiring a knowledge of chemistry and physics. She completed for publication several physiological communications in the Proceedings of the Royal Society and the Journal of Experimental Biology. By the time we left Cape Town, she had acquired a well-earned Ph.D.[4]

Besides a return voyage to East London when I spent a short working holiday at a native trading station, I made two other sea trips. One was on a hydrographic survey vessel of the Simonstown naval base, an opportunity secured because the commander was a former Cambridge man, very intelligent and usually drunk. My objective was to collect sea water samples for analysis to explore the possibility that circumstances other than temperature and the direction of currents contributed to the considerably different fauna of the two sides of the Cape peninsula.

On another journey the aim was to collect a gallon of octopus blood to round off work on the haemocyanins, abandoned after I left Canada. I went for a fortnight in a trawler as guest of a local firm with a large fleet. We dredged off the coast of Southwest Africa in the most stormy season. I had never experienced discomfort from the motion of a large vessel, but I did so on this one. It did not discredit me in the eyes of the crew or captain, all of whom vomited

PLATE I

figure 1   Portrait Head by Henry Meyerowitz, Cape Town, c. 1928. Now on display in the Medical School, University of Birmingham.

Figure 2 Alfred Russel Wallace, 1823–1913. Discoverer of the theory of natural selection and co-author with Darwin of *On the Origin of Species*, 1859.

PLATE III

Figure 3A The Hogbens, about 1910. Behind (*l. to r.*): Dorothy, Lancelot, Margaret. Front (*l. to r.*): Thomas Hogben, Bernard, Hamilton, and Margaret Prescott Hogben.

Figure 3B Bethune Rd; close to 91 Bethune Rd (demolished by bombs, together with several other houses, in WWII). The Hogben family moved into #91 and adjoining house in 1907.

Figure 3C Lancelot, 1915, Ambulance Corps.

Courtesy of Religious Society of Friends

PLATE IV

Figure 4A "The backs," Trinity College, Cambridge.

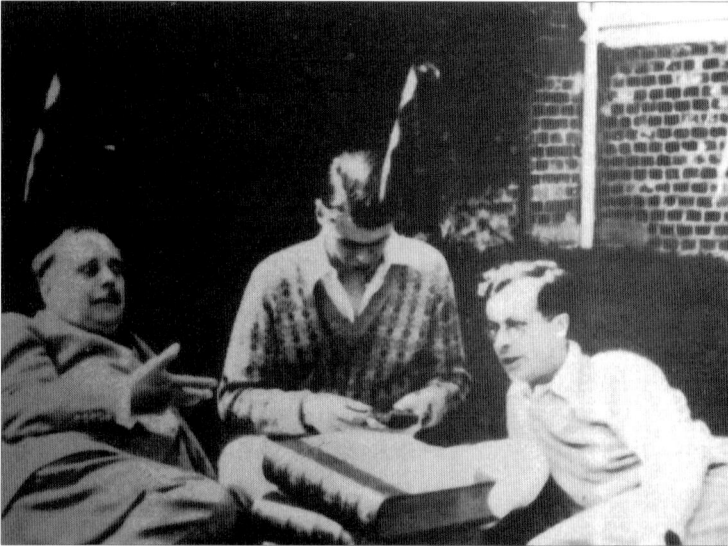

Figure 4B H. G. Wells, his son Gip, and Julian Huxley working on *The Science of Life* at Easton Glebe, Wells's home, in 1927.

PLATE V

Figure 5A T. H. Morgan. Nobel Prize 1933.

Figure 5B H. J. Muller. Nobel Prize 1946.

Figure 5C Two extremes of colour change in the common frog. From *Principles of Animal Biology*.

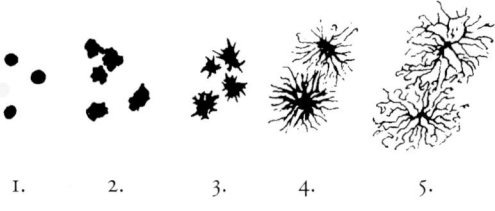

1.   2.   3.   4.   5.

Figure 5D Melanocyte under low power. Left to right, progression from extremes of pallor to darkening. (LH 1931b.)

PLATE VI

Figure 6A
Lancelot Hogben. Assistant Professor of Zoology, McGill University.

Marine Biological Laboratory, Woods Hole, Massachusetts, summer 1926.

Figure 6B
Carl Pantin. Marine Biological Assocation of the UK, Plymouth.

Marine Biological Laboratory, Woods Hole, Massachusetts, summer 1926.

PLATE VII

Figure 7A The South African clawed toad, *Xenopus laevis*.

Figure 7B Zoological Building, University of Cape Town.

PLATE VIII

If you are an ungodly child,
Rebellious turbulent and wild,
And organise a nursery strike,
You are the sort of child I like.

And if when visitors comment
Upon your features, you resent
A curious likeness to your father,
I'm sure that I shall like you rather.

Of course, if on the day of rest,
You freely chose to wear your best,
And always did as you were bid,
I'd think you were a hateful kid.

Figure 8A Dedication from *To Any Child*, by Lancelot Hogben, about 1928. Children (*l. to r.*): Sylvia, Adrian and Clare.

Figure 8B Drawings from *To Any Child*. Clockwise from lower left: "Form and Function," "The Species Problem," and "Future of Africa."

PLATE IX

Figure 9A
Frederick Bodmer.

Figure 9B Devon cottage. Moreton hampstead, 1933–37.

Figure 9C Keith Gold Medal. Profile: John Napier (1550–1617).

PLATE X

Figure 10A
Lancelot Hogben.
"New Statesman,"
1930s.

Figure 10B
J. B. S. Haldane.
"New Statesman,"
1930s.

PLATE XI

Figure 11A Living room, Inverdon, Aberdeen. (Left-hand door to greenhouse. Fifteen feet to rear of camera.)

Figure 11B Marischal College, University of Aberdeen.

PLATE XII

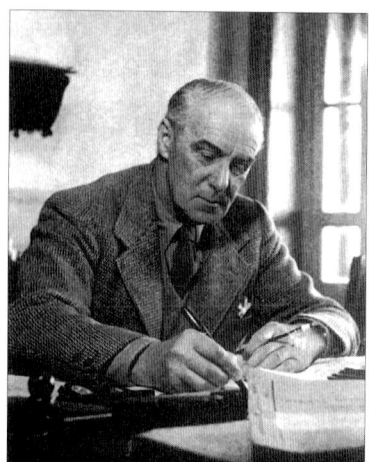

Figure 12A F. A. E. Crew.

Courtesy University of Edinburgh.

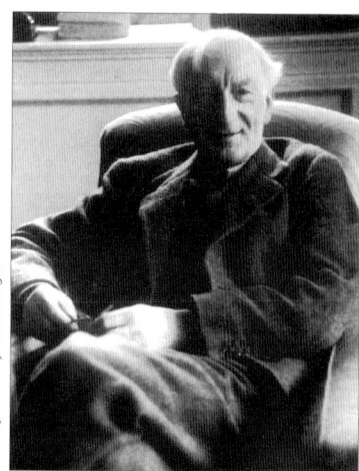

Figure 12B Lord William Beveridge.

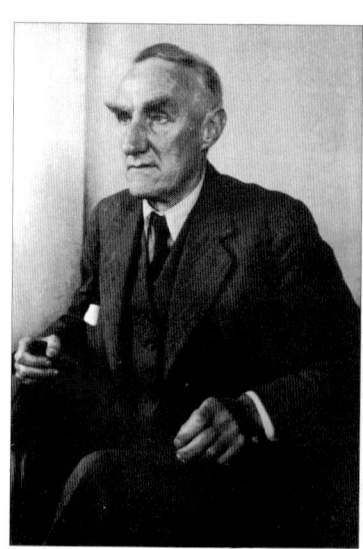

Figure 12C Lord John Boyd Orr.

PLATE XIII

Figure 13A Penrose home, London, Ontario, fall 1940. (*l. to r.*): Roger, Margaret, Oliver and Clare Hogben; B. Barman; Lionel and Jonathan Penrose. (Lionel Penrose sponsored Hogben immigration to Canada.)

Figure 13B The University of Wisconsin.

PLATE XIV

Figure 14A Chamberlain Tower, University of Birmingham.

Figure 14B   College of Medicine, University of Birmingham.

Figure 15A
Enid Charles.
Penybont, Wales.
About 1950.

Figure 15B
Lancelot Hogben.
Penybont, Wales.
About 1950.

PLATE XVI

Figure 16A   *Lloches y Fwyalchen* (Blackbird's Retreat), Glyn Ceiriog.

Figure 16B   Village of Glyn Ceiriog, Denbighshire, Wales.

intermittently over the side between hauls. The skipper was a Norwegian who was glad to have my company. Night after night I lay on my back close to the wheel, listening to a monologue of his experience in whalers or vessels trapping seals in the Antarctic. The recital might have come from the pen of Conrad, and could have become a literary masterpiece if tape recorders had then been available. It included a description of the grim rock face of Kerguelen Island at a time when its only inhabitants were a Scot and a German who never spoke to one another though they had settled within a day's journey of each other. It seems that they had come there to get away from human society.

Inescapably life in South Africa made a powerful impact on my preference for reading matter. I no longer had to read Somerset Maugham to discover what is the favourite indoor and outdoor sport of tropical wives or to read Louis Golding to learn what life is like in an orthodox Jewish family. If I wanted to explore the mental horizon of a remittance man, there was good enough case material within reach. A picturesque beachcomber, who supplied my laboratory with live lobsters, lived at Cape Point on the foreshore in a hut made of driftwood and flattened-out petrol tins. Before my own birth he had been to a public school and could still talk nostalgically about the curriculum.

While I was in Cape Town, my reading became increasingly restricted to historical and philosophical themes. I became interested in colonialism, in the contribution of Eastern civilisations to Western science and mathematics, in the new brand of Marxism that was emerging in the Soviet Union, in the psychopathology of race prejudice, in the rational credentials of theories of race superiority and in the population problem then coming to the fore. In an isolated community such as the English-speaking minority of Cape Town, intellectuals can, and then did, experience a constant terror of losing touch with contemporary thought in the distant centres of civilisation. Like most of my circle of this period, I was eager to sample any new book about which people were talking in Britain. When I returned to the homeland after five years abroad, the outlook of some former acquaintances I once regarded as sophisticated seemed to me insipid and drearily parochial.

CHAPTER XII

Dawn of Apartheid

So far I have not mentioned how we organised our home life when we came to Cape Town. We were able to rent a bungalow nearby the wooded slopes leading up to Table Mountain, and our children could thus lead an open-air life when not at school. We also had the good fortune to secure the services of a Swedish housekeeper so that Enid was able to devote herself wholly to scientific work. Doubtless, one circumstance which forced both of us during our years in the Cape to intense scientific activity was the fact that the tightening grip of apartheid overshadowed our social contacts and reinforced our determination to return to Britain when there was a favourable opportunity. We did not want our children to grow up in a country where a white man kicks a black man off the pavement. This was not yet true of Cape Town, but it was easy to see which way the wind was blowing when the clamour over the substitution of a national flag for the Union Jack died down. By 1928, a nationalist government had made Afrikaans a compulsory subject in all the schools, and, throughout my stay in Cape Town, South Africa was in a state of political turmoil without parallel in the first two decades after its attainment of Dominion status. In this setting, I seized at every available opportunity to understand the historical background of the battle between Boer and Briton. Eric Walker, later professor of Imperial History in Cambridge, was then head of the History Department in the University, and he was finishing his *History of South Africa*.

From conversation with him, from reading his book when it came out and from the official history of the South Africa Chartered Company, I learned much about the origins of the Boer War and its bearing on the nationalist policies then taking shape. Louis Herrman, the completion of whose book on the history of South African Jewry had forced him to delve into the unsavoury antecedents of some of South Africa's leading citizens, lent me a revealing book about the origins of the great South African fortunes. Prosecuted for criminal libel, as Afrikaners call candour, the author was at that time doing time on the breakwater, and it was an offence to possess a copy of his *chef d'oeuvre*. In Louis's house, I met an elderly Rand journalist who had lived through and covered events leading up to the Jameson Raid. One night I sat up with him till daybreak listening to a recital that deserved a more enduring fate than its mention here.

After I left, the *Cape Times* had a leader stating that there was at all hours of the night a light burning in my laboratory. This was not far off the truth. For both Enid and myself, it was a period of obsessional scientific activity. Nonetheless, we compressed an intense social life on a diminutive time ration. Aside from Eric Walker, my professorial colleagues were not intellectually stimulating; but several of the junior academic staff were more companionable, among them Benjamin Farrington, then a lecturer who taught Greek, and Frederick Bodmer, senior lecturer in the department of German.

Farrington awakened my interest in early Greek science and the Greek atomists sufficiently to make me read everything accessible about them—including the doctorate thesis of Karl Marx. Bodmer whetted my appetite for the French encyclopaedists. More than ten years later, we were to collaborate in *The Loom of Language*, the plan of which I drew up as editor. Oddly enough, I can recall during my stay in the Cape no interest in philology nor awareness of what it has methodologically in common with palaeontology. Not till a much later date did I assess the significance of the pressure for use of Afrikaans as a pointer to the many ramifications of linguistic differences in social tradition and practical politics.

Soon after arrival, we reinstated our Edinburgh Saturday evening for social intercourse. With Cape brandy at eighteen pence a bottle, this cost next to nothing. We soon assembled a weekly salon of the Cape Town intelligentsia.[1] The original nucleus was made up of my senior students and some of the non-professorial staff including Herbert Meyerowitz and his wife. Like my brightest students, most of the Cape Town medicos with consultant status were also Jewish. This brought within the orbit of my programme for buildup of a team active in physiological research several medical graduates for whom I had no need to provide an income. It also gave me a great deal of information about orthodox Jewry, and a new insight into the vicious cycle of persecution.

At that time, Cape Town was the first port of call for refugees from the ghettos of Central Europe. By the time the second and third generation had reached Johannesburg, they had shed much of their orthodoxy and many of them had assimilated the Afrikaner attitude of non-Europeans; but the first generation of immigrants in Cape Town and in the reserves, where they sought (and found) their fortunes as native traders, observed all the Talmudic proprieties. From such, I accepted an invitation to attend two circumcision ceremonies performed with Hebrew incantation by a ritual surgeon. Other than myself, the men stood around wearing top hats. The chief performer had no medical qualification, but was very quick at the draw with fingers and scissors. Though the last two mentioned were certainly not aseptic, I do not believe that he ever lost a patient. Nor was the victim vocally uncooperative. The anaesthetic was a lump of sugar in a muslin wrapping which the victim had no time to eject before the scissors had deftly done their worst.

Circumcisions apart, I had ample opportunities of observing aspects of orthodoxy usually unexplored by the unchosen. Unlike most, if not all, of my contemporaries in the field of endocrinology, I never made extracts of glands which I had not facilities for plunging in acetone within ten minutes of death; and in Cape Town, as in London and in Edinburgh, from which I travelled to the Glasgow abattoir for the purpose, I did not trust an assistant with the task. In the Cape Town slaughter house to which I repaired monthly to replenish my stock of pituitaries, there were three categories of killing: by so-called humane killer for so-called Christians, kosher kill for orthodox Jews and another variant of ritual slaughter for devout Moslems. The second was most convenient for my purpose. I perched myself on a five-foot-high cupboard by the slaughter pen because the half-wild native cattle sometimes broke loose and showed no appreciation of the advantages of a religious funeral.

Kaffir lads chased them one at a time into the pen, and danced around with ropes until one boy successfully looped a leg, thereby tripping the victim into a recumbent position. The others then speedily pinioned it with ropes, one of which stretched its neck rigidly for the officiating minister of religion, suitably attired in black and equipped with a long knife. Before a mumbled Hebrew incantation, part of the ritual was to toss a hair high enough to ensure that the razor edge could sever it by a swift stroke. Another swift stroke severed both carotids to ensure that the corpse was relatively bloodless before it reached the butcher. This performance always brought me back to St. Paul's counsel that even Gentile sinners should keep themselves from things strangled and from fornication. Once I travelled with one of my research team twenty miles each way during a thunderstorm in the Cis-Kai to see a local rabbi cut the throat of a chicken over an outside drainpipe lest peradventure unconsecrated hands had wrung the neck of the bird destined for our dinner.

This experience happened on my one holiday of more than a weekend while in South Africa. Some might call it a busman's holiday. My intention was twofold: first to take a look at the Cape fauna beyond the ancient track of the Dutch East Indies Company, second to grub up advances in atomic and molecular physics with little impact on the curriculum in my student days. It happened that I had seduced into biological research a recently graduated M.Sc. from the physics department. My protégé, Cecil Gordon, had authentically orthodox parents who, like so many others of their fraternity, were rich enough to send him to the South African *ersatz* Shrewsbury or Blundell's. When he offered to take me into a native trading station where we shared a bedroom, I welcomed the opportunity of what one now calls a *teach-in* to mobilise the resources of my not entirely neglected mathematical self-education. While staying with Cecil and his parents, I conformed to the respect one English non-conformist owes to another; that is to say, I borrowed a hat to sit through prayers suitably attired to face Jehovah.

Thunderstorms in eastern Cape Province are awe-inspiring. One may see a ribbon of fork lightning twenty-five miles long. During one such spectacle of dancing neon lights, Cecil and I sat drenched to the skin in subtropical rain merely making small talk which led me to mention someone in the periphery of my own circle in Cape Town. My companion said that one must take care not to talk about him at home. When I asked why, he astonished me by saying that the person mentioned had married a Gentile. Several years later, Cecil himself married a very charming Scots wife from the London School of Economics. By then, Hitler had transferred the doctrinal loyalties of so many young people like himself from Moses to Stalin.

Needless to say, the shops which provided nutriments for the Cape Town *goyim* could not accommodate all the prescribed taboos of the chosen people. To eat *Kosher*-wise, the orthodox must congregate in sufficient numbers to provide a viable market for permissible foodstuffs. If for no other reason, they must therefore isolate themselves from the society of their Gentile fellow citizens, and by doing so make themselves conspicuous as a social group with loyalties peculiar to themselves. The marriage taboo last mentioned put the spotlight on a second circumstance contributory to the conspicuous isolation. If one of the sons marries a Gentile girl, the orthodox family mourns at evening prayers for a considerable period after the event, and at each subsequent anniversary. In even mildly orthodox families of opulent South African Jewry, wedlock was in my time usually *mariage de convenance*, negotiated by a professional marriage broker who undertook the preliminaries of finding an acceptable and profitable match. In a profession such as medicine or the law, the fate of the impecunious male would depend on the size of the dowry his future father-in-law could offer.

In orthodox families which almost invariably saw to it that one of the boys had a university education leading to a learned profession, there was no such provision of higher education for the girls. It thus could, and often did, happen that the young Cape Town Jewish intellectual formed attachments with women students having cultural interests they were not likely to share with the marital partner of their parents' choice. The fact that such liaisons inevitably terminated without either church bells or a visit to a registry office inevitably invited resentment. It also accounted for an immense preoccupation with sex as a topic of polite conversation. I believe H. G. Wells went to the root of the matter when he said that Freud's obsession with the relevance of sexuality to neurosis was the by-product of a wealthy Jewish clientele not yet fully assimilated to the way of life of its Viennese neighbours.

As will be more clear at a later stage to readers with little knowledge of the antecedents and consequences of the Boer War, familiarity with another facet of the psychopathology of persecution and so-called *race* hatred forced itself daily on one's attention during my residence in South Africa. The admittance of large numbers of immigrants with a lower material standard of life entails both cultural and conspicuous isolation, as such a dual threat to the wellbeing of the community which admits them. It provides both a market for slum property and a reservoir of cheap labour which jeopardises the earning capacity of their neighbours.

If physical differences make the immigrant more conspicuous, the hostility evoked by the challenge of his presence is proportion-

Dawn of Apartheid

ately intense. Nonetheless, there is a pattern common to hatred of the Bantu by South African poor whites, anti-semitism in Hampstead at the end of the second World War and hostility of the Scottish and English protestant to the Irish Catholic in Glasgow and Liverpool. Alas, the muddleheaded attitude of the British Labour Party to unrestricted immigration from Pakistan and the West Indies during the fifties shows how reluctantly well-meaning people recognise the cause and cure of maladies they deplore.

At the time of my arrival, one could not remain long in Cape Town without feeling the impact of the mounting pressure for apartheid. Since Americans and most Britons do not use the word coloured and native in the same way as South Africans, I must here digress to explain the local usage. Coloured in South Africa stands for two categories of personnel. The Cape Coloured are a mixed stock with a basic stratum of descendants of Malay slaves brought in by the Dutch East Indies Company during the late seventeenth and the eighteenth centuries. Some of them mated with Hottentots and Bushmen, more with poor whites than Afrikaners care to admit. *Coloured* in the twenties was also the designation of the Natal Indian population mentioned earlier. In contradistinction to coloured, *native*, as Afrikaners use the term, signifies Bantu, Hottentots and Bushmen. By the provisions of the British South Africa Act (1910), only some of the Cape natives and a restricted number in Natal had the right to vote in elections for the Legislative Assembly. Elsewhere, they remained serfs on the farms or impoverished in reserves.

To understand what was brewing when a coalition of Afrikaner nationalist and white labour under J. B. M. Hertzog defeated the United Party under Smuts in mid-1924, one has to traverse a century of African history. After the abolition of slave ownership in British possessions overseas, many Afrikaners remained in the Cape and assimilated the antislavery tradition of British missionaries. It is worthy of comment that Jan Hendrik (Onze Jan) Hofmeyr, of Dutch descent, and Olive's brother W. P. Schreiner were most active in safeguarding the Cape Native vote when the provisions of the Act of 1910 were under discussion.

When the *Voortrekkers*, 12,000 or so who resisted abolition, left the Cape between 1835 and 1843 to found independent republics, they accounted for little, if any, more than a quarter of the Cape Dutch. They were simple farmers with no prevision of the discovery of diamonds—first in the Orange and Vaal rivers (1867), later in Kimberley (1870). Sixteen years later, when there was an unprecedented gold rush in Witwatersrand, the Boer leaders had neither the inclination nor the intention of accommodating the industrial Bantu proletariat, and the tycoons of the Rand could mobilise a source of cheap labour only by deposing them. This and no false sentiment of loyalty to the British Crown was why Britain bled itself to the accompaniment of Kipling's pop orchestra in a morally disastrous war, the evil consequences of which are now manifest.

Between the dates last cited and 1895, miners who came from all parts of Europe staked their claims, made fortunes overnight and lost them also overnight, at poker. Rightly or wrongly, I heard that Barney Barnato made and lost three six-figure fortunes in almost as many weeks. Be that as it may, the ownership of both the diamond fields and the gold mines soon consolidated in the hands of a small group of unsavoury cosmopolitan adventurers. In contemporary terms, they had therefore to pay exorbitant wages to the so-called poor whites who had gambled away their claims. So the main concern of the owners was to bring in cheap labour from beyond the northern frontier. Called by the Boers *Uitlanders*, they were mostly without a vote. This was a grievance they could eloquently exploit to their advantage. Since the ruling Boers refused to play ball, they were driven to explore the possibility of annexation by a European power sympathetic to immigration.

One eyewitness at meetings to petition the protection of foreign powers during the three years in the Rand before the Jameson raid assured me that devotion to the British flag was comically irrelevant. The promoters were equally amenable to proposals that the Kaiser, the King of the Belgians or the Queen of the Netherlands should undertake the role of Big Brother or Big Sister. At this juncture, Cecil Rhodes, who was well in with the Rand tycoons, found a sympathetic ally in the Colonial Secretary Joseph Chamberlain. Rhodes was at that time premier of the Cape and had controlling interests in three great mining concerns: De Beers Consolidated Mines, Gold Fields of South Africa and the South African Chartered Company with its concession north of the Transvaal. The last named had its private army, like that of the East India Company in the days of Clive, and under the command of a romantic Scot already corrupted by Rhodes's delusions of grandeur.

Starr Jameson entered the service of the Chartered Company as an Edinburgh graduate of medicine. In that capacity, he violated all the Hippocratic standards of professional ethics by extracting a concession at a nominal price from Lobengula, a local chief who was also one of his patients. The cosmopolitan crooks behind his ill-fated invasion of the Transvaal Republic had convinced influential persons in London that its intention was to rescue loyal British *Uitlanders* from an intolerable foreign yoke. That a man so evil as Rhodes was behind the plot is beyond dispute. That Chamberlain, so ostensibly rectitudinarian a patron of the Socinian heresy in its West Midland stronghold, did not connive at it is an article of faith among few other than his fellow Christians.

When the raid had ignominiously failed, the patriarchal president of the Republic behaved with astonishing clemency by handing Jameson over to the British Government to stand trial for infringement of the Foreign Enlistment Act. He spent only a year in Holloway before revisiting the scene of his crimes *en famille* with the chief instigator. Eventually, he received the K.C.M.G. in recognition of services to an empire on which the sun never set. As one of Rhodes's executors, he shared with Oxford University the exacting responsibility for whitewashing his memory.

After the failure of Jameson's raid, Rhodes and his associated tycoons manoeuvred more cautiously to bring about an act of war to force the hands of the home government to intervene on their own behalf and on behalf of the Birmingham small arms industry. The South Africa lobby had little difficulty in convincing the stronghold of nonconformity and arms manufacture that the Uitlanders and the Boers were engaged in the ideological struggle in which the antislavery tradition was at stake. Whether some don of vision in Oxford had as yet anticipated the payoff is problematical. What was in fact at stake was the sacred right of the native beyond the frontier to the privilege of sweating in the mines at lower wages than the expropriated European immigrants were willing to take. Such is the charity in aid of which our regulars fought a war which introduced the British to the term *concentration camp* and left behind it a load of hate for generations to come.

When the Boer War ended, the mining corporations had to face the challenge of an organised trade union of white workers on the Rand under the leadership of Colonel Creswell. From conversations with a Labour leader of the 1924 coalition, I gained the impression that racist ideology at first had no place in the programme of its promoters.[2] Their initial aim was to prevent the introduction at pitifully low pay of unskilled and illiterate Bantu immigrants from the North. When they failed to do so, the next step was inevitable. Creswell's followers demanded legal restriction of skilled work to persons of European descent. They had largely achieved their aim before the beginning of the first World War; but relations between their leaders and the chamber of Mines had become increasingly bitter owing to the intervention of Smuts in a strike of 1907, deportations he ordered in 1914 and the executions of 1922. By then, White Labour was behind a Nationalist party committed to further limitations of native civil rights.

In 1926, a Mines and Works Amendment Act tightened previous enforcement of the colour bar. At that date, most people in the Cape regarded the rise to power of the nationalists as a temporary setback to the party led by Smuts and supported by all South Africans of British descent; and I confess that I was slow to recognise on arrival in Cape Town the first compelling indication of the shape of things to come. The adoption of a national flag with no symbol of the British connexion evoked a furore in Natal where the Afrikaners were least influential. This is easy to understand. Its predominantly English-speaking voters anticipated their exclusion from public administration and higher education if the nationalists implemented—as they did—their intention to make knowledge of Afrikaans compulsory for civil servants and for university teachers.

Henceforth, civil rights had become a political issue which eclipsed every other, and those in opposition to racial discrimination sank all differences of opinion or belief about other matters. Thus I numbered among my personal friends the Anglican Dean of Cape Town, a Unitarian minister with a passionate dislike of vivisection, and the editor and printer of a South African communist party publication, Eddie Roux. The latter, an Afrikaner with a Cambridge degree, had set up a printing press to give lessons in English to natives whose only speech was a Bantu language such as Xhosa, with an infusion of Bushman clicks. After two years' residence in Cape Town my feelings were torn between a desire to exploit the unique opportunities it offered for biological research and a determination to leave the country at the earliest opportunity.

The arrival of the British Association in 1929 was propitious for a comeback. My team stole most of the limelight by putting on all-day demonstrations of our research work and advanced teaching curriculum, including physiological experiments on animals which most of our visitors had not previously encountered. Never behind as his own favourite ad-man, Smuts had manipulated the programme committee to get some publicity for a lately published and half-baked excursion into Teutonic mysticism with the title *Holism*. A symposium devoted thereto was the period piece of the verbal proceedings. As the principal opposition speaker, I advanced a viewpoint essentially like that of Ryle and Ayer later. On a voyage home, I elaborated the argument in a volume of essays called *The Nature of Living Matter*, 1930, in opposition to the thesis of Eddington's *Nature of the Physical World*, 1928.

In the ordinary sense of the term, neither Enid nor myself was at any time during our sojourn in South Africa politically active. That is to say, we did not take part in extramural political activity; but the relation between white and non-white intruded on every aspect of existence, not least within the university. Within a few days after my arrival, the admission of coloured students was on the agenda for my first attendance at a meeting of the University Senate. I spoke in a minority of three—with the support of Eric Walker and of Arnold Plant, then Professor of Commerce in Cape Town, later in the London School of Economics. From time to time, I also addressed meetings of student societies on the racial issue, and I never found it difficult to keep the attention of a student audience. Contrary to the timorous jeremiads of some of my colleagues, when there had been on my arrival no intake of coloured students, there was a sizeable number in the first year class in my department when I left. Students of both sets fraternised without affectation. The fact that the brightest ones were Jewish helped to create a standard of civilised conduct to which even Afrikaners from the Veldt conformed.

When I was not dealing face to face with the student body, Boer-backlashed mentality could make matters disagreeable. The lecturer whom I imported from McGill to replace the relict of my predecessor formed an attachment to one of the only two coloured medical graduates then practising in the Dominion, the other one being her brother-in-law, a leading light in the Moslem Community. Both held the Glasgow degree. When our young colleague confided in us that he was bringing his lady-friend to the University annual dance, both Enid and I scented embarrassment for both. Accordingly, we asked the pair to dine with us so that the lady could come as our own guest. My Jewish students clustered round and saw to it that she was never without a partner. Next day, the more rabid nationalist students held an open air campus meeting of protest.

In the course of it, one fanatical Afrikaner asserted that I had brought into the hall a native prostitute after leaving it in a state of intoxication. I heard of the campus demonstration on the same day and immediately consulted the leading civil rights lawyer, already mentioned as husband of Ruth Alexander, and the most influential member of the Cape Town synagogue other than my friend Bender the Professor of Hebrew. At his advice I threatened an action for slander against the Student Representative Council. The officers capitulated with the offer of a public apology read at a meeting convened for the purpose. I agreed on condition that I wrote the apology, an exercise in ironical prose with racial coexistence as its theme. They had to keep their promise.

By the beginning of 1929, the prospect was not at all healthy for university staff who openly opposed the Government's racial policy. That year the local press spoke of seven native bills.[3] One of these made marriage, and even intercourse, between a European and a native a criminal offence. Another tightened up the pass-system which restricted free movement of the native beyond the reserves, and imposed a period of forced labour on natives found squatting, in effect wandering, on land belonging to our kith and kin, an ex-European farmer. The most drastic of all provisions of the new legislation abolished the Cape native franchise and withdrew from the native anywhere in the Union the right of free assembly. The last two provisions abrogated safeguards in the British South Africa Act of 1910, any revision of which required a majority in a joint session of both houses of the South African legislature.

Herbert Meyerowitz and I sat in the equivalent of the British Stranger's gallery during the joint session. With the outstanding exception of J. H. Hofmeyr, nephew of the older Hofmeyr, the sentiments expressed by the followers of the incorrigibly equivocal Smuts differed little from those of government supporters.

There followed a personally memorable incident in 1930. During the week before free assembly of natives became illegal, a conference of natives called to protest against the new legislation met in Worcester, about a hundred miles north of Cape Town. Whereupon local farmers who had formed a posse of *vigilantes*, dispersed the gathering and forced into hiding two leaders they were out to lynch. A white man sympathetic to the native cause appealed for help to bring them to safety in District Six, the native and coloured quarter of Cape Town. Both Enid and I had learned to drive since our arrival, and our second-hand car had a capacious boot. The emissary of the natives assured us that the vigilantes would not allow without search a car driven by a male to enter or leave the district where the leaders were in hiding. On the other hand, they would not entertain the possibility that a white woman could have any truck with a Bantu male. Enid offered to drive by night over the range known as the Hottentots Holland to the place of hiding of the two native leaders and to smuggle them in the boot of the car through the outposts of the vigilantes. She brought them safely back to Cape Town by daybreak.[4]

One of the first cases for trial under the new law which prohibited miscegenation was that of a white doctor found in his car with a Bantu girl. The latter received a prison sentence of several years. The same Court on the same day, and after pronouncing sentence on the native offender, let the White off with a fine. There was nothing unusual about this. Soon after I came to Cape Town, a European farmer came before the bench for half flogging to death a native employee whom he threw into an ant-heap to finish the good work. In the Afrikaner press, there was an outburst of white-hot indignation when a Judge dared to impose a two-year prison sentence on a white man for an offence so trivial from the back-veldt viewpoint.

In a country whose white population is, as then, no greater than that of the present conurbation of Birmingham, university professors are highly vulnerable. By mid-1929 there were rumours that the nationalist coalition government was to take action to insist on the use of Afrikaans for lectures if a majority of the students attending so desired. What action they did eventually take, if any, in the predominantly English centres—Cape Town, Johannesburg and Durban—I do not know. I did hear that they had in preparation an ordinance giving the Minister of Education power to dismiss professors who expressed atheistic views in the hearing of students. This could directly concern no one except myself as president of the Students' Rationalist Society. More than any others of our academic set, I was now on the danger list. Accordingly, I decided to cash in on a favourable press during the meeting of the British Association by making a flying visit to London in the summer of 1929 at a time when academic vacancies are most likely to occur. I raised an advance of £100 on an outright sale as a textbook of my lectures for first-year students, and booked a second-class return on the Union Castle line with Frederick Bodmer for company each way.

A fortnight spent on a British liner largely in tropical waters is in many ways a socially educative experience. When on *terra firma* I am not the sort of internationalist who dislikes his compatriots; but beyond sight of land I find Englishmen intolerable. Most of them revert to the prep school. They elect a senior prefect to organise deck games, to pester any passenger who happens to be capable of sustained intellectual effort, and to give infantile pep talks on the need for competing teams to pull together and so on and so forth. At least, such was the pattern in 1929. My brief trip to and from East London for the busman's holiday at a native trading station had already prepared me for one feature of British social behaviour abroad, that of the female expatriate tropical wife on furlough. If one probes the protective cover of any one of the ship's lifeboats after sundown, one then disturbs a couple doing what frogs congregate to do at the edge of a pond in early spring.

One incident of my return voyage on the 1929 trip is mentionable. Bodmer had brought with him a copy of *The English, Are They Human?* a witty book by Renier, a 1917 Club friend of mine later to become Professor of Dutch in London University. Frederick left it lying in the smoke room, and next day there was a notice in the bar requesting the unpatriotic cad (*sic*) who owned the book to show his face by reclaiming it. The persons responsible were our kith and kin Rhodesian tobacco farmers, by and large the mental and moral scum of the planet. When I applied to the barman on Bodmer's behalf for return of the book I had to dodge, happily with success, half a dozen beer bottles aimed at my head.

At the end of two months, I came back from this voyage with a firm offer of a chair in London. On my return to Cape Town, the Governor General, then the Earl of Athlone, celebrated my appointment by inviting me to dine at the Residence. Other than himself and myself those present were his wife, Princess Alice, his daughter, Lady May Cambridge, and his *Aide-de-Camp* affianced to her. The last named was an amiable guardee of an immensely wealthy family of merchant bankers. At that time plain Captain he became, later, Colonel Sir Henry Abel Smith, Governor of Queensland. The proceedings were very formal as compared with meals I have had in later years from Colonial governors. On entry, the

Princess curtsied as befitted the respect due to the deputy of George V.

During the meal, conversation lagged. So far, I had been monosyllabic if articulate. I had been told that the correct convention at Government House was to let the Governor initiate vocal exercise. After the port, the Princess looked bored, and invited me to sit on a sort of tuffet beside her. She told me that she had never met a biologist before. So I brought the conversation *tête à tête* round to population control, whence by easy stages to birth control and reliability of contraceptives. A few months after my return to London, Dr. Edith (later Baroness) Summerskill organised a ball to raise funds for a birth control clinic. To the annoyance of court officials, Princess Alice allowed her name to appear as a patron. Conceivably I helped advance publicity.

As a family, we made the return voyage in a Dutch liner with no other English passengers to intrude on our privacy. We kept in sight of land as we entered Walvis Bay on the coast of South West Africa, putting into port at Lobito in Angola and in Grand Canary. Walvis Bay, as its name implies, is the site of a whaling station. I was prepared to experience the nauseating battlefield stench of whale meat, but not for such a depressing picture. The settlement in Walvis Bay was the most revolting spectacle I have ever set eyes on. Located on a desolate waste land without a blade of grass or other vegetation in sight, it consisted of huts and sheds made of flattened petrol or kerosene cans nailed on a wooden framework. The only other object in sight was a reservoir for fresh water replenished by visiting ships. It was an enormous tank, seemingly of galvanised iron.

While in Cape Town, I met J. B. M. Hertzog, the Nationalist Prime Minister, under odd circumstances. As a result of a series of public lectures I delivered on recent advances in genetics, the leading dentist had become one of my fans. He thought that I, as Professor of Zoology in the University, should have *ex officio* control of the National Zoo whose site adjoined that of the University and of the Rhodes Memorial at the foot of Table Mountain. With that hope he rang me up to meet Hertzog, gagged in the dental chair and therefore speechless. Still speechless, Hertzog listened courteously to the line of talk of my dentist friend. Happily it had no effect. Otherwise, I might have undertaken research projects with no prospect of reward before South Africa became too hot for me.

I look back on the time I spent in Cape Town with pleasure only because of the profusion of its fauna and the opportunity of making new friendships. Meyerowitz and I left South Africa at about the same time. He took on the job of promoting native arts and crafts under the aegis of the Colonial Office in the Gold Coast, and, in that capacity, left a permanent impress on the colony as it then was. Before our departure, he executed a bust of me, exhibited during the early thirties in Berlin.[5]

CHAPTER XIII

London School of Economics

IN 1919, the year in which he received his knighthood, W. H. Beveridge became Director of the London School of Economics and Political Science. Though nominally a college of London University, it then had little prestige in academic circles. The prevalent view was that it remained, as when founded by a group of Fabians, an institution dedicated to the propagation of a political creed. That it had begun by 1930 to attract students from the U.S.A. and substantial funds from the Rockefeller Foundation is largely attributable to the policy Beveridge pursued. At times his policy had scant approval from political activists of the academic staff. In particular, he strove to widen the curriculum and to break through the brick-and-mortar curtain which isolated staff and students from contact with the natural sciences of other colleges of the University.

One item of this programme was the creation of a chair of Social Biology. I was free to define its terms of reference, at first tentatively and not without embarrassment when asked to do so. The ostensible excuse for getting an endowment for it was that there was then widely current much rubbish about allegedly biological laws of population growth, a topic on which Beveridge himself was knowledgeable. My acceptance of the invitation was not without misgivings, one of which was the public image of the School as an academic institution.

Founded in the year of my birth, the London School of Economics and Political Science came into being as the result of a bequest of some £10,000 from an eccentric, wealthy Fabian, Henry Hunt Hutchinson of Derby, who named as his executors Sidney Webb and one of his daughters. His will, signed October 10, 1893, states that they should use this sum for propaganda of the Fabian Society "and its socialism." It names three other members of the Society, including the secretary Edward Pease, as persons to assist in the disposal of the fund. During its first five years, the School had no connexion with the University of London. It had a whole-time Director, paid only £300 a year. All its teaching staff were part-time and temporary. During the greater part of the first five years, its only accommodation was a house in Adelphi Terrace partly occupied by Miss Charlotte Payne-Townshend, not as yet the wife of Bernard Shaw. She helped substantially to pay the rent.

Meanwhile, Sidney Webb had secured grants from other sources, including the London County Council. After an Act of 1898 reorganised the University of London, he successfully applied for recognition of the School as the University Faculty of Economics. It became so in 1900. London was the first British university to have such a faculty. This gave a new impetus to fund raising, and it was possible in 1902 to open a building on a new site in Aldwych. By intelligent anticipation of a district due for slum clearance, the project benefited from the thesis of Shaw's *Widower's Houses*.

Its newly acquired status must seem to people familiar with academic matters somewhat remote from the intention of the donor whose will had made possible the creation of the School. Incredible as it may seem, neither of the Webbs could detect any inconsistency in the change. As I found in several weekends spent with them at Passfield Corner, both Beatrice and Sidney devoutly believed that lads and lasses who studied economics deeply would eventually become good collectivists. From the start both believed that a *mariage de convenance* between economic theory and factual social studies, if solemnised with a sufficient dowry to the latter, would advance the Fabian cause on a wide front. They continued to believe this despite the fact that at the time of my advent the School was the last stronghold of the most ultra-individualist metaphysical nonsense masquerading as economic science west of Vienna.

Needless to say, in academic circles the institution had still to live down the suspicion that it was an instrument of pink subversion when Beveridge took over at a salary commensurate with its need to expand. How or why I became the first, last and only professor of social biology must therefore have puzzled most of my professional contemporaries who knew me well. What weighed more heavily with me, when the first press notices inviting applications for the appointment of a Professor of Social Biology appeared in the summer of 1929, was the misgiving that the hierarchy of the Royal Society might suspect me of backsliding from biology into politics. This was about the time of my visit to London to explore the possibility of an escape from an ethically intolerable and personally menacing situation in Cape Town. Even so, I had no intention of jumping from the frying pan of apartheid into the cross fire between Viennese mystics and professional partisans of the left.

Till the press invited applications for the post, my sole contact with the London School of Economics had been through Ivor Montagu. It was at his aunt's house in 1920 or 1921 that I first met Harold Laski, then Professor of Political Science in the School. During the summer of 1929, when Laski heard that I was in town, he urged Beveridge to get in touch with me.

I surmise that Laski's main concern in inveigling me into taking the chair of Social Biology was that the brass hats of the Eugenics Society were already congratulating themselves on the prospect of one of their co-religionists getting the job.[1] At the time, the Society was truculently anti-socialist and a stronghold of racial prejudice. Unlike so many other leftists in the academic world of that time, Laski did not underrate the sinister significance of racist doctrines upholstered with bogus biology then gaining ground in Germany. He sensed that my appointment would insure that the new chair would not be a platform for racist propaganda of that sort. He was right. My inaugural lecture was a blistering attack on the scientific credentials of dogmas then sponsored by the Eugenics Society (LH 1931f).

When I first met Beveridge, I had just completed the basic work unequivocally demonstrating the control of the vertebrate ovarian cycle by the pituitary gland. Though anxious to leave South Africa, I was unwilling to accept an appointment which cut me off from laboratory work. Beveridge, who took to me from the start, as I to him, assured me that he did not wish the incumbent of the new chair to withdraw from the main current of biological research. He promised for me the use of a small building in Houghton Street, opposite the main block of the School, to equip as a laboratory with what funds I could raise from the Medical Research Council. It was somewhat like a dilapidated early-nineteenth-century Baptist Chapel but had a basement suitable for keeping tiers of rabbits and tanks of *Xenopus* for my unfinished work on reproductive physiology. This disposed of one obstacle. However, I should not have felt that I was pulling my weight in a post which carried no teaching responsibilities, unless prepared to give up some of my time to enquiries directly relevant to the title of the new chair.

At that time human genetics was a morass of surmise and superstition. It had as yet no sufficient theoretical foundation for firm conclusions about the results of matings necessarily beyond the range of experimental control. In short, no advance could materialise without further mathematical exploration of the postulates of experimentally established principles. At first, I was appalled by the prospect of engaging in a task so formidable, and one for which I could not formulate a programme on the spur of the moment. It was, however, a social as well as a scientific challenge. The rationalisation of race prejudice by appeal to biological principles was then plausible only because human genetics was so immature. Should I prosper in the Herculean task of cleaning the Augean stables of human heredity, I should be contributing to the overdue disposal of a manure heap of insanitary superstitions.

Conversation with J. B. S. Haldane jerked me out of indecision concerning my fitness for the task, but there was a remaining hurdle to surmount. Beveridge said that he could promise me the job if I applied. I had a little difficulty in explaining to him why a professor on the science faculty of one university does not apply for a chair at another. In disciplines that do not employ expensive equipment, lack of success involves only the *amour propre*. To a scientist, if unsuccessful, there is the certainty that his colleagues will be reluctant to endorse a request for additional expenditure when they learn that he has been contemplating a change. Getting an increase on one's annual grant is a skin game. Not being willing to take a risk of this sort, I told Beveridge firmly that I should not apply, but that I should accept if he could persuade the administration to invite me. I left London not knowing the outcome. Halfway back to Cape Town, I received a cable making a firm offer which I accepted. As a Lecturer, I did apply unsuccessfully for two posts before I obtained a chair, but thereafter I have been invited to every post which I have filled.

In the Houghton Street laboratory, Enid and I started an investigation into the duration of stay of the hen's ovum in the various regions of its oviduct respectively responsible for secretion of the albumen, of the shell membrane and of the shell itself round the ovum *sensu stricto*. With this end in view, it was necessary to carry out an autopsy at different intervals between ovulation and oviposition. Our results led to the conclusion that the eggs remain in the shell gland for only about two hours. If so, a simple calculation shows that shell secretion would exhaust the entire calcium content of the blood in a few minutes unless there were a very rapid concurrent mobilisation of calcium reserves from the bones. Accordingly, we repeated all our previous observations, but taking this time blood samples for analysis of blood calcium content immediately before autopsy. The outcome disclosed that the blood calcium level may rise to between three- and fourfold its normal level immediately before and during shell secretion. It drops sharply about the time of oviposition.

We therefore anticipated that the domestic fowl would provide ideal test material for bio-assay of parathyroid extract. In fact, we were not able to detect any increase of blood calcium from injections of such parathyroid extracts as we used.

Soon after I took up my appointment at the London School of Economics H. M. Fox, senior to me during my first year at the Imperial College and appointed to the Birmingham chair of zoology at the time of my move to South Africa, invited me to become his external examiner. This was the start of a long association with Birmingham, where I eventually succeeded Fox. In 1932 the Birmingham Medical Faculty invited me to give their William Withering Lectures. I chose medical genetics as the theme of the Lectures which I later published under the title *Nature and Nurture,* 1933.

By that time I had developed and published a non-commutative matrix algebra tailored to the requirements of the effects of different systems of assortative mating and inbreeding in populations of mixed genotypes (LH 1933e,f). I surmise that the kindly interest Turnbull expressed in it when received by the Royal Society of Edinburgh was largely responsible for the fact that the latter awarded me its Keith Gold Medal and Prize in 1936. I had sent my paper (LH 1933e) in typescript to J. B. S. Haldane, with whom I was weekly in contact when he was at Merton. It transpired that he had tackled exactly the same range of problems by a traditional and very laborious method. He published his own results several years later in a paper in which he confirmed all my results and handsomely acknowledged that my typescript had drawn his attention to an erroneous result in his first draft.

Haldane and I had several friendly controversies about minor issues with reference to human genetics, in one of which he eventually conceded to my view. In terms of the position I have later taken up in statistical theory, I would say that I was undoubtedly right if one concedes certain traditional assumptions I have since abandoned. From a more mature standpoint, I should say that neither of us was right. In *Statistical Theory*, 1957, I repudiated the still almost universally accepted assumptions of Fisherian statistics.

Though his best friend could not say that J. B. S. Haldane was easy to live with, his controversial etiquette was impeccable; and if an irritating arrogance, assumed as I suspect to conceal a fundamental modesty, might make him at times extremely irritating, no man I have known has at all times been more willing to admit that he could have been wrong and no one less reluctant to invite the opportunity of discussing the possibility.

With the £200 I received for the William Withering lecture and a 3-percent mortgage of £100 from my solicitor, I was able to buy an early-seventeenth-century thatched cottage in a delightful location near Fingle Bridge, a beauty spot on the fringe of Dartmoor. This made possible a new domestic setup. We had moved after arrival from Cape Town into a house facing Putney Common. There our children, now four with a second son, David, born in South Africa, fretted without the freedom they had enjoyed on the slopes of Table Mountain. Shortly after we bought the Devon cottage, Enid and I had the opportunity to rent a one-room flat in the Inns of Court, less than five minutes' walk from my department in Houghton Street. Before World War II one could get half-year season tickets to Exeter at an astonishingly low figure. We therefore decided to move the children to Devon after finding a suitable housekeeper. On Monday mornings, we ourselves went by car to Exeter to catch a fast train which reached London in time for lunch. On Friday we returned by a nonstop afternoon train.

This programme involved the absolute minimum of time wasted in travelling. Since the carriages on our line had tables, we could profitably occupy the entire time of the journey each way. On these weekend trips, I wrote the whole of *Science for the Citizen*, 1938. The change proved to be economical, especially when we started to keep hens, ducks and rabbits, and to grow our own vegetables under cloches throughout the year. When we returned to London on Monday, we could then bring with us fresh eggs, farm butter, a cooked bird with new potatoes and fresh salad—in short, everything needed for meals in the flat except fresh milk.

On Dartmoor, my eldest child Sylvia took to horse-riding. At the annual roundup, a Dartmoor pony could be purchased for a pittance at Widdecombe Fair a few miles from our cottage. During the thirties such wild ponies often mated with others of high pedigree let out by their owners to graze on the moor.

For the first time in my life, I genuinely enjoyed parenthood. There was a nearby station from which Adrian and Clare went to school in Newton Abbot. The children's new surroundings were highly educative. On the weekends, Adrian and I ran down local plants in Bentham and Hooker's. During the week, Adrian was responsible for the electric generator. With my help and with home-made apparatus, he and I were able to make a map showing the declinations and right ascensions of the brighter stars. With the same home-made apparatus, and before he was fourteen, Adrian had determined the latitude and longitude of the cottage by three different methods. We had intended to use a surveyor's theodolite to determine the orientation of the many stone avenues and other Bronze Age relics which abounded in our vicinity. Our move to Aberdeen intervened.

Gordon Childe, a friend of University Fabian days and, at the time, Professor of Archaeology at Edinburgh, often visited us en route to and from the cottage of Agatha Christie and her husband, Michael Mallowan, himself a distinguished archaeologist. Childe had already mapped three Iron Age forts which were accessible from our own cottage. We trudged together many miles of moorland to Bronze Age sites with which I was more familiar than he.

Our cottage was within 40 miles of the Plymouth Marine Biological Laboratory, where I could resume experimental work and keep in touch with younger biologists such as G. P. Wells during the summer vacation. Sometimes I took Adrian with me to see its aquarium or other exhibits.

At Newton Abbot, as elsewhere, my children attended state schools. I now view with cynical amusement the sacrifices endured by my professional acquaintances who beggar themselves to send their offspring to expensive prep schools and then to public boarding school or, no less costly, experimental ones run by cranks. If brought up in a home where books abound and conversation rarely degenerates into small talk, children of professional parents start, from the time when they can walk and talk, with an enormous advantage over their contemporaries reared in an intellectually less privileged milieu. I therefore make no claims to proficiency in parentcraft when I say that my four children were not handicapped by having nothing spent on them by way of school fees. As I write, Sylvia, mother of three, is a graduate of University of Wisconsin; Adrian has been chairman of the Department of Physiology at George Washington University and is now Professor and Head of the Department of Physiology and Biophysics at the University of Iowa; Clare, a mother of four, is a graduate nurse; and David, with a doctorate in mathematical statistics, has played a key role in the design of a computer language, Omnitab I and II.

Two considerations had dictated our earlier decision to rent a house in Putney when we returned to London. One was that I wrongly anticipated weekend outings to the Surrey, Kent or Sussex countryside. I had not foreseen the vast expansion of Greater London since I had known its southern periphery fifteen years earlier. Still less had I anticipated traffic congestion due to the increase of car owners. In 1920 there had been little Sunday traffic on the main roads to the South, and a British professor who owned and drove a car was either a celibate eccentric with private means or the husband of a wealthy wife. By 1930, traffic congestion had ended any prospect of a restful Sunday drive along any main road to the coast.

Another consideration was that Hyman Levy then lived quite near the Putney-Wimbledon boundary. Levy was now a full professor of mathematics at the Imperial College. He was the only friend who remained there with whom I had kept in continuous contact by correspondence while abroad. On Sunday mornings, we could take a stroll together on Wimbledon Common, and during the first two years after my return to London I often took advantage of his nearness for discussion of mathematical issues relevant to genetic theories. To that extent renewal of our friendship was, at least to me, stimulating.

Hyman could, however, exasperate me. Like so many left-wing British intellectuals, though they did not openly say so, he still thought of Canadians and Afrikaners as colonials whose local differences had little relevance to the weightier controversial issues of social policy in the homeland. Levy once remarked that too long residence in the back of beyond had encouraged me to concern myself with doctrines no one took seriously in civilised societies. What prompted him to say so was that I had dedicated to him my *Genetic Principles in Medicine and Social Science,* 1931. The main theme of the book was the biological credentials of the racist theories then so popular in South Africa and in Germany. Being himself

Jewish, though not ostentatiously so, Levy had good reason later to take them seriously when Hitler seized power in Germany.

During my residence in London, the editorial policy of the left-wing weekly *New Statesman* showed no interest in apartheid except insofar as it published in its correspondence columns letters from myself drawing attention to the true state of affairs in South Africa and in Southern Rhodesia where an ordinance legalizing flogging of juvenile employees received Royal Assent in the mid-thirties. I wrote on these lines from 1930 onwards till I left the London School of Economics in the spring of 1937, and I returned to the same theme when Smuts made a temporary return to power as prime minister. This brought South Africa into World War II as an ally of Britain on the tacit understanding that the Union would eventually gain control in Namibia. Meanwhile, British public opinion had changed little since the South African 1929 legislation. About 1950, when the *New Statesman* for the first time took cognisance of the resurgence of Afrikaner nationalism, few voices ventilated the claims of the disfranchised non-European majority. Besides my own, I recall only those of Lord Olivier, Fenner Brockway and Frank Horrabin.

Except insofar as I did try my best to force attention to issues of racial policy in the Dominion of South Africa, I took no active part in politics while I remained in the London School of Economics. I felt strongly that a party label would weaken my influence in the execution of a task which I regarded as an ethical no less than a professional responsibility. It therefore seemed to me that a person with unique opportunities for moulding the outlook of his fellow citizens should accept certain restrictions which would rightly be intolerable to others with no such outlet for exercise of civic responsibility. So my sympathies were more with Beveridge than with Laski, when there was friction between them over some of the political publicity the latter invited. Nonetheless, I retained a warm regard for Harold as a person.

On returning to Britain, I had renewed my friendship with Frank Winton, Frank Horrabin and Frank Crew. Soon after I arrived, I renewed contact with the Wedgwood family and gained access through their Museum to correspondence from which I extracted valuable information about the link between Midland industry and Scottish science during the lifetime of the founder of the Wedgwood dynasty. I had also opportunities to cement an enduring friendship with three people I had met casually in a Cambridge club to which Ivor Montagu had invited me before I left London for Edinburgh. One was Kingsley Martin, who became Editor of the *New Statesman*. One was Barbara Wootton, later a life peeress. The other was H. W. Dickinson, then a lecturer at Leeds on economic history, later a professor at Bristol. Through Dickinson I made the acquaintance of his father, formerly Director of the Science Museum in South Kensington and author of several key biographies of prominent figures of the scientific renaissance in eighteenth-century Birmingham and Edinburgh.

My long-standing friendship with Hyman Levy cooled off when he became a member of the Communist Party with all the enthusiasm of the newly converted. At one time, he used to rag me for taking Marx too seriously. As a matter of fact I had never regarded as other than rubbish the hodgepodge of Teutonic mysticism, phrenology and mid-nineteenth-century naturalism defended by Engels in *Anti-Dühring*. Shortly after the rise of Hitler, and now a convert to the Faith, Levy borrowed this book from me and did not return it. Though he himself had not previously read it, he made his debut within a few weeks as Number One Party Theoretician by a publicly advertised lecture on Dialectical Materialism. By then he had all the patter which conveys the esoteric truths of the thesis-antithesis-synthesis triad, the interpenetration of opposites and the passing of quantity into quality.

During the years immediately after the Nazis seized power, I numbered among my acquaintances several scientific workers who were members of, or sympathisers with, the Communist Party, but I recall none who had any enthusiasm for the Labour Party. Part of the explanation of this may be the bungling futility of the first two Labour governments. Of more importance in my view was the indifference of the Labour Party intelligentsia to technological innovation and their total failure to conceive nationalisation as an instrument for technological progress. When they advocated state ownership, the pundits of the Labour Party envisaged no attempt to create new sources of wealth. Their concern was largely to perpetuate moribund industries for the benefit of their employees. Meanwhile, the Soviet Union was making a serious effort to mobilise scientific discovery for greater productivity. Many of the younger scientists in Britain and in France regarded the restrictions of one-party rule as a small price to pay for this.

I myself had considerable respect for the communist minority in South Africa where the non-European majority, having no political rights, could not conceivably obtain social betterment by recourse to democratic restraints on arbitrary power. However, I found Marxist dogma dished out as dialectical materialism deeply distasteful and wholly incompatible with my own criteria for intellectual integrity. Having off-loaded one brand of religious fanaticism, I had no inclination to submit to another. About the time I left London for Aberdeen, the great purges began. The nauseating humbug with which British Communists rationalised Stalin's appetite for murder made me little disposed on my frequent visits to London to renew contact with friends who were Party members.

One of the old Bolsheviks liquidated was Bukharin, whom I had met while still living in Putney. Shortly before the family settled in Devon, I had accepted an invitation to be a member of the organising committee of an international congress on the history of science, meeting in London. For this a Russian contingent, headed by Bukharin, arrived during the first session, having given no advance notice of their intention. Bukharin appealed for my help. I was able to see that his delegation had at their disposal a morning previously set apart for sightseeing. He himself impressed me as a charming and humane man. He visited my home and presented us with several books written by him in Russian, one inscribed in his own handwriting to Enid. The news of his execution came as a painful shock.

The star performance at this conference was that of Boris Hessen, a professor of physics. His paper dealt with the technology of Newton's lifetime, and I made myself responsible for its publication as part of a paperback with the title *Science at the Crossroads*. During the early thirties, one of the few compensations of my chair was that it brought me into contact with economic historians with a lively appreciation of the scientific basis of technological advance. First and foremost among such was M. Postan, then a lecturer at the L.S.E., later Professor of Economic History at Cambridge. I also benefited from contact with Abraham Wolf, then Professor of Logic and engaged in writing his two treatises on science and technology in the seventeenth and eighteenth centuries. Through Eileen Power, appointed Professor of Economic History soon after I came to the L.S.E., I met G. N. (later Sir George) Clark, author of *Science and Social Welfare in the Newtonian Age*. At that time, he was Professor of Economic History at Oxford.

Apart from Wolf and my colleagues from the Department of Economic History, I recall few with whom I had much in common. I regarded, and still regard, as a mental exercise comparable with astrology, economics as taught by Frederick von Hayek and Lionel Robbins in what an early Fellow of the Royal Society called 'the notional and disputatious manner of the ancient philosophers.' Laski's conversation was at all times wittily erudite, if somewhat self-consciously so. One might say the same of Branislaw Malinowski, appointed as Professor of Social Anthropology in the year when I myself joined the staff. Both Laski and Malinowski had some appreciation of the difference between authentic science and argumentation. I should have enjoyed the company of Malinowski more had he not been wooing the Colonial Office with a recipe to justify the *pax Britannica* in Africa at minimum cost by bribing local chiefs to dispense justice and otherwise manage affairs within the tribal boundaries. During the Great Depression of the thirties, this was a welcome relief to civil servants under fire for excessive government expenditure.

As applied to the African scene, Malinowski's functionalism was a plea to leave the native content with leprosy, malaria, protein deficiency, other diseases and illiteracy. The effect of indirect rule was to stabilise tribalism and to relinquish responsibility for promoting a high standard of health, nutrition and education.

CHAPTER XIV

Mathematics for the Million

ON accepting an appointment in this unfamiliar milieu, I had to dispose of misgivings of three sorts: raising funds for purchase of equipment, providing salaries for post-graduate research assistants, and attracting such in an institution where there was no provision for biological instruction at the undergraduate level.

Fortunately, I had as a physiologist a substantial claim for support on the Medical Research Council. Soon after taking up my appointment I was co-opted as a member of its endocrinology committee. I also prevailed on its Secretary, then Sir Walter Fletcher, himself a physiologist of good repute and an ex-fellow of Trinity, to create a new committee to promote research in human genetics. Aside from grants from the M.R.C., including a research fellowship for Enid, I was able with the help of Beveridge to obtain a substantial maintenance grant from the Rockefeller Foundation. By the end of my first year, I had two laboratory assistants and all the equipment I needed for physiological research of the sort which interested me.

Although I continued experimental work throughout my stay in the London School of Economics, I kept faith with Beveridge by devoting part of my own time to mathematical investigations bearing on human genetics. Enid was a tower of strength during this period. Though she had obtained her doctorate for physiological work, she found in the study of population growth a new and congenial field of enquiry in which to exploit her mathematical training. By 1939, she had made an international reputation as a demographer and received an invitation to work in the Dominion Bureau of Statistics at Ottawa. Since the main concern of Beveridge in promoting a chair in social biology arose from his preoccupation with population problems, her newly found interest was highly gratifying to him.

Also gratifying to both of us was the arrival in London as a refugee from Nazi Germany of R. R. Kuczynski, then the leading

European demographer. Beveridge obtained for him a research fellowship in which capacity he became a member of my department. Before I resigned, the partnership of Kuczynski and Enid Charles in promoting the study of differential fertility by new statistical techniques had made the Department of Social Biology a centre of demographic investigation well known both in western Europe and in the United States.

Differential fertility is a topic to which Beveridge himself had made a short but pioneering contribution. Henceforth there was no need for embarrassment either by him or by me when asked to define social biology. I myself directed some enquiries into the utilisation of young people aspiring to an education, in particular the wastage through lack of educational opportunity of ability, as measured— rightly or wrongly—by so-called intelligence tests. Working under me, Louis Herrman had completed a large scale investigation into responses of monozygotic and dizygotic twins to the same tests. To celebrate my exit, the output of the Department on demographical and cognate enquiries such as the last mentioned were republished collectively in one volume called *Political Arithmetic*, 1938, after the seventeenth-century pioneer work of Sir William Petty.

Despite all efforts of Beveridge, there still clung to the London School of Economics during my tenure an atmosphere reminiscent of a Liberal, Fabian or Young Conservative summer school. A comic incident, which concerned myself, illustrates what Beveridge had to contend with in his endeavour to raise its academic status. On my arrival I assumed that a Professor would, as elsewhere, have a department. I had indeed accepted the assignment only when Beveridge agreed to give me a building. In conformity with academic custom elsewhere, I ordered notepaper with the designation *Department of Social Biology, University of London* printed at the top. Somehow, a specimen reached Graham Wallas, an ex-schoolmaster and Fabian Founding Father of the School. As one of the Board of Governors, he demanded withdrawal of the issue of my departmental notepaper. When asked why, he replied that the intention of the Founding Fathers had been to ensure that students should have the opportunity to hear every point of view, that they could do so only if every member of the teaching staff were free to disagree with every other about everything, and that the teaching staff could not enjoy such freedom if organised as departments, each with its own head.

Beveridge and I both enjoyed the joke. So organised, a medical school would have separate professors of authentic medical science, Christian Science, Herbalism, Hydropathy and Homeopathy for every course in the curriculum. A few weeks after this incident, Eileen Power, as head of the Department of Economic History, issued her own Departmental notepaper and others followed suit. Eileen was an exceptionally charming woman, though intellectually far less gifted than her second in command, whom she married after his promotion to a chair at Cambridge.

My appointment carried no obligation to teach, but C. P. (later Lord) Snow had, if I rightly recall, introduced a general science paper into the Higher Civil Service examination syllabus, and Beveridge asked me to give a course tailored to its ostensible requirements. I assented and *Science for the Citizen* took shape laboriously as a by-product of the assignment.

I came into contact with undergraduates in another way. Students at the L.S.E. often invited members of the staff to take the chair at meetings of their Societies—mostly political. On one occasion when I took the chair at such a gathering, the guest speaker was John Strachey, later Minister of Food in the third Labour Government, and as such responsible for the deplorable collapse of the African groundnut scheme. Strachey struck me as a mentally irresponsible politician. He had lately terminated a brief flirtation with Mosley's Black Shirts and was now earning his Party card. After the announcement of the Stalin-Hitler pact, he left the Communist party and wrote one of those books claiming that Marx would have joined the Labour Party if alive when it promulgated its 1918 constitution. Possibly he would have, but being by then a centenarian, his political acumen would have been past its best. The blue-eyed boy of the Labour left wing in 1945, Strachey finished as a pillar of its right.

Hitherto, my relations with adolescents with whom I came personally into contact had always been stimulating. The same was true in later years at Aberdeen and at Birmingham, but I cannot say that I took to my heart students I encountered in the London School of Economics—either those who attended my *Science for the Citizen* lectures or those I met when in the chair as requested at student meetings. A sizable and truculent minority of them had Communist Party cards. When citing some of the more intelligent sayings of Marx, they were rattled to hear that Bacon had expressed the same views more eloquently in *Novum Organum*, 1620. What evoked my distaste for their outlook and demeanour may well have been a by-product of the disputatious attitude to learning encouraged both by the Hayek-Robbins circus and by Harold Laski. Much as I admired Harold for his generosity and much as I respected his versatile erudition, I did not feel that his teaching technique evoked from his audience the eager curiosity which is an essential ingredient of what I myself would call science.

My own reaction to the student body may reflect some of the difficulties that Beveridge experienced in dealing with it. Some of his difficulties may, however, have arisen from lack of teaching experience and his consequent reluctance to give reasons for directives when there were indeed good ones. This was certainly true of an occasion on which the students touted the staff to sign a protest because he had prohibited a meeting with Tom Mann as the principal speaker. Tom Mann was at that time a leading figure at protest rallies of the unemployed. It was widely known that a contingent of medical students from King's College had threatened to march on Houghton Street with the intention of breaking the windows of the School if he spoke. I explained to the student delegation that the outcome might be a disastrous increase of insurance against damage and that Beveridge, who was in general a staunch upholder of free speech, was responsible to the Board of Governors for avoiding financial risks to property. Somewhat reluctantly those I talked with recognised the cogency of the case for the prohibition, and I believe that they would have done so more readily if Beveridge had taken them into his confidence.

Among the more agreeable consequences of coming back to London were the frequent invitations Enid and I received to spend weekends at Passfield Corner with Beatrice and Sidney Webb. We also spent several weekends at the cottage of Beveridge near the Savernake Forest and the Woodhenge site in Wiltshire. Beveridge was the least ostentatious of men. Some of the most interesting conversations I had with him happened when we were washing up together after dinner.

Beveridge visited us once at our cottage in Devon. So did Eileen Power and Julian Huxley. Julian had always been a brilliant raconteur with an endless fund of new stories or limericks. So was Laski, but, unlike Harold, Julian never gave the impression that he was out to impress. He would chuckle when telling a story or reciting a limerick as if he were doing it only for his own amusement.

Visits to Passfield Corner were never boring. Conversation was non-intermittent. Indeed, Beatrice would trot down the drive beside my car, delivering her last word on the last argument as we drove through the gate. Hospitality was unpretentious and an ample libation of Scotch preceded retirement to one's bedroom. We invariably celebrated the Sabbath between breakfast and lunch by a walk over that endearing confluence of ecological incompatibilities in the Hindhead sector, where a richly chalk fauna and flora meet in the low-level calcium content of typical ericacious—heather— moorland.

Repeatedly it has been said that Sidney had no sense of humour. Near Hindhead I can recall at least one item for the defence counsel. The great man was recalling the days when the annual lectures of the Royal Institution produced models of lucid writing on scientific topics in the Davy and Faraday tradition. I mentioned that I had read the lectures of T. H. Huxley with so unlikely a title as *The Crayfish*, and that some of the most noteworthy of these had been given to audiences of working men in the Victorian sense of the term. Sidney Webb then told me that he had attended Huxley's lectures and that anyone eligible to attend had to fill in a form stating his craft. When I asked him how he had surmounted this obstacle, he answered that he gained admittance as a wood carver. This did not register till he explained that he would carve, if he could.

To me these visits to the Webbs are particularly memorable. In the words of the Welsh Bible, I felt myself to be *mab nid yn ol y cnawd ond yn ol yr ysbryd*[1] adopted by two elderly foster parents who had made higher education possible for me by introducing London County Council maintenance grants for winners of open scholarships to Cambridge or Oxford. My admiration did not blind me to their limitations. They had regarded the Boer War as a trivially peripheral incident irrelevant to the more pressing claims of municipal milk supply. Before they went to the U.S.S.R., their political horizon rarely extended beyond the Isle of Wight. This would have been less regrettable if Sidney had not undertaken in the second Labour government a role for which he was not fitted and one which must have been uncongenial to him.

Our first visit to Passfield Corner occurred when Sidney Webb was Secretary of State for Commonwealth Relations. When we arrived, Beatrice was as gushing as she was capable of being about the charm of their most recent guest, J. B. M. Hertzog, then prime minister of South Africa who had laid the foundation for apartheid. To Enid and myself, this had the familiar ring of all one used to hear about the courtesy of the gentlefolk of the Southern states when Stonewall Jackson led them in the fight for the freedom of white men. Whether we ever got into the head of Beatrice or Sidney Webb that Hertzog was indeed the architect of apartheid, I do not know. Sidney Webb had made no lasting impact on Commonwealth relations when the second Labour government went out of power to the echoes of Ramsay MacDonald's resounding adverbial prepositions inviting one and all to go forward and onward and up and through and on and on.

Like the Webbs, Beveridge was an endearing host both at his country cottage and when entertaining the staff of the School at his flat in the Inns of Court. At that time, some of our colleagues commuted twenty miles or more to work, so the customary formal evening dress could be a prohibitive inconvenience. I dined more than once in Beveridge's town flat. Each time Lloyd George was the only other guest, and we all wore lounge suits.

Neither Enid nor I dined out often. On one such occasion, Eileen Power was our host and the guests, with one exception, did not wear evening dress. The exception was Hugh Gaitskell. It was our first encounter, and I never found reason to revise my initial impression of him as a woolly-minded, emotionally shallow, self-satisfied and pompous careerist, totally devoid of a sense of humour.

Looking back on this period of my life, I recall with pleasure my contacts in the London School of Economics for enlargement of my knowledge of the history of science through sources of information placed at my disposal by Postan and Wolf. Otherwise, I could never have undertaken so laborious a task as entailed by the writing of *Science for the Citizen*. When we moved to Devon, our London flatlet was near Bloomsbury where Eileen Power, C. K. Ogden and Arthur Waley then lived. I saw Ogden often, and our many discussions about his *Basic English*, 1930, kindled an interest in comparative linguistics. I got to know Waley better when he came to Aberdeen where we conferred on him an honorary doctorate for his translations of Chinese poetry and Japanese fiction.

Chinese culture was in those days a common bond of interest between Eileen Power, Ogden and Bertrand Russell. I believe it was in China that Dora Black, a Cambridge contemporary of Enid, came to know Bertrand Russell. She had married him before our return from Cape Town. I have never been able to forgive her for making a fool of him to compensate for her own childish frustrations. Following publication at the end of World War I of *A Dominie's Log* there occurred a highly profitable pullulation of private schools kept by cranks to protect the children of the rich from the cruelty of having to learn anything. Dora's Beacon Hill School was one of them, and she made the best of Bertie's name and reputation as bait for victims. Enid and I had an invitation to visit it. The other guest when we arrived was our old friend Sylvia Pankhurst.

Apart from the fact that I retain an almost schoolboyish admiration for Bertrand Russell even past my three score years and ten, I had a less personal reason for accepting the invitation. I looked forward to learning how Bertie's *a priori* approach to early education and his axiomatic viewpoint as a pure mathematician stood the test of practice in the day-to-day work of a school. On arrival, I could scarcely wait to deposit my grip before putting the question tactfully to our hostess. Bertie, she said, had ceased to interfere. He had discovered that children do not like mathematics. At the end of our stay, I confessed to Dora that I was unable to discover what they taught the children. She replied that as a modern educationist her concern was what the children could teach her.

I recalled this episode vividly a few years later, while having lunch at Simpson's in the Strand on the expense account of W. W. Norton, the American publisher of my book *Nature and Nurture*. To my query about whether he had any special mission this side of the pond, he replied that there would, in his view, be a big market for a book if it could do for mathematics what Wells had done for world history in his *Outline*. When I asked whether he had any prospective author in mind, he mentioned Bertrand Russell as his best bet. I reminded him that Bertie tells us somewhere how, as a boy, he read through all the books of Euclid in one stride and decided that Euclidean geometry was too easy to merit further study. Besides, I added, Bertie had discovered that most children dislike mathematics. Warder Norton's disappointment was so patent that I said something to the effect that I had already written the book he wanted, and that I might be able to find it for him.

About two years earlier, I had had a nearly fatal streptococcal septicaemia following tonsillitis and a tonsillectomy, followed by operations on my antral and frontal sinuses. While in hospital, I had written *Mathematics for the Million*, 1936, to pass away the time and with no immediate intention of publishing it. At that time, I was still a candidate for the Fellowship of the Royal Society, and its hierarchy frowned formidably on what they regarded as scientific popularisation.

I had never had any intention of becoming a *populariser*. Both of my best-sellers were write-ups of assignments taken on as education commitments without any ulterior aim. Both *Mathematics for the Million* and *Science for the Citizen* were, as far as I know, the only so-called popular books with exercises and answers—several hundred in *Science for the Citizen*. When I called them self-educators, I meant it; and that may be the secret of their success. Either way, I put into the writing of both of them the fruits of a teaching career from which I gained much joy and self-education.

Actually, I did offer the script of *Mathematics for the Million* as a gift, free of any financial recompense whatsoever, to the Left Book Club of Victor Gollancz on the understanding that it should appear pseudonymously. Gollancz declined to accept it. He said in as many words that mathematics is a worst seller. Thereafter, the typescript lay in a drawer till the day on which the foregoing conversation with Norton took place. Warder's reaction to my flippancy was to beckon a waiter, pay the bill and rush me into a taxi from which we alighted at the room I occupied with Enid in the Inns of Court during the working week. There I fished out the script. Next morning, he returned before 9:00 A.M. with a contract printed on blue paper. Stanley Unwin's memory was at fault when he claimed in *The Truth about a Publisher* that he was the first to recognise the saleability of the book. The fact is that I signed a contract with Norton before Stanley Unwin heard of its existence, seeing no prospect that it would prejudice my professional aspirations if it appeared in America only. When I agreed to its publication in Britain, I already knew that my election to the Royal Society was sure.[2]

I doubt whether Norton would have been so enthusiastic if the script he sat up all night reading had lacked illustrations. Though his entries in *Who's Who* cite my friend Horrabin as the illustrator of both *Mathematics for the Million* and *Science for the Citizen*, the truth is that he had merely to copy, with line thickness and shading suitable for the printed page, figures which I had myself drawn to scale. With the exception of photogravure reproductions from historical sources, this was true both of the 206 illustrations in the shorter book and 498 in the longer one. Horrabin was reluctant to take on the assignment, and would not have done so had he had other than what was for him merely a mechanical task. I was well aware of the publicity value of his name on account of his highly popular maps and comic strips, and I was all too familiar with what the appearance of a book owes to thickness of line and of shading appropriate to the amount of reduction the original undergoes in reproduction for block-making. I did not therefore hesitate to offer him 40 percent of the royalties due to the author in all editions and translations. To my gratification he accepted this offer.

My recollections of life in London during the early thirties would be incomplete without mention of the Tots and Quots, a fortnightly or monthly—I forget which—dining party in a Soho restaurant.[3] It was Solly Zuckerman who mobilised its first meeting. I had met him in Cape Town on a visit to his parents shortly after he obtained in London a conjoint diploma to practise medicine. He had then, I believe, already secured an appointment as Prosector to the Zoological Society in Regents Park, and had not yet shed an eager and boyish curiosity about the behaviour of baboons. During his visit, I drove him to their haunts, and watched with him their antics through a pair of binoculars.

All members of the Tots and Quots except J. G. Crowther, a pioneer of scientific journalism and then science correspondent of the *Manchester Guardian,* had academic appointments. Other than Solly and myself, the original members included J. D. Bernal, P. M. S. Blackett, later President of the Royal Society, J. B. S. Haldane, Julian Huxley and Joseph Needham. Our common bond of interest was the right use of science for human wellbeing. Some of the group—Bernal and Haldane—were confessedly communists. Others like Huxley and myself were not, but none of us harboured the forlorn hope of converting the Labour Party intelligentsia to a realistic appraisal of nationalisation as a means to planning for plenty.

In what circumstances I first met Ritchie Calder—later a Labour Life Peer—I cannot remember. While I was in London only during the working week, he was subeditor of a London newspaper with an office in Fleet Street very near my Inns of Court flatlet. He had received no formal instruction in natural science, but had thrown in his lot with John Boyd Orr as an unpaid publicity agent for the National Malnutrition Crusade which the latter launched when unemployment was at its peak. From familiarising himself with the jargon of calories and vitamins, Ritchie developed an insatiable appetite for further physiological information and, thereafter, for scientific information in general. He was the first reader of *Science for the Citizen*—chapter by chapter as I finished them. After his paper had gone to press, we often walked together along the Thames Embankment which lies scarcely more than a stone's throw below what was then his office. Late at night, when the Embankment and the Inns are deserted, London is at its least intolerable.

Ritchie's great service to me was to bring me into personal contact with John Boyd Orr, then Director of the Animal Nutrition Institute at Aberdeen. In the early twenties, Frank Crew had asked me to go with him to the inaugural dinner of the Aberdeen Institute. I recall it vividly as the first occasion on which I tasted an aperitif, and I also witnessed a highland-style fancy dress feast complete with pipers and with a chief piper to take the first sip from the loving cup. Such again was the occasion on which I first shook hands with both John Boyd Orr and with Walter Elliott. As a medical graduate, the latter had been one of Orr's students in Glasgow. At the time of the inaugural dinner, he was working part-time under his former teacher for the Aberdeen doctorate of science which he eventually obtained for work connected with dietary deficiency.

Walter Elliott was a brilliant talker, a dedicated careerist and had been a leading member of the Glasgow University Fabian Society before the outbreak of war in 1914. He returned from active service in 1918, covered with military glory and disillusioned. Before demobilisation, he received by cable a request to stand as a member of Parliament for a Scottish constituency in the election of 1918. Rumour relates that he wired back briefly: 'Yes, but which party?' It turned out that the offer of a candidature came from a Conservative office. His devotion to his former teacher remained untarnished, for which reason I liked him. As I once said to him, when he was Secretary of State for Scotland, he had earned his first-class ticket into Heaven by getting John Boyd Orr his knighthood.

The great depression of the thirties had a calamitous effect on the financial resources of Crew's Institute. John Orr was more fortunate. If backing for agricultural research was minimal, mounting poverty made the need for medical research into the nation's food more imperative. Orr reoriented the research programme of his Institute accordingly. Henceforth, he and his co-workers concentrated their efforts on the study of human nutrition. By this change of policy, he was able to see the kingdom of heaven and be paid for it. Before 1937 he had gained, with the help of the High Commissioner of Australia, the ear of the League of Nations and was laying the groundwork for the creation of the Food and Agriculture Organisation of the postwar United Nations. It was his good luck to have the support, as Secretary of State for Scotland, of a medical graduate who was also a devoted friend.

CHAPTER XV

Aberdeen

By the time I became a Fellow of the Royal Society, early in 1936, I was eager to concentrate all my energies again on experimental research. Beveridge would have given me his blessing because the Department had delivered the goods from his own point of view. However, there was one insurmountable obstacle to concentrating on physiological problems if I stayed longer at the School. When I came to London some former Cape Town pupils of mine, studying for higher medical qualifications, had worked in my laboratory. Since there was no place in the curriculum for teaching experimental biology, I had no means of enlisting new recruits for teamwork when this source of supply inevitably dried up. I also had no day-to-day contact, as I should otherwise have done, with colleagues of kindred interests in a medical faculty. For both reasons I was already toying with the idea of changing my job when I learned through the grapevine that Beveridge, for whom I had such high regard, would probably become the new Master of University College, Oxford. I saw little likelihood that I should get on as well with his successor as with him. Rumour had it, and rightly, that the next Director would be Carr Saunders,[1] an intellectually second-rate bore whom I had met at Oxford in the early twenties, when staying with Julian Huxley. Saunders had been prominent in the Eugenics Society and, unless my memory plays tricks on me, served as Secretary or as editor of its journal.

At this juncture, two highly attractive chairs came on the market. Beveridge prevailed on Lord Macmillan, then one of the Governors of the School, to invite me to lunch with the intention of persuading me to stay. Beveridge himself entertained no ill feeling when I was unmoved. Of the alternative opportunities for profitable change, one was the chair of zoology at Edinburgh. Frank Crew was eager to promote my claims, and I had other support since I had kept up my association with the Royal Society of Edinburgh. I have little doubt therefore that I could have had a firm offer, which I should have accepted if there had been no other opportunity for full-time research in experimental biology. Other than myself, the only candidate in view then held a chair in Aberdeen. I judged that this would almost certainly become vacant if I declined to take advantage of the support I might have had from my Edinburgh colleagues. My surmise turned out to be correct.

With the exception of Edinburgh, the universities of Scotland date their origin before the Protestant Reformation, and the names of several departments have an antique flavour. Physics is *Natural Philosophy*, Pharmacology is *Materia Medica*, Physiology is the *Institutes of Medicine* and Zoology is *Natural History*. The chair of Natural History in Aberdeen is a Regius appointment. The full title of the incumbent is Regius Professor of Natural and Civil History. The epithet Regius signifies that the Crown makes the appointment, in Scotland on the advice of the Secretary of State, at that time Walter Elliott. The wording of the Royal Warrant one receives is mediaeval. Too late to exploit my privileges, I learned at my farewell dinner from the Dean of the Faculty of Law that a Regius professor, by an unrepealed Act of the Scottish Parliament in the last decade of the sixteenth century, is ex officio a minister of the church of Scotland.

In September 1936, Ritchie Calder was staying with us in our Dartmoor cottage when he received his marching orders from the Associated Press Agency to take a plane in pursuit of Mrs. Simpson en route to her hideout in France. Since I had already learned from him that my new appointment was in the bag, I expected my own warrant to carry the signature of Edward VIII. The date cited therein is exactly three weeks after the passage of the Abdication Bill, and there is little doubt that the warrant was one among a mountain of other accumulated documents awaiting a reluctant Royal pen when his brother came to the throne. Several of my friends used to say that I was Mrs. Simpson's nominee. The truth is that John Boyd Orr wanted me to come to Aberdeen as an ally on the governing board of his Institute. I never discovered how much the Secretary of State approved of me, but what John Boyd Orr wanted was good enough for Walter Elliott. During his December visit, it cheered me greatly to learn from Ritchie Calder how much the scenery of the countryside around Aberdeen resembles that of my beloved Dartmoor.

It would be a gross exaggeration to say that Aberdeen is, from the standpoint of material for teaching biology, as memorable as Cape Town. As elsewhere in Britain, climate sets forbidding limits on what species are spawning for the convenience of the curricular timetable. Nonetheless, it had advantages which no other university city could offer me when I settled there. Because it is bounded by a sea front, a supply of rock pool fauna is easily accessible. Sandwiched between the Dee and the Don, it confronts the ecologist with the unique situation of two rivers less than twenty miles apart. Each has a fresh water population peculiarly its own, though climate conditions are much the same. The sources of the Don provide ample spawning ground for salmon, and the Dee teems with eels of all sizes.

My only visit to Aberdeen before I received the Royal Warrant had been on a wet and cold winter day in 1923, but when I returned for a few days in January 1937, what I saw did not dissipate the more favourable impression that Ritchie Calder had given me. At his residence in Old Aberdeen I stayed with the Vice Chancellor, Hamilton (later Sir William) Fyfe, a man of great charm—witty and highly civilised. His brother was at that time editor of *Reynold's News,* the left-wing Sunday newspaper owned by the Cooperative Movement. At Oxford, he himself had been a Greek scholar and at one time a proctor. Though far less influential than Beveridge, he was always entertaining outside office hours. The main object of my stay with him was to explore what domestic accommodation was available. Hitherto, Enid and I had never bought a house other than our Dartmoor cottage. It seemed that I had now at last found a permanent foothold, for it was my intention to remain in Aberdeen till retirement, as I probably should have done if there had been no second world war.

Experience of house hunting in London in the thirties had taught us that large and comparatively old houses, built for a period in which families were large and domestic labour abundant, are less costly than much smaller new ones. This was equally true of Aberdeen. For £1,500—less than the price of a lately built suburban villa—I was able to purchase a rambling house on the fringe of Old Aberdeen, just above the Brig of Don, less than two miles from my department. It stood in two acres of garden, sloping down to the river on one side. On the other, it faced a stretch of moorland. The main lounge, thirty feet long, opened into a heated greenhouse with a spreading camellia as its centrepiece.

The grounds had a capacious stable. My research assistant Frank Landgrebe, subsequently Professor of Pharmacology at Cardiff, converted the upper floor into a flat for himself and his wife.

We paid for our new home *Inverdon* with the royalties of *Mathematics for the Million* and sale of part of our property on Dartmoor. Since my elder son was due to qualify for university entrance at the end of the summer term, we decided not to move the family as a whole till after his examination. Enid remained with the children in Devon when I went north at the end of the Lent Term, this time in a second-hand sports car which travelled on a clear road at ninety. Frank Landgrebe, for whom I had obtained a salary grant from the Medical Research Council, came with me. We made the journey leisurely in three stages. After a detour through the Lake District, which neither of us had visited before, we spent a night at Carlisle.

Scenically, the Lake District seems to have suited Wordsworth, Coleridge and Southey. To me it was disappointing. I recognise that grass is useful for grazing sheep, cattle and horses, but it is ruinous to enjoyment of the landscape if one's preference is for moorland glens and brown burns. Our next stop was Blairgowrie in Perthshire, where we learned on arrival that the mountain road to Braemar was snowbound and impassable. In the morning, the radio announced that snow ploughs had cleared it, and we stuck to our original plan. At the Devil's Elbow, we made our way through a narrow lane bordered on either side by a vertical wall of ice higher than the roof of a car. As we descended to Braemar in brilliant sunshine, we drove beside a trout stream fringed by mountain ash, and a herd of deer basked in the sunlight of the wooded country beyond.

On arrival, I was fortunate to find a cooperative skeleton staff. My second in command was older than myself, but he, like the only other lecturer, had been too overloaded with teaching duties to get any work published. The evening after my arrival, the three of us went out to the pub patronised by the University, the press and the legal profession. There I outlined my plan for reducing teaching duties to one-third of what they had been. This was practicable by the simple expedient of arranging the three-year curriculum as a sequence of one-term courses in rotation instead of a threefold repetition of the same lectures and laboratory work for students of successive years. Within three years, both members of my skeleton staff obtained their doctorates for work I had encouraged.

I say 'skeleton staff' because I was able to add three others already experienced in research and three research fellows. That I succeeded in doing so was largely due to the fact that I could claim to attract from other sources far more than the total cost of my laboratory—including my own salary. For recurrent maintenance, I obtained grants from the Rockefeller Foundation, the Medical Research Council and the Agricultural Research Council amounting to more than ten times my departmental appropriation from the University chest. A Rockefeller grant also provided a salary for Enid to continue her work as a demographer. I took over a department that had published no research for fifteen years. Within five, its publication list numbered about thirty items.

I could not have mobilised so large a team if I had had at my disposal only the floor space available for my predecessor. It was my good fortune to arrive when there was a general exodus of preclinical teaching departments from Marischal College, the Science Faculty building, to the Forrester Hill site of what was then probably the most up-to-date hospital building in Britain. I lost no time in staking a claim to what had been accommodation for the departments of pathology, bacteriology and pharmacology.

I was then interested in eels, of which abundant supplies are available in Aberdeen. Having ordered appropriate tanks as at Cape Town, it was a matter of a few hours to discover that the eel is chromatically sensitive, and I tried one afternoon with Harry Waring the experiment of removing the pituitary, because the reaction time of the eel is very prolonged in comparison with other Teleosts whose melanophores are under direct nervous control. After that Harry took over and established that the eel, like Elasmobranchs, conforms to the amphibian pattern of my younger days.

In Aberdeen, Landgrebe sewed up all the loose ends of the pregnancy diagnosis story. He also cooperated with me in, as I recall, the only publication in which my name appeared singly or jointly as an author at this time. I was interested in following up the differential role of the upper and lower halves of the retina of aquatic animals capable of chromatic response when the control mechanism is nervous, as in Teleosts other than the eel (LH 1940a). The minnow was the test material and had led to a rather interesting discovery, developed in greater detail in a study of the salmon's eye by R. M. Neill, who was my deputy on arrival in Aberdeen. The lens of the eyes of fishes has two zones, the outer one whose refractive index is almost exactly that of water, and a core whose refractive index is somewhat higher or about the same as glycerine. This means that it can see both in air and in water. After a little friendly scepticism over lunch with the Professor of Physics, now Sir Antony Carroll, this led to the making of a model camera with a water *plus* glycerine lens which would produce a clear image of an object if half submerged. At a meeting of the Society for Experimental Biology at Plymouth, I had an opportunity of demonstrating the refractive properties of the lenses of several widely different species of fishes in the tanks without need for further confirmation.

I had taken a look at the littoral Isopod *Ligia*, which is a very good type for study of colour change in crustacea; and the fact that in some Arthropods there is a morphological differentiation of the upper and lower halves of the compound eye suggested to me that it would be a good subject for investigating the contrast effect. I put Smith, one of the junior members of my staff, onto this for a doctoral thesis, and the results were as convincing as anticipated. Here I should say without undue immodesty one thing about my Croonian lecture. Though I never referred to myself except by reference to a publication on which my name appeared, perhaps half the authors quoted were my own pupils, and I refrained from comment on how much work I myself had already done in the background.

Perhaps I am wrong, but I attach very great importance to another long-term enquiry in which R. M. Neill collaborated with me. By the outbreak of war we had convinced ourselves, though with insufficient reason to put confidently on record, that the alleged immature testis of the silver eel known as Syrski's organ is in fact an immature ovary. If so, there is abundant indication that the eel, like the gall wasp *Cynips kollari*, is a perpetually parthenogenetic species of which the male is extinct. In retrospect and for several reasons I shall not mention here, I deem it extremely unlikely that our conclusion reached in the summer of 1939 was incorrect.[2]

To build up practical genetics, I had invited Cecil Gordon to join my department. I had earlier engineered a fellowship to extradite him from South Africa, and he had found a niche with J. B. S. Haldane. One outcome was what I still regard as the most important contribution to the Nature-Nurture issue. This emerged from Cecil's own discovery of the Drosophila mutant *Antennaless*, followed up in a very congenial partnership which I nursed between Gordon himself and James Sang, who joined my staff later. In this, my only useful role was to foresee more clearly than they did the immensely important theoretical possibilities in Gordon's initial discovery with reference to the role of variations of the nutrient medium vis à vis the exhibition of the relevant gene. I urged on them the desirability of withholding publication until they had placed on a firm foundation what were to be some of the most important features of this investigation. Unhappily, the finished performance dragged on till war had broken out, and the publication of their results did not occur till 1943, whence it never attracted the recognition it should have had in a peacetime situation.

My inaugural public lecture at the beginning of my first summer term did nothing to disclose my intention to create, as in Cape Town, a substantial school of research. In writing *Science for the Citizen*, I had become fascinated by the efflorescence of scientific activity in Birmingham and Scotland during the second half of the eighteenth century. As the theme of my inaugural, I chose the interrelations between Birmingham industry and Scottish science during that period. The occasion was the start of several friendships. In *Science for the Citizen*, and in my inaugural lecture based on the same material, I had quoted extensively from the work of Henry Hamilton on the Scottish Industrial Revolution, not knowing that he was at that time Reader in Economic History at Aberdeen. After the lecture, he greeted me cordially and disclosed his identity.

Over drinks at his house in Old Aberdeen during the evening, Hamilton Fyfe asked me if the Henry Hamilton I had spoken of so highly was, in his own words, any relation to our little Hamilton. Till then, Henry Hamilton had been a prophet without honour in his own country, though by no means elsewhere. A year previously the University Court had turned him down as a candidate for the Chair in Economics to which they appointed a garrulous minor Oxford don. Perhaps due to my influence, Henry Hamilton eventually succeeded to the chair.

Resplendent in kilt and sporran worn by several of the staff and students at that time, one of my audience at the same gathering was Archibald Clow, who became director of science talks for the London B.B.C. He was then engaged in chemical research, as his wife had been before marriage, and my narrative of the origins of industrial chemistry through the work of Scotsmen domiciled in Birmingham quickened an interest in a hitherto too little explored aspect of the history of science. Archie himself was a junior lecturer and his wife, Nan, at a loose end. I was able to help them to get a grant which enabled them to complete the researches embodied in their important book *The Chemical Revolution*, awarded the Senior Hume Brown prize by the University of Edinburgh. After my family moved into our new home near the Brig of Don, the Clows became the nucleus of a younger set who foregathered on Saturday nights to drink Scotch or sherry with my own staff and post-graduate students.

Other than two or three of the medical faculty the professorial staff were mostly dull, and pretentiously so. In the thirties they shared no social life with their non-professorial colleagues and spent their evenings dining with one another in rotation. These dinners were six-course proceedings at which the men wore white tie and tails. The excellence of the conversation did not match the quality of the cooking, which was admittedly unexceptionable. After one acceptance, I resolved never again to expose myself to so tedious an evening. However, our Saturday *soirées* brought us into touch with some colourful personalities, several being ardent Scottish nationalists and a few survivors of the vintage in which Eric Linklater was the dominant figure among Aberdeen undergraduates.

The circle of friends who came to Inverdon on Saturday evenings included research workers of one or other of the local research institutes. Aberdeen had four. One was the Institute of Animal Nutrition already mentioned, a second that of Soil Research. Two others were concerned with fisheries, one financed by the Scottish Ministry of Agriculture, the other by the Department of Scientific and Industrial Research. Shortly after I came, I organised a monthly colloquium bringing together, for discussion of current research, personnel of the institutes and of the University biological departments—physiology, pharmacology, anatomy, bacteriology, botany and zoology. Doubtless because of a hitherto unfulfilled need, the attendance exceeded my expectations. Owing to the expense of visiting London for gatherings of national scientific societies, younger research workers in Aberdeen had hitherto experienced little impetus from the sort of discussion such meetings promote. Before I left, I persuaded the University to pay the travelling expenses of non-professorial staff to attend scientific conferences in the deep south.

In Aberdeen, John Boyd Orr and I were at that time the only Fellows of the Royal Society. He attached me to the governing body of the Institute of Animal Nutrition, and our friendship ripened into reciprocal affection. It also made a lasting contribution to my subsequent *Weltanschauung*. While at the London School of Economics, I had met several people, notably M. Postan, who helped me in the search for sources of information, but no one who made an appreciable impact on my values. John Boyd Orr influenced my outlook profoundly and in more ways than one. By making me alert to the Scottish cultural heritage, he forced me to recognise the difference between a cosmopolitan and an internationalist. He also impressed on me the need to recognise how imminent was the demand of hitherto undeveloped territories to a voice in power politics at an international level.

The local milieu was propitious to a new look at the national scene. To the overwhelming majority of Englishmen, Aberdeen is a foreign city. It would seem more so if they came to live there. It is indeed almost exactly halfway between London and the southernmost tip of Iceland. Those who worked in the major industry, fishing, were far more at home in Icelandic waters than they would have been in Billingsgate. Its ubiquitous gray granite is forbidding, but its situation, facing the sea between the estuaries of the Dee and the Don, is pleasing. The centre of no British city of comparable size is so near such stupendous scenery as that which extends from its outskirts to Braemar sixty miles inland. Perhaps the most vivid impression gained by the southerner who visits it for the first time is the length of the summer nights and the short span of winter daylight.

Londoners, who meet only nostalgic Scots emigrés, rarely realise the vast gulf which separates Scottish and English social tradition. Very few Englishmen know anything about Scottish history. Being, at Aberdeen, the only Englishman on the University staff, I could scarcely fail to take stock of it. Scottish national culture differs from that of England more fundamentally than does that of Wales. Insofar as the Welsh language is very much alive, Wales has in one sense admittedly a more distinct culture. In other respects it is an outlying group of English counties. Wales, unlike Scotland, was not to attain a capital or a Minister of State, and its laws are still the laws of England. What is more significant is that, for two centuries, those laws included the Test Acts which excluded nonconformists from public office or entry to the universities. Indeed, the Welsh language would have become extinct, as the Cornish dialect became extinct, had not the lay preachers of the Methodist revival, itself an English movement, given it a new lease of life.

Aberdeen

At the date when Parliament repealed the last of the university Test Acts, Wales had no university. Scotland had universities which antedate the Protestant Reformation, and the severance from Rome took place more smoothly and more drastically than in England. Whereas the defeat of Owain Glyndwr extinguished Wales as a political entity, the union of the crowns of England and Scotland in 1603 came about by consent without recourse to arms, as did the union of the two parliaments a century later. The final settlement left the Scottish legal system and the Church of Scotland intact. This being so, Scotsmen were not subject to religious tests which excluded English and Welsh nonconformists from so many avenues of employment. This explains the large numbers of Scottish recruits to English medical practice and to the English civil service for more than a century and a half after the union of 1707.

Unlike Wales, whose only non-bardic culture is nonconformist, and as such English, Scotland has never had a nonconformity. Though there have been many defections from, and returns to, the fold of the Kirk, they have rarely been about deep doctrinal differences, being mostly about money. At the time of which I am writing, Scotland had its own Law Lords of Appeal, and separate departments of Agriculture and Fisheries, Education, and Health under its Secretary of State for Home Affairs. It also had its own Registrar General. Enid's work brought her into frequent contact with the Registrar General of that time, and mine brought me into contact with the Ministries of Health and of Agriculture and Fisheries.

We had indeed come to a country which shares with England and Wales only a Parliament, a language and the armed services. Perhaps, if only because we came in a more privileged position and with a feeling of greater security, we also came prepared to make a more sympathetic appraisal than at first acquaintance fifteen years earlier in Edinburgh. At that time, I had been a cosmopolitan, ready to welcome white, black, red or yellow people as brothers if they were willing to conform to my own cultural standards. I now began to see Scotland through the eyes of John Boyd Orr with his enjoyment of kilt and sporran, piper and loving cup. The man then laying the foundations of what was to be the Food and Agriculture Organisation of U.N.O., and who was to become its first Director, respected the right of other people to cherish their folkways as he cherished his own. In short, he was an internationalist.

In late evening, I frequently visited John at his Aberdeen home near the Institute. He spent weekends on a farm he owned at Edzell near Montrose. For weekend use I myself rented a croft in well-wooded moorland country near Tomintoul, off the main Aberdeen to Balmoral road. When I had foreign guests, I sometimes drove with them on Sunday afternoon over the mountain pass via Cairnamount to Edzell. When at ease in his own home, John always talked in his broadest Ayrshire Doric. The contrast between it and the dialect of Aberdeenshire forced on my attention the very large contribution of Scandinavian words to the more northern vocabulary. Some are words which did not exist in the low German of Great Britain before the Norse invasion; for example *bra*, a bank or hillside. Others such as *bairn* for child and *quaen* for woman—in Norwegian, *kvinne*—perpetuate in their original sense words once common to all the Teutonic languages. Thus Anglo-Saxon *cwen* survives as queen only for the king's woman.

Some of my students came from the Orkneys and Shetlands. In their dialects, the Scandinavian influence is very noticeable. Up till the end of the fifteenth century Old Norse was the vernacular of the Orkneys, and there were still those who spoke an Old Norse dialect in the outermost Shetland Isles at the beginning of the nineteenth century. What was in my time still characteristic of the dialects of North Scotland was partly the persistence of vowel values, as in *hus* for house. This was common to the language of the Vikings and that of the earlier Teutonic settlers when there must have been a considerable measure of intercommunicability between them. Equally noticeable was the survival of consonantal Anglo-Saxon combinations represented in modern English by *wh* and *gh* but no longer pronounced as such.

Contrary to what many people assume, the influence of Gaelic is noticeable only at the western fringe where a remnant still spoke it in recent times. Today, there are few who do so. In Wales, of course, many can speak their native Brythonic (P-Celtic). At the time when the Scots (Q-Celts) from Ireland penetrated the Western Isles and the west coast of the mainland, there was a large Brythonic community throughout the Lowlands and P-Celtic infiltrated far to the North. Aberdeen, like the Welsh town Aberystwyth, is itself an authentically Brythonic place name.

How much the dialects of the Scottish countryside since the time of which I am writing have successfully resisted the impact of radio and television, I do not know. When the chair of English fell vacant,

I pleaded with the Senate of the University to appoint a professor with the phonetic expertise to put them on tape before submergence by mass communication media. I was not successful. The Faculty of Arts was then ultraconservative. When a proposal with the flavour of innovation was under discussion, the Arts Faculty invariably had the support of the professors of theology, themselves about as numerous as those of medicine. The applicant who was appointed had made his name by a commentary on some little-known letters of Wordsworth—or something equally pedestrian. In my efforts to attract financial support for the Arts Faculty from American foundations, I suffered yet another reverse. There exists in the Reykjavik public library considerable material about rebel refugees from Scotland, and there was already in the late thirties a direct airline from Aberdeen to Oslo. When the chair in Spanish fell vacant, I therefore urged the University to replace the Spanish Department by one of Scandinavian studies. The Science Faculty, in a minority as usual, supported the proposal unsuccessfully.

Aside from discussions about Basic English with C. K. Ogden, whom I continued to see when in London for conferences or committees, my interest in linguistics of any sort had hitherto been negligible. Contact with students who spoke different Scottish dialects quickened it as did my friendship with Gunnar Dahlberg of Uppsala.

It was on journeys to and from London that I got to know Walter Elliott. The routine was always the same. The London train left before eight, in time for dinner. It arrived about 7 o'clock, when one could shave at leisure in one's sleeper. I could then proceed by taxi to the Zoo of which Julian Huxley was Secretary, with a flat on the top of the administrative building overlooking Regent's Park. I usually arrived in time for a bath before he was up. The homeward journey began at midnight. The breakfast on the train was equal to a whole week's ration in wartime. I would reach my laboratory as usual at about 9:30 A.M.

I went to London about once a month and only on business. Since I had first-class fare, sleeper, meals and taxis as expenses, the journey cost me nothing. My travelling companions with whom I dined on the London train were invariably one of the trio Orr, Elliott and Ritchie Calder. As a medical student, Elliott had learned all the verses of the pornographic *Ball of Kirriemuir*. He once recited them to me en route with his customary gusto, a rare accomplishment for a Secretary of State.

While my friendship with C. K. Ogden and the dialects of the local milieu were quickening my interest in language, an unexpected event reinforced their impact. Without warning, Gunnar Dahlberg came to Aberdeen to see me. He was then Director of the *Statens Rasbiologiska Institutet* in Uppsala and, as such, Professor of Medical Statistics. We were each familiar with the work of the other in the field of mathematical genetics, and we shared the same viewpoint with reference to the racist theories officially endorsed by the Nazis. It happened also that Sweden was then in the forefront of countries seriously interested in the problems of differential fertility, the field of work in which Enid Charles was making a name for herself. We therefore both jumped at an opportunity to combine serious work with the chance for foreign travel when Gunnar invited us to stay for a week or more with himself and his charming wife, Stina. I purchased an elementary grammar of Swedish in preparation for the visit.

This visit prompted several others by myself alone. On the second, I travelled by boat from Newcastle to Bergen and back via Stavanger, then by sleeper through Oslo to and from Stockholm. On the outward journey, I met Dagny Vemmestad, a Norwegian school teacher who was intelligent and altogether delightful. This led to a pen-letter friendship which introduced me to the secrets of the Norwegian spelling reform, *nyeste rettskrivning*, then about to come into force. Under the impression that it was still, as in the time of Ibsen, the language of the educated Norwegian, I had already taken up Danish in my spare time. Since there is less difference between the three principal Scandinavian languages than between the Buchan dialect of North Scotland and the dialect of the Somerset countryside, the effort of learning all three together is minimal. After eighteen months, I could give press interviews in Swedish, Danish and Norwegian.

About the time of my third trip to Sweden, I must have come across Max Müller's *Lectures on the Science of Language* delivered at the Royal Institution in 1861 and 1863. This introduced me to a new approach to the study of language, much like the study of the origin of species. At school I had found French tolerable with my mother's help. As I have already said, I detested Latin but did not dislike the little Greek I had to learn for Cambridge Littlego. Later, when I had to master enough to translate set pieces for the London Science degree, I disliked German even more than Latin. I still feel that no one who has been proficient in academic German can hope to write readable English. Against this unpropitious background, I had now made a new beginning with study of the Scandinavian group. Arguments with Ogden about the semantics of Basic English had infused a new interest in the acquisition of an alien vocabulary adequate for self-expression. Understanding of the role of sound change in the creation of linguistic barriers between formerly intercommunicable dialects is comparable to the story of evolution from the fossil record of the rocks. Comparative linguistics and palaeontology are close relations, and palaeontology was one of my earliest sources of intellectual excitement.

It was in this frame of mind that I welcomed Frederick Bodmer, when he arrived from Cape Town on a sabbatical year. The Cape Town chair in German had fallen vacant, and the University had turned down his candidature in favour of a truculent Nazi. By then *Science for the Citizen* had become a best seller. I put to Bodmer an alternative to an otherwise, for him, intolerable situation. The plan was this. Could one not bring the dead bones of language learning to life by expounding both the art of memorising a vocabulary sufficient for making oneself intelligible and the requisite minimum of grammar in the light of what modern philology can teach us about the evolutionary process? I drew up a synopsis and used the security of my royalties from *Science for the Citizen* to procure for Frederick a publisher's advance to guarantee him for two years a competence sufficient to keep body and soul together while he got on with the good work in my highland croft near Tomintoul. He moved in during the early spring of 1939.

Though the intention was different, I had benefited during the previous summer from an opportunity to view a unique linguistic situation. Being short of foreign exchange owing to loss of her Spanish market for fish, Iceland was then intent on a boost for tourist traffic, and I booked for a fortnight trip to Reykjavik from Leith. My main concern was to get more insight into the technology of early Norse navigation. When I arrived the principal, and so far as I know only, bookshop on the island displayed *Science for the Citizen* as its major exhibit.[3] Perhaps this was because I had included a map of the Vinland voyages. The bookshop proprietor was Snaebjørn Jonsson, a former translator for the Icelandic government and author of what was then the only primer of contemporary Icelandic.

In the thirties of the nineteenth century, Babbage was the Lucasian Professor at Cambridge, inventor of the first mechanical computer and foremost among Royal Society fellows who broke away to start the British Association. He had declared with some justice that Iceland might become the powerhouse of Europe. The houses of Reykjavik had central heating from hot springs in which the girls of the farms could do their winter washing out of doors. To generate electricity, there are abundant waterfalls of the type they call a *foss*, a sheer torrent in contradistinction to water tumbling over rocks at different levels as when we usually speak of a waterfall in our own island. In Britain I know of only one such—at Llanrhaiadr ym Mochnant in North Wales.

Fifteen years before my visit, Iceland did not have a railway, an automobile or a hydroelectric generator. By the mid-thirties, the internal combustion engine and electrical power plants had become a feature of everyday life. Happily the island had thus sidestepped the ravages of the coal age. Its greatest handicap was that denudation of forests from Viking times onward had removed all traces of a windscreen from its forbidding volcanic landscape. I saw no trace of vegetation higher than three feet above ground level during drives which took me to the Great Geyser and the largest power station, built turretwise with a circular corridor on the walls of which hung pictures by local artists. The outstanding character of such local art, a riot of colour, is a protest against the climate. During a July fortnight, I did not see the sun once.

I sought to find out how the Norse navigators of the tenth and eleventh centuries threaded their way through sunless seas in latitudes where the vagaries of the isomagnetic lines ruled out reliance on the use of the lodestone. I believe I found the answer in the national *Bibliothek*, to the chief librarian of which Snaebjørn Jonsson had introduced me. One of its records, composed at about the time of the Vinland voyages, tells us that the pilot used a crystal of Iceland spar to locate the sun when the sky was overcast.[4] At home one thinks of this double-refracting transparent mineral as a rarity. It abounds on the Icelandic seafront like mussel shells on a British beach. I brought back with me a paperback copy of *Eiriks Saga Rautha ok Graenlending-athattr*—the Saga of Eric the Red with its account of the discovery of Greenland and of Vinland on the continent of North America. Though highly inflected like Anglo-Saxon, more so than modern High German, Old Norse is not difficult to read if one knows one or other of the contemporary major Scandinavian dialects. With the help of the Icelandic vocabulary of Snaebjørn Jonsson's primer I was able to make an otherwise tedious sea journey tolerable by reading the story of Leif Erikson's exploits.

In conversation, about the time when I first came to Aberdeen during 1937, John Orr had assured me that I should find it more restful to work in a place where there was no temptation, as in London, to go outside to buy one of the editions of the evening papers published hourly from eleven o'clock onwards, as news of German rearmament became increasingly ominous. War was not then the only spectre that haunted one's social conscience. Maybe the hunger marches to London from Jarrow and from South Wales did more to promote the ethical education of England than the preceding forty years of socialist propaganda. From the South Wales coalfield came columns of unemployed miners singing in harmony, as only Welshmen can do, the minor refrains of *Yn y dyfroedd mawr a'r tonnau* and *Gad i'm deimlo awel o Galvaria fryn*.[5] Though little recorded as such, one of the most moving moments of Labour's third term of office was the celebration at the final vote on the nationalisation of the coal industry. The members from South Wales stood and sang, as still Welshmen sing in the local pub of Llanrhaiadr ym Mochnant on a Saturday night, harmonising spontaneously the hymn, ending with the refrain O *am aros yn ei gariad ddyddiau foes*.[6]

Fortunately for my sanity, I had a heavy research programme to absorb my energies during the five years which ended with the first phase of what one then called the phoney war. I could respect the integrity of those who volunteered for service in Spain with the International Brigade, but I could not share their optimism about the outcome. Those in an age group too young for call-up in the first world war had no recollection of the unreflecting optimism which impelled Rupert Brooke and others like him to suicidal enlistment without foreseeing the colossal wastage of life at the Somme and Verdun that left half the continent of Europe prey to military dictatorships. To those in their late thirties or older, it was self-evident that war on the same scale would henceforth be at least as destructive in terms of human life: indeed, far more so for women, children and old people. It was equally self-evident that it would be incomparably more destructive to the material resources of western civilisation. On the other hand, it was difficult to dismiss the likelihood that the aftermath of a Nazi victory could well accomplish a retreat to barbarism without parallel and with little prospect of a return to decency.

In the late thirties, there was an organisation named Federal Union founded with the aim of confronting the Third Reich with a United States of Europe embracing the Scandinavian democracies, Holland, Belgium, Czechoslovakia and Britain. Beveridge and I were members of the first executive, and Barbara Wootton gave it active support. Being more wise, John Boyd Orr would have nothing to do with it. He probably felt, as did the bulk of Labour Party supporters, that any such proposal to promote a federal structure was locking the stable doors after the horses had made their getaway. His assessment was more realistic than that of most of us, but for a different reason. Our preoccupation was with the fate of our white Commonwealth, with that of Europe and of the U.S.A. Orr's contacts with the League of Nations to promote a worldwide campaign against hunger and malnutrition had convinced him that the outcome of a second world war would have repercussions which would destroy the colonial system and lead to the emergence of an Afro-Asian bloc as a major force in power politics. We all know now how right he was.

Discussion with John Orr about the future of hitherto underdeveloped territories called to my attention how exclusively the linguistic habits of people whose native tongue is one of those included in the Indo-European family had bounded the horizon of proponents of an international auxiliary language. The recognition of this influenced me greatly while finalising the plan of *The Loom of Language* for Bodmer's agreement in 1939. In the last chapter, which I myself wrote a year later, I outlined a project I completed while fire-watching at night in Birmingham during 1941–42 and later published as *Interglossa*.

In retrospect I now regard my brief flirtation with Federal Union, which was after all merely a forerunner of the movement to bring Britain into the Common Market, as a soporific for my social conscience. I was caught between horror at the prospect of colossal carnage and hatred of the moral values of German National Socialism. More than a few people branded with the trademark of appeasement had been of military age in 1914, had lively memories of disillusionment after an earlier conflagration and found themselves torn between the same conflicting emotions.

From the beginning of the civil war in Spain, I did my best to avoid thinking about politics. Aside from my association with Federal Union, and with one infringement of my resolve, I continued to do so while I remained in Aberdeen. Ritchie Calder and I made an approach to Ernest Bevin to suggest the usefulness of a Scientific Advisory Committee for the Trade Union Congress. Bevin liked the idea. I made myself responsible for recruiting the members, twelve Fellows of the Royal Society, one of whom, P. M. S. Blackett, became in 1966 its president. With an equal number of Trade Union leaders, our first meeting took place in the Holborn Restaurant. I recall it chiefly because John Boyd Orr, as spokesman for our side, revealed one of his most endearing characteristics. He took as his theme malnutrition in the Glasgow slums and spoke unselfconsciously with a compelling compassion which captivated the attention of even the most hard-boiled. This is something I have never been able to achieve. In the highly charged emotional situation I lived through while in Cape Town, I acquired the habit of communicating my most cherished convictions in a scorn-proof carapace of irony. Thereafter this became a lifelong habit.

Now, thirty-five years later, I cannot reconstruct a reliable account of the sequence of events during the mounting tension following Neville Chamberlain's trip to Munich. I do vividly recall that in the spring of 1939 my elder son left Aberdeen to embark on the study of medicine at the University of Wisconsin. Perhaps I remember the farewell chiefly because I had good reason to congratulate myself later on the confidence I had in his ability to look after himself, then 17 years old. I sent him off with $5,000 from the American royalties of *Mathematics for the Million* and *Science for the Citizen*. The sum was sufficient, with care, to see him through the course. I took this action before transfer of funds from Britain to any other country became illegal.

My eldest child, Sylvia, who was to come of age in December of 1939, had been somewhat disorientated by change of schools on three continents, and she decided that she would like to take a secretarial job before proceeding to university entrance. It happened that my department was then in need of a secretary. Though it is risky to employ one's relatives, she proved to be highly and congenially efficient. Being able to drive a car, she offered her services to Frank Crew as a social hostess to cope with an influx of foreign delegates when the International Congress of Genetics met under his presidency in Edinburgh. This was during the ill-fated September of 1939.

Before the Congress ended, the nationals of countries bordering Germany, Austria and Italy had received from their several consulates or through the radio their marching orders to return. Sylvia ferried them in our car in groups of five to Waverley Station. The partings were lachrimose. Gunnar Dahlberg was among the last to leave and pressed her to return with him partly in a secretarial capacity and partly as a guest who might provide practice in English conversation for his daughter Ragna. Sylvia accompanied him on his return journey. Less than six months later, her mother and I were to take a less cheerful view of the likelihood that Scandinavia as a whole would remain neutral. Part of the attraction of Gunnar's offer was that Otto Mohr and his wife had invited Sylvia to spend a long Christmas holiday in Oslo, likewise to talk English with their offspring. There is nothing odd about this. No Scandinavian can hope to get by in the upper reaches of business or in higher learning unless fairly fluent in English at best or, at worst, in German. I came to know the Mohrs, though briefly, at the September Congress. Otto Mohr was then Professor of Anatomy in the Medical Faculty at Oslo. After the liberation, he became its Rector. His consort was then the leading gynaecologist in Norway. They were a lovely couple, civilised like Gunnar Dahlberg in the Scandinavian way, if less adept in the vein of ironical humour comprehensible to intellectuals of all nations.

The next few days after the declaration of war faced the residue of the family with undelayable decisions. Enid had relinquished her research fellowship, intending to take up a temporary assignment in the Dominion Bureau of Statistics at Ottawa. The Canadian equivalent of the Registrar General's Office had invited her for a year in an advisory capacity involving a unique opportunity for work in a setting so diverse as the Protestant prairie provinces at one extreme and Catholic Quebec at the other. This promised unique opportunities to extend her studies on differential fertility and she had given enough lectures on a tour in the U.S.A. to pay her way for a short preview visit early in 1938. It confirmed her intention to make the best of the offer. Accordingly, we had decided to send our two younger children, Clare and David, to a Quaker boarding school. At the outbreak of the war, Enid cancelled her passage rather than leave them behind to a problematical fate.

This is why, about the end of what one later called the phoney war, we sold Inverdon before its mini-size crystal palace annex and outer greenhouses became a target for the Luftwaffe. This was a wrench for me. Enid and I still had a *pied-à-terre* in our weekend croft. During the working week, we shared rooms in a two-storey house of Old Aberdeen with one of our younger colleagues.

There is, after that, little to tell of the tail end of our common association with Aberdeen. In Britain the prevailing attitude to the war was one of confident, but somewhat indifferent, optimism. Few, even among the more educated of the community, had any premonitions of the scale of military operations or the horrors of Belsen. A widely indulged-in phantasy was that the French would remain fast in the Maginot line while Britain blockaded the sea. Eventually, Germany would exhaust its resources of food, gasoline, rubber and other raw materials. There would then be a revolution. Hitler would be deposed by his generals and the great siege would come to an end. One hoped that wiser counsels would then prevail to prevent a repetition of Versailles, and that genuine collective security based on a federation of democratic states would be built into the framework of the settlement. Meanwhile, there was nothing to discredit the British bulldog *sang-froid*. Evacuation was working according to schedule, and everyone had gas masks. If the Nazis did try an invasion of the Low Countries, so much the better. Germany would only increase her embarrassment by extending the theatre of war, hastening the inescapable penalties of defying the principles of sound finance and of substituting autarchy for international trade.

CHAPTER XVI

Scandinavia

WHEN I made a decision which irrevocably broke up our family, the phoney war was approaching its abrupt end in the blitzkrieg of April–May 1940. Sufficiently worried about Sylvia's vulnerability, I accepted an invitation to lecture on the genetic credentials of Nazi race theory in the Universities of Oslo and Copenhagen with the intention of bringing her back to Britain.

My last lecture in the Anatomical Institute of the University of Oslo was on the evening of April 8, celebrated by an informal beer party of medical men, professors and post-graduate students. We were all very cheerful, and there was no sense of imminent inconvenience. We broke up about midnight, when some of us stopped to read the late-night news posted in the office window of *Tidens Tegn* or one of the other Oslo dailies. Nobody attached much significance to the report of an unconfirmed rumour that transport ships had been sunk off the Norwegian coast. Next morning, Fru Lois Mohr drove Sylvia and myself, seemingly with few misgivings, to the Grand Hotel where the *luftbil* awaited to take passengers to the airport to catch the plane to Copenhagen. The bombing of the airport began. Bombers were cruising low above the housetops, firing less with destructive intention than to terrorise. Road transport in Oslo came to a full stop.

Sylvia and I made our way on foot to the British Legation located in a suburb on the far side of the city. The entire staff other than an aged butler had retreated into the country, leaving the American Consul in charge. While we discussed our next move with the Consul, he received a phone message from his French opposite number to the effect that German troops were in command of the harbour. He therefore advised us to make tracks with utmost speed to the Swedish frontier. He had good reason. A lorry of Nazi troops in gray uniforms with steel helmets, machine guns pointing in all directions, was patrolling the street outside the Legation when we emerged. The city had been lulled to a false sense of security by a radio announcement that a German ultimatum to the Norwegian government did not expire till evening, and we had no time to take stock of other possibilities.

The night before, I had refused a lecture fee at Oslo, relying on a handout from my Danish publisher on arrival at Copenhagen. We therefore returned to the Mohrs. Happily, Otto had ready the cash without which we would not have had enough to pay our rail fare to the frontier. Our next objectives were to get a Swedish visa and to regain our luggage left at the Grand Hotel for Thomas Cook to collect. We found the railway station closed and staff at police H.Q. too bewildered to endorse our passports. Its building is only five minutes' walk from Karl Johans Gaten, which is the Parliament Street of Oslo. When we turned into it, there was an ominous silence punctuated by the clicking of boots. The march of triumph was in progress.

From the steps of the Grand Hotel where two American journalists gave us the latest news, we watched the pageant over the heads of the onlookers who lined the sidewalks in rigid speechlessness. From what I had learned from our American friends about the number of troops, I surmised that the Germans could not post guards at all roads leading out of the city. We set out with an air-transport handbag for my shaving kit, a Norwegian dictionary and a valise. We soon found the valise too heavy and dumped it in the entrance of a shop, where I bought a map of Oslo and its environs. Sylvia and I worked our way on foot to the outskirts of the city. When we saw a Nazi soldier posted at a corner, we went round a block, taking a zigzag course towards the main road to the Charlottenberg frontier. Some distance out of town, we came upon a gas station where the driver of an empty lorry was filling up. When I told him why we had to get out of town, he was at first incredulous. Eventually, he agreed to give us a lift to one of the railway stations on the main line from Oslo to Stockholm.

Along the road, we passed a hospital with windows which had been raked by machine gun fire. Any remaining doubts our driver benefactor may have harboured evaporated when several Nazi lorries and military motorcycles passed us. It was now evident that the occupying troops had sealed the main road to the frontier. Conversation was difficult because the driver spoke *landmål*, a hayseed dialect, but I got him to see that we might get into Sweden if we made our way to one of the smaller frontier villages south of the main Charlottenberg road. This necessitated returning through Oslo to a suitable exit. Sylvia and I adjusted our clothes to present a plausible aspect as members of the driver's family, and we doubled in our tracks, facing a stream of armoured cars with more pressing commitments than vetting civilian traffic.

We passed through Oslo before darkness fell. The sun was setting over snowbound wooded hills. Our driver took us to his cottage in the mountains. Having had no food since seven o'clock in the morning, we were grateful to stop off for tea and bread with shrimp paste. After coaxing the driver's wife to let him carry on, we then continued our journey. Apart from the fact that it was bitterly cold, that the conveyance was almost devoid of functionally active springs and that our driver expertly skidded or skated round hairpin bends separated from a sheer drop of several hundred feet by no fence or hedge, we finished the trip without incident. After several hours of night driving, we saw a barrier across the road to mark where the frontier lies. A few miles further on we were at the *tullstation* of the frontier hamlet Hån. There we gratefully parted with the driver and our remaining cash—a hundred Norwegian crowns—pitifully inadequate to recompense him.

Luckily a Swedish law student working his way through university had taken a temporary job as an official in the customs office at Hån. He had recently read a Swedish translation of one of my books, and press cuttings I had with my passport left no room for doubt about my identity. Since the radio had alerted all military installations along the boundary with news of the invasions of Norway and Denmark, it was not difficult to explain my presence without a visa. When we entered the *tullstation*, a senior official in charge was on the phone, reporting to the police at the nearest sizeable village, Tjöckfors, a description of a German plane hovering above. The officer who immediately drove out to take down further details of the plane undertook, with the utmost consideration, the formalities of taking Sylvia and myself into custody for illegal entry. After receiving our passports, he put us in a comfortable car and deposited us in the bedroom of a guest house about six miles inside the frontier. The next day Gunnar Dahlberg telegraphed a remittance for the journey to Uppsala, and the police turned up at our guest house to say that our visas had come through. They charitably arranged for a car to take us to the nearest railway station at Arvika fifteen miles inside the frontier.

While in Sweden, we stayed at Uppsala in the apartment of Gunnar Dahlberg and his wife, visiting Stockholm about once a week. With Gunnar's help I got commissions for translations of scientific books or articles from Swedish into English at a rate of remuneration that I had not expected. From what I earned, I was soon able to replenish an exhausted wardrobe and provide for air travel from Sweden.

Days dragged on while we waited for our Russian visas. Meanwhile, Finland refused to grant visas to foreigners without tickets to show that they were in transit. If Sweden had been invaded, there would thus have been no egress for a British citizen, and I would have no reason to suppose that my university would continue to pay my salary indefinitely. If not, I had plenty to worry about. Thus I urged Enid by cable to take Clare and David to Canada, where she would be able to continue her research with adequate means of support for the three of them.

During the weeks of waiting, my friendship with Gunnar mitigated a claustrophobia reinforced by lack of motor transport or a pair of skis. At the best of times, Uppsala has few attractions other than the magnificent mediaeval castle where Greta Garbo abdicated in the role of Queen Christina, and its university library, which has on public exhibit the impressive original of the *Codex Argenteus* of Bishop Ulfilas, a Gothic version of the Gospels and, as such, the earliest extant Teutonic document. Till I met Gunnar, I had always thought that no one other than myself was as cheerfully anti-sport, but I did take advantage of winter in the Aberdeen countryside by equipping myself with a skiing outfit, too late in life to acquire proficiency. I had to leave it in Oslo when we escaped. I once asked Gunnar whether he felt no impulse to ski. He replied that he had no intention "until they change that law." To my query *what law*, his answer was "the law of gravity."

Gunnar had an oddly professional rationalisation for no excessive muscular activity other than shaving and conversation. The terms of reference of his Chair embraced Vital Statistics, and his researches had put the spotlight on the low expectation of life of professional sportsmen, more especially owing to coronary disease. To forestall early demise from undue physical effort, he kept a couch in his office. He rarely wielded a pen except for algebraic exploits and otherwise dictated everything he published to a secretary, in a recumbent posture. Unfortunately, he died when scarcely more than sixty from a pancreatic disorder diagnosed too late. A few weeks before his death he had written to tell me that he was preparing a brief for his Faculty of Medicine recommending me to receive an honorary M.D.

To discuss at length our common interest in so technical a field as mathematical genetics would be merely tedious and largely unintelligible to those who may try to work their way through memoirs so personal as these. Briefly, the position was then that the exponents of what the Germans called *Rassenhygiene* and what their British counterparts called Eugenics presented pedigree charts with circles and squares of white or black as evidence of the role of heredity vis-à-vis human behaviour.[1] When exhibited in stud books of farm stock, such charts do indeed convey information about genetic differences, but only because the breeder operates within the framework of a highly standardised environment. That of different families in a human community is not a comparably fixed framework. The human family is a unit which transmits to the next generation a particular environment no less than a peculiar assortment of genes. We can, however, recognise genetic differences by the ratios in which individuals of diverse types turn up in matings between parents distinguishable in one way or another. Such ratios are easy to compute when we can select the parents themselves for breeding. If we cannot, as indeed we are never free to do when the parents are human, we have to work out the consequences of mating at random. The rationale of a scientific approach to human inheritance therefore calls for more mathematical sophistication than the science of animal or plant breeding.

I shared with Gunnar Dahlberg an ethical outlook no less than an intellectual attitude, and each of us had reason to feel isolated before we met in the late thirties. J. B. S. Haldane, with whom we both participated in theoretical explorations of mathematical genetics relevant to the racial issue, loyally gave me his support when obstacles to publication came my way. Haldane's later acquiescence in the apotheosis of Lysenko and his reticence with reference to the fate of Vavilov[2] were consonant with his avoidance of any public denunciation of the bogus genetic credentials of *Rassenhygiene*. Insofar as we were its outspoken opponents from a scientific, in contradistinction to an emotional, viewpoint, Gunnar and I were very much alone on our side of the Atlantic.

Since we approached the existence of antagonism to minority

groups as a pathological phenomenon to the prevention of which an understanding of its aetiology is prerequisite, our common approach isolated us also from sympathy with well-meaning people who advocate ostensible remedies which can only aggravate the disease. When I once asked Gunnar why Swedes were comparatively free of race, or so called race, prejudice, he succinctly replied that they discouraged immigration.

Prior to my enforced stay in Sweden, I had been invited by the Nobel Prize Committee to represent Britain in connexion with nominations for a 1940 laureate for the medical, that is the biological, sciences. In that capacity, I prepared the brief for the choice of H. J. Muller—a friend of long standing, foremost among the architects of the Theory of the Gene and the first to produce mutations by radiation. The invasion of Norway and Denmark delayed a decision until the Liberation, but it was gratifying to renew my friendship with H.J. when he spent a few days in Britain en route to receive the award in 1946.

The first stage of our trip to Moscow was somewhat nerve-racking. At the Stockholm airport, passengers awaited their turn in the same queue for two planes, each Russian, destined respectively for Berlin and Riga. When we reached the plane, we discovered that the Russian attendant did not understand English, French, Swedish or even my atrocious brand of schoolbook German. While I tried to get an intelligent verdict about our destination, a fellow passenger pushed us in from behind and the door closed on us. Until we reached Riga, where we changed planes, we were not certain that Berlin might not be our first stop. At Riga, we comforted ourselves with vodka in the company of a fellow passenger who had unhappily booked to Britain by way of Moscow, Bucharest and Rome. He was thus destined to walk into an Italian internment camp.

On the second lap of our journey we flew below the cloud belt, sufficiently low to take stock of the scenery and architecture. Inside the Soviet frontier, we touched down at Velikiye Luki. Our fellow passengers were members of a Swedish trade delegation and speedily got their clearance from the customs officials. Our own dealings with them were more protracted, and we were to find when we reached the far eastern limit of the Soviet Union, that their consequences were almost disastrous. At its Stockholm office *Intourist* had assured us that one of its guides who spoke English and/or German would shepherd us when we reached Soviet territory. None turned up and the Customs Officer at Velikiye Luki understood no English, German or Swedish. We had to disclose our foreign currency and our passports in which the corresponding amounts had been stamped by the Swedish authorities. It was obvious that our examiner did not know the difference between a dollar bill and a traveller's cheque, and had no idea of the value of the Swedish coins we had kept to buy roubles for petty cash expenses on the journey. He destroyed several receipts and eventually gave us for signature one on which we could read only the numerals. It turned out to be wrong when we got to Vladivostok. At first I objected to signing it because we could not read the text, but since he made it clear that he had no intention of letting us through till we had done so, I gave in. Until we reached Vladivostok, we did not realise that we had, in effect, parted with all the currency needed to face the next phase of our homeward trek.

We had not known we should have any communicable companions on the journey from Moscow to Vladivostok and thence to the Japanese port of Tsuruga. It was a pleasant surprise when a party of fellow travellers—mostly from Stockholm—turned up at the Hotel Metropole on the night before departure. The Stockholm party, as I shall call them, consisted of about two dozen people, including several children. Most of them were Jewish refugees who had found asylum in Sweden and had decided to take no chances on current and insistent rumours of an imminent invasion. They included an agricultural engineer bound for the Argentine, to which he hoped to bring his Swedish wife; a German novelist with his wife, a dress designer; the Viennese wife of a refugee physician in England; and two families of which the male representatives were engaged in trading of some sort. One of them intended to start a frozen egg business in Shanghai. The other was going to Mexico. On the same train there were two Chilean diplomats, one accompanied by his wife; an ex-captain of the Swiss army, leaving behind him a business in Sweden to start life again in Costa Rica; and our only English-speaking fellow sufferer, a wealthy Australian lady who had divorced a Norwegian husband just before the Occupation.

The Chilean trio conversed in French. Otherwise, Swedish was the *lingua franca* of the party. Perhaps the fact that few of us conversed in our own languages during most of the journey was responsible for our success in getting along without any quarrels in circumstances which were not propitious to cheerful companionship among a rather odd assembly of bedfellows. More probably the chief reason was that *Intourist* bungled everything which human ingenuity and incompetence can conspire to mismanage.

The Russian landscape had no redeeming features such as gardens. The only decorative efforts along the Trans-Siberian railroad were faded photographs of Stalin fixed in bright scarlet frames, nailed above the front doors of the log houses.

Somewhere near Omsk and Irkutsk the Steppes fade into the luminescent loveliness of snowcapped mountains around Lake Baikal. The Steppes of Russia in Asia had been for me, since boyhood, a symbol of desolation. The reality is far less forbidding. With the exception of a stretch we traversed while we skirted the shores of Lake Baikal, the landscape was remarkably uniform from the Latvian frontier to the far eastern border of Siberia. Evidence of human interference, which gives variety and grace to the countryside in Massachusetts, in the west of England, and in Japan, was entirely lacking. If monotonous, as is commonly true of scenery which does not disclose the imprint of human occupation, it was not unpleasing. Almost everywhere along the route, the surface was flat, covered with good grass and clumps of silver birch sometimes mixed with pine or, more rarely, larch. I saw no stretches of trees sufficiently dense and extended to earn the title of a forest, nor clearings as bare as Salisbury plain. As far as the eye could reach, the general effect was mild, mostly woodland of a type common in some parts of Quebec province, in the Middle West, and in eastern France. Occasionally a river meandered near the line, without appreciably affecting the character of the vegetation. I can recall the sight of few birds or butterflies, and scarcely any signs of agriculture.

The people collected near every wayside station were as homogeneous as the vegetation. Though we skirted the Mongolian border for three days, we saw few typical Mongol faces before we boarded the *Harbin Maru* in the port of Vladivostok. Uniform, like their inhabitants, the small towns or large villages of which we got a glimpse throughout our trek from the Latvian frontier to the Pacific Ocean were assemblages of log cabins of a sort common in the backwoods of Canada. In their natural setting among the silver birches and early summer flowers of the surrounding country, the picture might well have been one of attractive simplicity. As they emerged to view along the railroad, the effect was quite otherwise. Wherever a settlement came into sight, the land for half a mile around had been divested of every trace of vegetation. The bare earth which separated one hut from its neighbours formed a dusty cake of dried mud, or a quagmire where rain had recently fallen. Roofs had no gutters or rain pipes. During a shower, water dripped down into puddles through which the owners or tenants waded in wooden clogs or bare feet.

During each of nine days' travel between Moscow and Vladivostok, we stopped at three or four such settlements, and others of the same type had been visible below as we flew from Velikiye Luki to Moscow. Most of the houses were weather-worn, often dilapidated. Usually there were some, occasionally many, of the same pattern in course of construction. At Irkutsk there were buildings of concrete, brick or stone, grim and unadorned, including barracks of a type presumably used for housing factory workers. These tenements reminded me of the buildings you can see inside the walls of Dartmoor prison, as you approach Princetown from Two Bridges. From the outside, the factories at Irkutsk, as elsewhere visible in the course of our itinerary, were all of an 1890 pattern, built without regard for the surroundings in which the working population has to live. Omsk, where the dark satanic mills are supplemented by rectangular erections of concrete, was the only other considerable town visible by daylight between Moscow and the end of the journey. I saw it in the morning twilight of June, a hideous combination of negligent modern and decaying Muscovite architecture.

We reached Vladivostok on the night of the thirteenth, due to board the *Harbin Maru* for Japan early on the fifteenth, but later were told that it would not leave till the seventeenth. As an extenuating token of Russo-German friendship, the explanation innocently offered to the German-speaking Jewish refugees from our party was that the harbour was too full of Japanese ships bringing goods to Germany to handle the discharge of cargoes according to schedule.

At four o'clock in the afternoon of the third day of our internment in Vladivostok, we had word that our ship had unloaded its cargo and would sail at six o'clock that evening instead of at noon on the following day.

On foot, with our luggage, we reached the Customs Office about two and a half hours after the ship was ready to sail. We waited without food till midnight, when life in Russia at that time really began. The customs officials then turned up with Ogpu personnel to examine our luggage. The latter were told to check any reading matter, presumably for political content. I myself had left Oslo with nothing but the clothes I stood up in, and most of the luggage I brought to Vladivostok consisted of books and manuscripts. Thus I monopolized most of the attention of one out of the six members of the police force. One of the others spoke English fluently and all of them were courteous. What is more remarkable, they showed a quick grasp of, and apparently an intelligent interest in, the contents of my baggage which included a pile of photographic illustrations of scientific diagrams for a book. We chatted in a friendly way in English, helped out by my atrociously bad German.

Before we left, and by that time almost penniless, I sustained the worst shock I had experienced since watching the German march of triumph down Karl Johans Gate. The customs officers got around to our valuta. The official who had examined our passports at Velikiye Luki had erroneously listed as in dollar bills all the American currency which Sylvia and I had brought in traveller's cheques; and we had no authority to take dollar bills out of the country. We had to give up one hundred and thirty dollars and, what was worse, about $300 worth of traveller's cheques. When the *Intourist* interpreter returned from a session at the telephone, we were able to show that the numerical quantity of American currency which we had hoarded for the next stage of our journey agreed with the Swedish endorsement on our passports. She did her best, but without success, to get our traveller's cheques back. Fortunately for us, we had just enough to see us through to the Kobe consulate when we reached Tsuruga. There awaited us an introduction from the British legation in Stockholm to the Embassy at Tokyo.

CHAPTER XVII

Madison, Wisconsin

WHEN we boarded the *Harbin Maru*, we had before us three days in surroundings of spotless cleanliness before facing what we expected to be the most hazardous part of our homeward voyage. For it seemed likely that an explosion in the Far East was imminent, and a Swedish lady had offered three-to-one odds that we would get to Japan in time for the occupation of Hong Kong. The one stop we made en route was at Rashin in Korea. There the Japanese Police boarded our ship to interrogate aliens in English. The performance was less a questioning than a sequence of astonishing misstatements seemingly proffered with the intention of alarming the passenger into an admission of espionage. Among other things, they asked if we did not know that the British Government with the royal family had left London to continue the struggle from headquarters in Ottawa. Since we had no reliable information of what had happened after we left Moscow, we received these disclosures with polite interest and gave a factual account of why we were in transit.

We docked at Tsuruga on the noon of a day near the summer solstice, and I can still luxuriate in the recollection of our first experience of a Japanese June twilight. I had no anticipation of the artistry still immanent in the everyday life of the nation. Tsuruga was then a fortified town and the police were punctilious. Every passenger had to go through a more thorough interrogation than had been our lot when in dock at Rashin—both to disclose his or her reasons for coming to the country and intentions with respect to residence during the period for which our transit visas were valid. Our interrogators were courteous, and I soon detected that the English they had learned was Ogden's *Basic English*. This gave me an opportunity to commend their linguistic expertise and to divert their devotion to duty into congenial topics for discourse.

Tsuruga itself was scarcely more than a large village with, I surmised, about 10,000 inhabitants. The railway station was over a mile from the dockside, and the way to it lay through narrow, colourful streets of small shops of a type then still common in a town as large as Kobe, from which we were provisionally booked to sail for America. As we were to notice more vividly in Kobe itself, such streets were commonly decorated with paper lanterns and flags, which might well seem garish in the mechanised milieu of urban life in Europe, but in their own setting were delightful. Wherever there was a gap between buildings with paper walls supported by wood frames, a garden came into view, and where there were no trees or shrubs planted against the wall, exquisitely pruned and tended dwarf conifers set out in tubs of earth softened the red and blue of flag and lantern with the urbanity of the village green. By the entrances to the shops, one saw stone troughs or glass bowls with radiant tropical fish. Cages for birds, fireflies or stridulant insects hung from the lintel.

Beyond the shops, we found ourselves before the *tori* or painted gateway of a Shinto shrine. We had our first glimpse of landscape gardening as we started out on the path across the rice fields where the young green shoots stood a few inches above the flooded surface of the soil. Blue-gray mountains filled the sky beyond, while a chorus of bullfrogs and cicadas signalled the approach of midsummer night. Having turned along another street in carnival colours which challenged the sunset, we eventually reached the railway station.

Through the open windows of the Kobe train, moonlight flickered in the steely radiance of the water lying low on the young rice shoots. At the raised edges of the rice fields, the foliage of the cedars was silhouetted in fretted ebony. Beyond them, as far as the eye could reach, jet-black mountains towered towards an iridescent sky. Shortly after midnight, we had left behind us the earthquake-proof skyscrapers of Osaka, and we reached Kobe by one o'clock. There we took a taxi to the Tor Hotel and enjoyed the luxury of a hot bath before retiring. The hotel had copies of two of the half-dozen Japanese dailies then printed in English and produced like an American or British newspaper. During the whole period of the French collapse we had been almost completely cut off from the outside world. Before we closed the mosquito net curtains round our beds, we had a mountain of foreign news to digest.

We were able to spend two idyllic days in Kobe and enjoy the hospitality of several delightful meals with the Consul General and members of the Consular staff. The residence of the Consul General stood in a spacious terrace garden halfway up the mountain, overlooking the harbour and sharing the stillness of the neighbouring Shinto shrine where the only sound in the late June evening is the chirping of the cicada. Two of the Consular staff had a Japanese house furnished with the attractive simplicity found in a Japanese interior. Before crossing the threshold, the guest had to observe the local custom of changing from shoes or boots into grass sandals kept in the porch for general use, a custom I should like to have enforced in the porch of the Welsh cottage in which I have retired—especially after rain. During our first lunch, we watched large swallowtail butterflies flitting among the shrubs while lizards darted out of the crevices in the rock garden.

On reaching Kobe, I had received instructions from our Embassy to come to Tokyo where I was to be a guest of honour at a luncheon of the Japanese-British Society. We were now able to travel with a clear conscience at public expense. On the way to Tokyo we broke our journey at Kyoto. With its 400 shrines and 1,400 Buddhist temples, Kyoto was for many centuries the Japanese capital. It occupies about 240 square kilometres in a roughly rectangular basin surrounded by famous mountains. There we had time to visit the temple of the Thousand Buddhas, the temple of Havi with its mammoth cedar pillars hauled by ropes woven of human tresses donated by its votaries, also the great Shinto shrine of Heian-jinga, and the Buddhist monastery of Chionin. Accessible to people of all social levels, Japanese gardens may extend over areas as small as the communal plot of many squares in Bloomsbury or larger than the barren waste of Hyde Park, but there is little in common between the garden of a shrine or temple and anything to be found in an English town. They enfold and protect the visitor in a privacy which is the product of luxuriant growth through centuries of solicitude and design. Indeed *gardening* is too narrow a term for the common thread which runs through the design of a Japanese street, the pattern of a kimono, the water colour painting on the wall, the charming *Bon-Kei* or tray landscapes used as objects of interior decoration, or the communal serenity of temple and shrine.

The effect for which a Japanese gardener strives is at once natural and highly artificial. Everything in a Japanese garden has the appearance of having been there from time immemorial. The Japanese gardener cherishes the large butterflies which flit in the sunlight no less than the bright and tuneful birds. Rock pools for ornamental fish, kept fresh and cool by fountains and miniature cataracts, are an indispensable as well as conspicuous feature of the large-scale garden.

In Kobe I had one good reason to be thankful for the mistake of the customs office at Velikiye Luki. If the Russians had not confiscated our dollar reserves at Vladivostok, we should have sailed from Kobe to Seattle on the twenty-first of June. In that event, we should not have visited Kyoto, nor stepped ashore at Honolulu. I should also have missed the opportunity of meeting some of the Japanese members of the Japanese-British Society and should not have had the privilege of learning something about Japanese culture and language from its most famous European exponent. Sir George Sansom, then a leading authority on both, had recently retired from the Embassy staff to take up a professional appointment at Columbia, but rejoined it temporarily in an advisory capacity after the outbreak of war in Europe. When Sylvia and I stayed at the Tokyo Embassy, it was our rare good fortune to have Sir George as our host. Aside from so congenial an opportunity for further education, the visit to the capital solved my most immediate financial difficulties. Through the good offices of the Consul General, who optimistically accepted my cheque on an Aberdeen bank, we managed to get permission from the Yokohama Specie Bank to take away the bare minimum to satisfy the American immigration authorities and keep us going in San Francisco till a credit arrived.

Within half an hour of my arrival at the bungalow he occupied in the Embassy compound, Sansom had plunged into a discussion on the possible role of Jesuit missionaries in the efflorescence of Japanese mathematics during the latter half of the seventeenth century when Wallis, Brouncker, Newton and Leibniz were the leading European mathematicians in parallel developments.[1] The possibility had not escaped me. My interest in Japanese culture had been awakened while at Aberdeen for two reasons. It was there my privilege to make the acquaintance of Arthur Waley, and I had read his lately published monumental translation of the novel of Lady Murasaki in anticipation of his visit. Also, at about this time, I was drafting the programme of Bodmer's *Loom of Language* and the light shed by the history of the Japanese on the transition from so-called ideographic to a phonetic script intrigued me not a little.

While in Tokyo, I noticed that a Japanese clerk, like his opposite number in Stalin's Russia, still relied on the use of the counting frame for computation. However, his instrument was very different from the abacus of classical antiquity or of Russia at that time, and he used it with a speed which has astonished European mathematicians.

Sylvia and I left Yokohama in the *Tatuta Maru* on June 29. It was with great relief that I had received the day before our departure a cable from Enid in Liverpool, stating that she hoped to land in Canada with the children about the time when our ship was due to dock in San Francisco. After fourteen days, we passed through the Golden Gate. When the pilot boat brought on board the Immigration officers, I received a welcome response to one of three cables I had dispatched from Tokyo. My elder son, then about to start medical studies at Wisconsin, had wired a loan adequate to take Sylvia and myself to New York, where I was confident of further assistance from my publisher, W. W. Norton. I received no acknowledgment, then or later, to my request that Aberdeen University should persuade the Treasury to issue a permit from my bank for release of sufficient cash for the boat fare back to Britain.

The day spent in San Francisco was pleasant. A fellow passenger invited us to join him at lunch with his brother, a professor of mathematics at Berkeley, and to visit the world's fair then in session, after a drive round the Berkeley campus. The latitude of San Francisco is within two degrees of that of Tokyo, and its climate suitable for the cultivation of comparable flora. The floral layout of the University of California campus and of its residential environs for academic staff showed ample evidence of Japanese influence, and I have visited no university of the Western world set in comparably colourful surroundings.

Sylvia and I travelled to New York by rail, a route through Nevada, Utah, Nebraska and Iowa to Chicago, where we had to change. At each state boundary, we had a new restaurant car and an entirely new budgetary problem. While passing through a dry state, no liquor was obtainable. It was therefore a great relief to step off at Chicago, the more because it gave me a chance to meet Count Korzybski in the flesh.[2] Just before the outbreak of war, Korzybski had invited me to become a Vice President of his *Institute of Semantics*, and I had agreed. I put through a call to him on arrival and took a cab. On reaching the Institute, I was pressed into addressing a seminar impromptu. After that, Korzybski took us out to a very liberally lubricated lunch. When he saw us off on the New York train, we were all but anaesthetised.

Madison, Wisconsin

At New York my publisher, Warder Norton, entertained us at his flat in Gramercy Park off Lexington Avenue. His partner Storer Lunt, who proved to be an equally congenial companion, took us next day to the New York World's Fair, where I sampled the safety parachute. The layout of the New York fair was more pleasing than that of its California twin, but I recall little of general interest.

My first concern in New York was to settle my debts and to earn enough to pay my fare back to Aberdeen. I secured with little difficulty an advance for a travelogue, *Author in Transit*, which I had written on the *Tatuta Maru*. The advance gave me time to look around while still hoping to get word by cable of Treasury permission to pay for my homeward ticket from my Aberdeen account. I was also anxious to see that Enid and our two younger children had enough to live on while she settled into her job at the Dominion Bureau of Statistics in Ottawa. It was therefore good news when I received an invitation a few days after reaching Manhattan. It was from the President of the University of Wisconsin asking me to discuss the offer of a semester's visiting professorship. With as yet insufficient means for a return journey to Britain, I decided to accept. The summer vacation was on, and my elder son, Adrian, had rented for a few weeks a lakeside cabin in the wilds of Wisconsin.[3] There Sylvia and I joined him. We arrived by Greyhound bus. Travel by bus was to give me, throughout the next few months, an otherwise unattainable glimpse of one-horse-town life.

I have mentioned how I date successive episodes of my life story by the thrill of first seeing in the field, or as a microscopic preparation, an already familiar textbook illustration of an animal, plant or part of one. One of my most vivid recollections of late July, 1940, is of alighting at the Greyhound bus stop nearest to Adrian's cabin. There, for the first time, I saw a field of buckwheat in full flower. Buckwheat (*Polygonum fagopyrum*) is an Asiatic plant which has spread across Europe through Britain to the U.S.A. Though it is not rare in Britain, British farmers have never bothered to cultivate it as a crop. In the U.S.A. and in some parts of Canada, pancakes made of buckwheat flour served with maple syrup are a staple breakfast fare.

I can no longer reconstruct the authentic sequence of events during what was otherwise a very full schedule in the late summer of 1940. I negotiated a lecture tour which included a few commitments in the Christmas break. Throughout the remainder of the academic summer vacation, New York was my *pied-à-terre*. Until term began, I could always get a bed in the Gramercy Park apartment of Warder Norton, who commuted from his rural residence in Connecticut during the hotter months of summer. This gave me opportunities for visiting professional colleagues at Columbia University, at New York University and at research institutes on Long Island. It was a period in which I could recover from the enforced claustrophobia of my stay in Sweden and the journey across Siberia. Happily, I had already arranged for Sylvia to start work as a student in the University of Wisconsin, where her brother could introduce her to a circle of congenial friends.

I had therefore no domestic distractions, and was in a mood to see America of the New Deal through rose-coloured spectacles. If one must live in a city, Manhattan would still be my first choice. As the streets are laid out in a rectangular grid except where Broadway intrudes, one can become more familiar with its layout in a few days than with that of London or Birmingham in a lifetime. It is relatively smokeless and some of its thousand-foot-high buildings, in particular Rockefeller Center, have to my taste a unique geometric beauty. Throughout my summer visit, housekeeping was easy. There was fresh seafood in abundance and a ready-made meal of hot dog or hamburger at coffee stalls within a few minutes' reach of almost every habitation other than those on Riverside Drive.

My lecture tours took me as far afield as Kansas State University, where there was a party fixed for my benefit by the *Kansas City Star*. On one such journey, I took the opportunity to visit scientific colleagues of long-standing acquaintance at the Woods Hole Marine Biological Laboratory on Cape Cod. In Long Island and elsewhere in New York State, I had refused alternative offers of academic appointments. In Woods Hole, Thomas Hunt Morgan, founder of the Columbia school of genetics, was convalescing from a sickness at the time. He flattered my vanity by an undeservedly generous offer. He not only urged me to remain in the U.S.A. but also offered to lend me £1,000 [sic] so that I could look around for a suitable job. Before the summer ended I had several firm offers of permanent positions, and I am heartily glad that I turned them all down.

In doing so, I knew well enough that there would be little prospect of return to Britain if I remained away while hostilities lasted. I had reached the age at which one does not make deep friendships easily. While the New Deal was still on, I was able to sample the United States in its finest hour and the University of Wisconsin was itself a hothouse of Franklin Roosevelt's brain-trusters. Nonetheless, I could not convince myself that the ideological marriage of Henry Wallace and Eleanor Roosevelt had made any lasting dent on the hard core of the ad-man conscience or lack of it. In Canada, I had seen enough of witch-hunting in the mid-twenties to make me harbour doubts. My misgivings proved to be a counsel of prudence. Few years were to pass before McCarthy's congressional committee revived the Salem tradition as never before in this century. Reimbursed with the first fruits of a lecture tour, I contrived to pay a fleeting visit to see Enid and my two youngest in Ottawa. Though overclouded by the uncertain future of Britain, my semester in Wisconsin was otherwise singularly happy. At no time in my life have I felt less a misfit. I had the double satisfaction of intellectually stimulating colleagues with versatile interests, and agreeably picturesque surroundings. The state of Wisconsin has only one large city, Milwaukee. Its capital, the seat of the Legislature, is at Madison, comparable in size to Cambridge, England. Like Cambridge, it is a university town. Its campus occupies a lakeside setting with a nearby forest maintained as a public park.

My initial assignment at Madison was to give a post-graduate course on mathematical genetics in the Department of Genetics within the Faculty of Agriculture. The Department of Political Science pressed me on arrival to give an open course on the social background of science. An impressive gaggle of campus wives attended it. Some of the staff of the Department of Political Science had served in the Tennessee Valley Authority in an administrative capacity. Without my prior knowledge, they had implemented a proposal I had made in a lecture published while I was at the London School of Economics. In it, I had stated the need for a niche in the curriculum of social studies for *social technology*—that is, the impact of scientific discovery and new techniques on social institutions. I shared a room with the first incumbent of the post, William Beard.

William Beard, a delightful companion with a specialist training as an engineer, was the son of Charles and Mary Beard whose authoritative work on the American Constitution I had sampled while at McGill fifteen years earlier. When invited to lecture at the Johns Hopkins medical school in Baltimore shortly after the end of the war, I had the pleasure of meeting his mother. His appointment was one of the many congenial features of Wisconsin. There was no need to mourn lack of understanding between what C. P. Snow has called the two cultures. One of my newly found friends was William Ellery Leonard, head of the English Department and author of the Everyman verse translation of Lucretius's *De Rerum Natura*. Another professor in the English Department was completing a study of the Lunar Circle in the Birmingham of Boulton, Watt and Priestley.

Wisconsin had two visiting professors. My stablemate was Sinclair Lewis, a superb conversationalist with whom I spent several enjoyable evenings. He was gratified when I told him that I greatly preferred *Elmer Gantry* to *Main Street* and *Arrowsmith*. It was, he told me, the one he had most enjoyed writing. Among other well-known people I met, other than faculty personnel, the most memorable was Henry Wallace, at that time candidate for Vice-President. His son Bob attended my mathematical lectures in the Department of Genetics. His father is primarily remembered as a statesman of sincere humanity and enlightened sympathies, but few people know that his earliest passion, after graduating from the Agricultural School of Iowa State University, was the genetics of maize. During the historic third-term campaign for Franklin Roosevelt, Henry Wallace broke his journey at Madison. To my immense gratification, he turned up without warning at my flat in the Faculty Club and took me off to a respectable speakeasy where we spent the afternoon discussing the problems of integration in the deep South. I found him to be a warm and thoughtful conversationalist. Friends who took me for rides in the Madison countryside pointed out to me many examples of the early work of the architect Frank Lloyd Wright, who studied civil engineering at the University of Wisconsin. He made history by using the floating cantilever principle in the construction of the Imperial Hotel at Tokyo, the first earthquake-proof building. When I had visited it during my stay at the Tokyo Embassy, I knew nothing of his work. After seeing it for myself, it was easy to recognise Japanese characteristics in so much of his later work. When I visited the University of Minnesota at the invitation of the Mathematics Department to conduct seminars on Biomathematics, I stayed for a week with Dean Willey in one of Lloyd Wright's famous domestic creations.

A highlight of the Minnesota visit was a performance of *Androcles and the Lion* at the University Drama Center. The theatre itself was an attractive example of cubist interior decor, and the acting of the student cast of a quality as high as any I have seen at the Birmingham or Plymouth repertories. Like Minnesota, Madison had its school of dramatic art. That it could stage a different play each weeknight might seem incredible if one were not familiar with the scale on which Wisconsin, like many of the better state universities, operated. In such institutions all full-time higher education is on one campus, and size alone makes possible cultural activities for which a large audience and a large reservoir of talent are alike prerequisite. At the time of my visit, there were about 11,000 students on the Madison campus with a network of extramural courses in the highways and byways embracing a registered total more than twice as great.

Extramural classes held examinations, and students with a certain minimum of credits in them could complete a degree qualification with a much-reduced period of residence. Among the cultural and productive activities which linked the University with the community as a whole, two set a pattern some of our British universities might well follow. One was the Home and Farm Radio. The other was the role of the Agricultural Faculty as the controller of maize for sowing on the farms. The rationale of the last mentioned communal responsibility is that the best varieties of maize are hybrids produced by cross-fertilisation of highly inbred but less productive strains. They can therefore be propagated for seed production only by a programme of perpetual cross-fertilisation.

The industrial Lake Michigan port of Milwaukee has a large population of descendants of Polish Catholics, but a high proportion of the rural population of Wisconsin and Minnesota are of Scandinavian descent. This may partly account for the long liberal (in the American sense) tradition of Madison. There the progressive La Follettes[4] were still influential on the University Board of Regents during my stay, and I met both the brothers socially. An incident, while returning from Minnesota to Madison by Greyhound bus, is eloquent. As we approached our destination, I found myself talking Norwegian with an octogenarian from Trondheim. By the time we reached it, all the passengers were singing in unison Solveig's Song from *Peer Gynt*.

My semester at Wisconsin was due to end in late January 1941. Without my knowledge, the University President wrote to the Vice Chancellor at Aberdeen requesting the Senate to second me for the remainder of the academic year. At the time this was flattering, but it was a source of annoyance when I got back to Aberdeen. My Aberdeen colleagues assumed that I wanted to remain in America out of harm's way. I had in fact already booked a homeward passage. In anticipation, Enid was able to come from Ottawa for a farewell visit of two or three days during the short Christmas break. She stayed with me in the Faculty Club for a family reunion with Sylvia and Adrian. Before resuming teaching duties, I spent two other nights on a trip to Ames, Iowa, where I lectured at the alma mater of Henry Wallace.

By New Year, when I booked a passage back to Britain, I had paid all my debts. Sylvia was now twenty-two. On departure from Sweden, I had arranged for her to have by deed of gift all my American royalties, whence an income sufficient to see her through college. With no pressing worries about parental responsibilities, I thus left Wisconsin for New York in a warm glow of friendship after a round of good-bye parties. Part of the entertainment at one of these was my introduction to Paul Robeson's rendition of the *Ballad of America*. The night before I boarded the *Georgic* on what was to be its last voyage, several friends on the editorial staff of the since defunct but then influential *New York Herald Tribune* gave me a last farewell party. For the next few years my professional and social life were to be a protracted anticlimax.

CHAPTER XVIII

Birmingham

The last voyage of the *Georgic*, before it became a casualty of submarine warfare, lasted over a fortnight. We cruised in the Arctic waiting for the all clear for full speed southward out of danger into territorial waters between Skye and the Outer Hebrides. There were two minor discomforts. We had to bring our life jackets into the saloon at meals, and all the portholes throughout the ship were closed and blacked out. The deck was out of bounds, offering no scope for fresh-air fiends or sports addicts. The only relaxation was small talk. For me, companionship of Canadian air pilots who had learned their navigational astronomy from *Science for the Citizen* helped mitigate the boredom. Happily also, one of the passengers was Geoffrey Bing, whom I met years later as Constitutional Adviser to Nkrumah and first Attorney General of independent Ghana. He had a repertoire of limericks better even than Julian Huxley's.

After an absence of nearly a year during which I had traversed more than 20,000 miles to cover the 500-mile gap between Oslo and Aberdeen, I reached the bomb-battered dockside of Liverpool in late February 1941. Back in Aberdeen, I had a bed in my department. For the time being, I had decided to sleep there in order to record my basal metabolic rate under resting conditions, with the help of my laboratory assistant. The reason for this was that I had begun to experience more acutely the inconvenience of a retrosternal goitre, which had been discovered while I was at Madison. My hope was to use myself as a guinea pig to follow up an observation I had made many years earlier. I had shown that extracts of the posterior lobe of the pituitary gland contain a component able to antagonise the anterior lobe hormone which stimulates growth and activity of the thyroid of salamander larvae. Because it was no longer easy to obtain supplies of fresh glands for making extracts, the attempt was abortive.

I had come back to find my return unexpected, and half of my staff dispersed on war work. Shortly thereafter I met the Labour member for North Aberdeen, Garro Jones (afterwards Lord Trefgarne), and had his assurance that he could have obtained overnight a Treasury permit for my return if the University authorities had had the sense to approach him. However, my main reason for accepting an offer from Birmingham to assume the Mason Chair of Zoology in January 1942 had nothing to do with this. Between myself and Philip Sargant Florence, then Birmingham's professor of Economics and Social Science and a Cambridge friend of long standing, there was a tacit understanding that there would be a significant job for Enid Charles in Birmingham when it became convenient for her to return. Aside from that, I had had long and pleasant associations with Birmingham University, then the only English university with a campus in the American sense of the term.

During the last months of my tenure at Aberdeen, I spent the weekends at my croft, editing Bodmer's chapters for *The Loom of Language*. My own interest in constructed auxiliaries had received an impetus from my discovery in the University library of *The Essay towards a Real Character* by Bishop Wilkins, commissioned by the Royal Society to find a remedy for the confusion of tongues. While firewatching twice weekly throughout the night during my first six months at Birmingham, I explored the possibility of assembling a universal vocabulary built on the Latin and Greek roots that form the basis of the language of science. For instance, *earth*, *air*, *fire*, *water* are recognisable as *geo*, *aero*, *pyro*, *hydro*. Admittedly, someone with little scientific knowledge would not immediately make a lively association to every such vocable. The resulting language, which I called *Interglossa*, was published as a Penguin paperback. The compositor who set the book in type wrote me a letter in *Interglossa*, suggesting some emendations which I gratefully accepted.

Upon my arrival in Birmingham, a young graduate in Physics, R. L. Kirk, sought my patronage because he happened to be a conscientious objector, and it occurred to me to round off my work on the chromatic function by finding an answer to the question: is it of any use to an animal? So far as this concerns the frog, the only residual question, at least as I see it, is: does the change protect against overheating by absorption of solar radiation? An answer to this involved both sensitive measurement of the temperature of the lymph sacs under the dorsal skin and measurement of radiation intensity as recorded in the final communication (LH 1944a) of the *Pigmentary Effector* series. The technical problem of this enquiry led us to look further into temperature regulation in so-called cold-blooded animals and confirmed a conclusion then somewhat recently recorded by Mellanby with less sensitive methods than we then had at our disposal. So-called cold-blooded animals fall into two sharply distinct groups: (a) such with a low thermal death point normally in a moist environment as maintain a body temperature well below that of their surroundings by a wet bulb thermometer technique; (b) such with a high thermal death point as equilibrate with the temperature of their external surroundings and can therefore live in a dry hot climate. Our test materials were the frog, slug, garden snail, earth worm, lizard and alligator (LH 1944a; 1946a). One interesting outcome of comparing the rate of equilibration of the two species last named is a plausible explanation of why large Dinosaurs became extinct in the Cretaceous (LH 1946a).[1]

While in Birmingham, I was invited by the Royal Society to deliver the Croonian Lecture (LH 1942a) on Chromatic Behaviour, 18 June 1942. I served on the Council of the Society the following year.

During my first year in Birmingham, my goitre progressed. Alternating spells of lassitude and excitability with concomitant tachycardia made increasing demands on my strength and on the tolerance of colleagues. In endeavouring to keep myself on an even keel, I was becoming alarmingly tolerant to barbiturates. In December 1942, I decided that thyroidectomy (in Britain at that time an operation with a high fatality rate) was the only alternative to a long period of rest. Happily, the professor of surgery in the Birmingham Medical School had a good record of success. Because of the depth of hypertrophied tissue, I was in the theatre for five hours. Not surprisingly, pleurisy and pneumonia supervened and I was in the hospital for two months.

When I came out, I received a letter from Frank Crew, who was in charge of the so-called Directorate of Biological Research within the Medical Directorate at the War Office. In it, he asked me to overhaul army medical statistics. I came to London with that assignment, nominally as his deputy. As a result of the report I prepared, the Directorate of Biological Research changed its name, and I stayed on as Acting Director of Medical Statistics to carry out a drastic reorganisation of Army Medical Documentation. In that capacity, my activities were essentially humanitarian and did not call for the agonising moral reappraisal of some of my less privileged contemporaries. In London I stayed with my brother Hamilton, Medical Officer of Health for Tottenham, at his home near High Barnet. Hamilton was eighteen months my junior. As a hospital orderly in Belgium in World War I he had been, with Kingsley Martin and others, a member of the Friends Ambulance Unit.

One of the compensations of my assignment to the War Office was that I had to make trips by air to Malta, Naples, Sicily and Cairo in search of missing reports. Most rewarding of these was the Egyptian visit. The military airport was near Gizeh, and the first sight which met my eyes when our plane descended below the cloud belt was the Sphinx and the Great Pyramid of Khufu. I had time one afternoon to see the inside of the Great Pyramid, with its layout of ventilating shafts exactly as I had expected them to be. Another afternoon I spent at the Royal Museum, seeing the Tutankhamen exhibits. On the return journey we flew above the Nile in sight of land. A few miles beyond the twentieth-century metropolis, we looked down on a scene of mud-hut villages and strips of cultivated land, the pattern of life little different from that in the Neolithic period more than 5,000 years earlier.

I remained at the War House till the end of 1946 in order to complete an official monograph on Army Medical Statistics. I left it with one particular achievement which was perhaps unusual: six of the officers I had picked for my team gained doctorate degrees for work carried out under my direction.[2] Two discoveries we made, both connected with venereal disease, did not get much recognition then or later. We established how the therapeutic efficacy of sulphonamides for treatment of gonorrhoea had been reduced by 40 percent in the Naples sector. What had happened was the selection of resistant strains of *Neisseria gonorrhoeae*, due to the Nazi Medical Authorities' policy of distributing free packets of sulphonamides as a prophylactic measure to prostitutes likely to entertain German troops. The medical profession as a whole was slow to learn the lesson Naples taught Army V.D. specialists. Fifteen years later, surgeons were dismayed by the incidence of postoperative sepsis attributable to resistant strains of microorganisms which had developed following indiscriminate prescribing of sulphonamides and antibiotics.

Our work also disposed of a current misconception about 'serum' hepatitis (as we called it) following injections to cure another of the penalties for escape from military boredom. We were able to show conclusively that jaundice following injection of arsenical compounds for treatment of syphilis is not attributable to the virus responsible for 'infectious' hepatitis, then a major health hazard in the Forces. Alas, we did not find out why the latter has been peculiarly prevalent in military campaigns or establishments since the time of Napoleon.

All in all, I was not such a misfit in the War Office as my more intimate friends might have forecast. Thanks to a former colleague temporarily assigned to one of the personnel-selection branches, I assembled a team of uniformed disciples grateful to be able to work in a unit run like a university research department. Among people nearer my own age, the temporary brigadiers were men of consultant status, and several already knew of me as a physiologist. The major generals were regulars, not a few of whom, as Scottish medical graduates from humble homes, had preferred secure employment in Army service to the prospect of paying by instalment for entry into private practice. They regarded an Aberdeen professor with some awe.

During my years at the War Office, I kept in touch with my department in Birmingham by taking the late Saturday night train thereto, returning to London late on Sunday. Sunday apart, a twelve-hour working day, ending at the Cafe Royal in Piccadilly if an air raid was on, left me with little time for other preoccupations.

In the War Office and later as Professor of Medical Statistics at Birmingham, one of my major concerns was the conduct of therapeutic trials. While in London, I had been in day-to-day contact with the Directorate of Psychiatry. As a physiologist and thus a behaviourist, I had long ceased to regard Freud's methods and vocabulary as authentically scientific, without having dismissed his therapeutic claims out of hand. Lazily, if unduly charitably, I had been willing to concede that the new Messiah from Vienna might perform miracles of healing.

When circumstances forced them on my attention, I began to recognise that the therapeutic claims for Freud's approach, as well as those of Jung, Adler and Ernest Jones, rested entirely on case reports with no standardisation of data and no control groups. More rigorous validation is now regarded as essential in scientific therapeutics and cannot be achieved by examination of records attributed to what patients said upon the couch. Case histories collected in this way tell one nothing about whether the patients would have recovered without treatment or, if they did so, whether treatment expedited recovery.

If one turns from curative claims put forward by psychoanalysts with so uncertain sources of confirmation to examine the aetiological rationale advanced to explain the origin of mental sickness, psychoanalytic doctrine is wide open to another criticism. The psychoanalyst studies the verbal behaviour of a human subject. The assumption that this has a one-to-one correspondence with events which may have, or not have, happened is a violation not only of the principles of scientific medicine but equally of reputable historical enquiry.

Now that experimental methods with statistical safeguards have displaced consulting room case notes as a means of validating curative procedures, the teachings of Freud and his disciples are of only historical interest to medicine. Yet it seems that no review of a new work of fiction in the highbrow weeklies can be taken seriously unless it includes reverential mention of their revelations. I should be grossly dishonest if I pretended that when I left Cambridge, and till many years later, I was not bemused by the Freudian mystique. Much of what passes for freshness of outlook and originality of thought in a protracted adolescence is merely the gullibility with which youth embraces the ephemeral fad. When I left Cambridge I had become, like so many Fabians, a vegetarian perhaps for no better reason than that Bernard Shaw was one. As research assistant to Joseph Barcroft, I was also a practising vivisectionist—to Shaw an abomination. An integrated intellectual outlook comes, if at all, in middle age.

Towards the end of the war, that is to say when the German armies were in full retreat, Harold Laski, then Chairman of the Labour Party, approached me to revive the defunct Science Advisory Committee of the Labour Party as its chairman. My understanding was that the condition of eligibility should be unassailable professional credentials combined with the will to work for a planned economy. (Such was the condition accepted by Ernest Bevin when he enlisted Ritchie Calder and myself to recruit the Trades Union Congress Scientific Committee in the late thirties.) I named individuals who would be willing to serve, all of them eminent.

The tribal chief of the Labour Party at Transport House was at that time a fellow called Morgan Phillips. He shared his sole claim to notoriety with J. Edgar Hoover of the FBI. Like his American twin, he could smell a potential red lurking behind every rhododendron in a public park. Two of the names I put forward, both Fellows of the Royal Society and one a Nobel Laureate, had been members of the Party or fellow travellers. Morgan Phillips refused to accept my nominations. After two altercations, I refused to go along with Transport House unless I had my way about who was or was not sufficiently expert to make a useful contribution. The outcome was that I resigned.

After the Japanese surrendered and Labour gained an overwhelming majority in the House of Commons, the General Medical Council and the Whitehall bureaucrats had agreed on the chief innovations of the proposed National Health Service. It was clear that planning the details intelligently called for a fund of statistical information not then available. Secondly, it would be possible to prescribe the pattern for making it available only by a pilot project in a propitious situation, a region with a relatively stable population. Sir Leonard Parsons, then Dean of the Birmingham Faculty of Medicine, came to see me in London with the assurance that the Ministry of Health was willing to finance a Chair of Medical Statistics and Human Genetics in Birmingham if I would take on the job. It was a difficult decision. I was now fifty years of age with little time to make a fresh start as an experimental biologist.

I had also mastered a new technique. The need for up-to-the-minute information in a war economy had greatly speeded up the use of mechanical devices for sorting and tabulating statistical data. By devising my own self-coded documents, I had reduced from eighty to twelve the clerical staff needed to handle the requirements of machine translation of raw data. The construction of codes had for me an intellectual fascination like that of fabricating *Interglossa*. The invitation confronted me with another challenge. For some years, I had witnessed a retrograde movement in experimental biology, especially in the domain of animal behaviour.

To cite an extreme example, a biological journal might publish a record of cockroaches offered choice-chambers at different humidity levels leading to the result that 45 percent went to one, 55 percent to the other. The author of an experiment of this sort would regard it as worthy of publication if he could announce that the difference was "statistically significant at the 5-percent level." Statistical jargon apart, what the record proved was that the author could not say one thing or the other about most of the insects tested. Few psychologists and biologists who adorn their publications with so-called significance tests have the remotest idea of the assumptions latent in the mathematical rationale of the statistical theory involved.

On receiving the offer of a Chair in Medical Statistics, I had therefore realised that acceptance would commit me to undertake a critical evaluation of the credentials of current mathematical statistics, that no one else with an understanding of experimental biology was likely to accept the challenge and that a younger man equally or better equipped for the task would find it well nigh impossible to get an editor or publisher willing to print his conclusions. Having taken up the challenge, I set about writing an introduction to probability using visual models (LH 1950b; 1955b). This provided me with what William Blake called mental work for Jerusalem.

Early in 1946, Enid had announced her intention of resigning her research appointment in the Dominion Bureau of Statistics at Ottawa in order to return to the UK. The likelihood that Birmingham University would develop research in demography had receded since I had made my decision to leave Aberdeen, and I urged her to delay her departure so that we could jointly explore possibilities of employment near to one another. Enid did resign, and many months of frustration followed her return that year until a suitable vacant post became available in Birmingham. In 1948, the Birmingham City Council decided to set up a Statistical Office like those of Prague and Stockholm. Enid became its first Director, with an Honorary Readership in the University.

Readjustment was difficult for anyone so long absent from Britain and in such a situation. Rationing of fuel, clothes, food and petrol remained in force for five years after the end of the war. Those who had been in Britain throughout the war had learned to live with the changes. More formidable was the readjustment for husband and wife after such a long separation. In retrospect, it seems to me to be tragicomic that two reasonably intelligent people—at least by academic standards—could reach no common footing of communication.

Enid's remedy for disillusionment and frustration was work to the exclusion of all other interests, and this was the last thing I had hoped for when she announced her decision to come back. The wear and tear of life in London during the blackout and incessant bombing had left me with a desire to recuperate in the small cottage we had retained in Devon when we moved to Aberdeen. Moreover, thyroidectomy had curbed my gluttony for sustained work, and I wanted to gratify the only intellectual satisfaction I derived from my postwar assignment as Professor of Medical Statistics by a regular retreat into mathematics in the countryside. The prolongation of petrol rationing and Enid's inability to play truant precluded any prospect of visiting Devon together.

In the early thirties, when there was no separate Inland Revenue assessment of spouses, Beveridge had suggested that married couples like ourselves get divorced and live in sin. At the time when Enid returned, wife and husband could make separate returns as we did in the belief that separate assessment covered surtax as well as income tax below the surtax level. It did not. The situation in which we found ourselves, during a period when my royalties brought in more than our joint salaries, was well above the surtax threshold. In effect therefore, my royalties were paying Enid's salary. Meanwhile, the severity of postwar taxation was a source of worry for a different reason. During the war, and on the advice of my solicitor, I had let my royalties accumulate with my publisher on the understanding that income is not income till it has come in.

Inland Revenue's special enquiry branch went into all my accounts for the statutory seven-year period. After the investigation had dragged on for three years, they settled for an £800 penalty for my failure and that of my solicitor to grasp the meaning that the Commissioners of Inland Revenue attach to the word *income*. If a publisher who owes an author a thousand pounds goes bankrupt, it is still the obligation of the author to include this sum as income in his tax return. His only consolation is that the Inland Revenue may refund the money after months of exasperating correspondence.

The real value of my endowment policies, once sufficient to ensure us an agreeable retirement in Devon, had drastically declined. We could make no adequate financial provision for retirement in Britain, let alone America, if we were to make annual trips by air to the U.S.A. to see our four children as Enid wished. We did in fact go to see them at Christmas 1949. Enid returned in time to resume work when the Christmas leave was at an end.

To make provision for David to continue his university studies, I remained in America throughout January 1950 for a lecture tour partly arranged by the United World Federalists.[3] I had one invitation from the University of Indiana at Bloomington, where H. J. Muller was my host. Kinsey, of the Kinsey Report, then one of the faculty, arranged a cocktail party for my benefit and for my instruction concerning the sexual mores of the natives.

I had previously taken an active interest in the Movement for World Government and brought back a letter from Einstein in support of a Birmingham candidate, who successfully fought his election campaign on the issue. Unhappily, a promising beginning with support from M.P.s of all three parties came to nothing when the U.S.A. refused to recognise the de facto government of continental China. Since that time I have taken no active part in any political movement.

I returned from New York to learn that a satisfactory purchaser had been found for our property in Devon. At that time, my official responsibilities for Medical Statistics in the West Midlands extended to the boundary between Shropshire and Denbighshire. I could therefore use my extra petrol ration to get as far as the border of North Wales. Before the visit to America in December of 1949 I had explored a valley within twelve miles of my last hospital outpost in the border country. A cottage in the district with an acre of land was for sale on my return. It stood near to the fast-flowing Ceiriog tributary of the Dee, well stocked with trout. I lost no time in the purchase and arranged with a local builder to add a study-library and to modernise the interior. The surroundings were reminiscent of Dartmoor and Aberdeenshire, my favourite sort of countryside. If it lacked the rich Bronze Age monuments of Devon or the Ogam relics of North Scotland, it was culturally unique in its own way. Almost all the inhabitants of the Ceiriog valley were Welsh-speaking, a few of them monoglot.

Our riverside cottage was ready for occupation by Whitsun. Without advance notice in the press, we heard on the Whit Monday of 1950 that petrol was henceforth off the ration. This was good luck. The distance between the cottage and the Queen Elizabeth Hospital which housed my department was less than eighty miles, a two-hour drive. So all seemed set for spending Saturday and Sunday in restful surroundings with opportunities for cultivating new interests. My own extramural intellectual interests in latter years had shifted increasingly to comparative linguistics, and I looked forward to learning Welsh. Enid's first language had been Welsh. As a child, she had walked barefoot over the Denbighshire moors. She also liked rock gardening, for which the situation of the cottage close to an abandoned quarry offered unusual scope.

Such sentimental hopes did not allow for the fact that Enid herself had reacted as strongly against the Welsh way of life as I had against the evangelicalism of my own upbringing. She still insisted on working at the Birmingham Statistical office every Saturday morning. Her view was that a woman needs to do her job twice as well as a man.

For a year we had this limited opportunity of relaxing in our Welsh mountain valley. Then I developed thyrotoxicosis, followed by a second thyroidectomy. The surgical colleague who did the job remarked that the time to operate is when the patient becomes unbearable to live with. Subsequently, my need for relaxation was greater than ever. So was my consumption of Scotch. I often went to the cottage for weekends with one or other of my postgraduate students as my only company.

In the years since our trip to the U.S.A., Enid and I had failed to find a community of interest strong enough to keep us together. In 1953 she had the offer of an appointment with the World Health Organisation of the United Nations in the Far East, a gratifying professional opportunity. Initially the assignment was temporary. After a year, she became Director of Statistics for the South East Asia Division of W.H.O. When we parted, I had already resigned myself to the impossibility of a common life without recurrent disillusionment for one or both of us. The parting was not as painful as it might have been if the war had not kept us apart. If two people can learn to do without one another for six years, as we had because of World War II, they are capable of doing so for a longer period.

There were no material obstacles to divorce, or responsibilities to be shouldered. Enid had a high-level United Nations post with a tax-free income equal to at least half our joint life savings. All our children were self-sufficient, married and with children of their own. Accordingly, I wrote to her persuading her to divorce me.

CHAPTER XIX

Wales

IN Denbighshire I had become increasingly attached to a pen friend from whom I was getting Welsh lessons. Jane was then headmistress of a little school on the mountain above my cottage, in a scattered sheep-farming community which was wholly Welsh-speaking except when dealing with the Inland Revenue. She had an infectious gaiety which gave her companionship special attraction. She also talked intelligently about Celtic history and Middle English grammar. When we first became acquainted, she had an invalid husband and two children, one going through and the other about to enter University. There was then no question of marriage.

I had bought as a bargain a second cottage from the owners of the abandoned quarry nearby. With it, I acquired six or seven acres of land which I thought of developing as a smallholding. Later, to provide light employment of a supervisory sort for Jane's husband, Arthur, I persuaded them to take over this guest cottage at a peppercorn rent. The smallholding did not materialise. Before the introduction of myxomatosis, the rapid growth of the local rabbit population ended any immediate prospect of growing vegetables, and Arthur's health deteriorated rapidly. He died of cardiac failure within a year of moving in.

For the two ensuing years, I kept Jane company at the weekends. During that period she continued to teach. In 1956, I had the offer of an official tour in what was then the Gold Coast. Jane, who had not previously travelled outside the British Isles, was willing to accompany me—nominally as my private secretary.

Jane and I left London Airport for the Gold Coast at the end of November 1956 and returned by boat to Liverpool a few days before it became, as Ghana, an independent sovereign state on March 6, 1957. During that period we travelled by car about 6,000 miles along all the main routes into Ashanti, Northern Territories and what had been German Togoland before 1918. My initial assignment was to write a descriptive book commissioned by the Colonial Office to celebrate the country's independence,[1] but a more congenial prospect greeted us on the day of our arrival at Accra. A few hours after we set foot in the town, Geoffrey Bing called on us at the Government Hospitality Centre, henceforth our base. Geoffrey, who later became Attorney General of Ghana, was then Constitutional Adviser, and as such *Eminence Grise*, to Dr. Nkrumah the Premier.

On hearing about my impending visit, he had suggested to Dr. Nkrumah that I should prepare a comprehensive report on the needs of scientific research and higher education after independence. Accordingly, I saw the Premier next day and accepted the offer. I was to have the use of an official car with driver and a room at the Cabinet Office with secretarial assistance.

My mission called for a survey of natural resources, language barriers to educational progress and problems of health. It took me into the cocoa plantations and into the Unilever hardwood forest concession. In Ashanti, I had to visit the open cast mines for manganese and watch the elaborate process of extracting gold from seams of the metal in quartz. I had an opportunity of seeing different styles of tropical architecture designed for ventilation by trapping solar energy to create convection currents. In one or other of half a dozen agricultural experimental stations I saw for the first time coffee and rubber cultivation, once also a tea crop (Camellia) resplendently in flower.

Aside from the enjoyment of exploring, if merely in a superficial way, a rich fauna and flora largely new to me, the journey through Ghana was memorable because of the atmosphere of adventurous hopefulness of a people then exulting in new opportunities to shape their own future under a leadership not as yet corrupted by power. A dynamism, shared by not a few dedicated colonial officers who remained in office, permeated a diversity of new welfare services including medical field units, self-help housing projects, a drive for adult education to abolish mass illiteracy, and information services to promote improved methods of agriculture, pest control and introduction of new crops.

When I left Ghana, I did not anticipate how rapidly the infectious dynamism of the period of self-government would wane after Ghana became a sovereign state. Nor did my brief impression of Nkrumah's personality lead me to forecast his acquired appetite for personal wealth and ruthless treatment of friends who had brought him to power. On the contrary, he seemed to us a man of thoughtful modesty, as we chatted about George Padmore, whom I had met in Britain. It was he who advanced Nkrumah as organising secretary for the Pan-African Congress at the conclusion of the second world war. Like many other leaders of the revolt against British colonialism, both Padmore and Nkrumah had come under the influence of Palme Dutt and of Laski. Freedom from colonial rule was to some the road to socialism. To others, socialism was a useful war cry in the campaign for independence. While we watched the coast of Ghana disappear on the sea voyage homeward, Jane and I were debating which mattered most to Nkrumah—his self-styled undenominational Christian Marxism or his Pan-African dreams of a United States of Africa. Subsequent events have answered the question.

Marriage to Jane in the autumn following our journey through Ghana took place in 1957 two months before my sixty-second birthday. I had published my academic swan song, a critique of statistical theory (LH 1957a)[2] in the same year. I occupied myself during the greater part of 1958 and 1959 in the production of a small monograph on design of medical records for mechanical analysis and a major educational project which fulfilled a long-standing ambition to enlist the fullest use of colour in production of visual aids to mathematical exposition. My friend W. Foges, who published the outcome as *Mathematics in the Making,* 1960, put at my disposal a team of artists and book designers whose intelligent co-operation ensured a gratifying outcome.

In Birmingham, the retiring age for professors comes at the end of the academic session in which the sixty-fifth birthday occurs. Since the session ended in September and my birthday is in December, actual retirement for me was not due till the summer of 1961. My university marked the event by paying me a gratifying compliment. I retired with the title of Honorary Senior Fellow in Linguistics.[3]

No biologist who is also at heart a naturalist can be happy if condemned without respite to town life. Certainly I could not; and luckily I have had access at least to a weekend country cottage during nearly the whole of my professorial life. Nonetheless, there are some drawbacks to retirement in a panoramic Welsh mountain valley. Having to do small chores such as carrying coal buckets and carrying buckets of ice-cold water from the river when the water pipes freeze up is tiresome. With us, the winter of 1962–63 was more than usually irksome. Our piped water supply gave out in early December. The fast-flowing river below my study window froze solid before the New Year, and we had to take refuge in a nearby fishing inn till the beginning of March. Such was our plight when I received a cable from Cheddi Jagan, then Premier of British Guiana, inviting me to become Vice-Chancellor of its projected university.

At the time, I could not reply with an unconditional affirmative. Jane had lately stood as County Councillor for our Valley, and had come head of the poll, her vote handsomely exceeding the combined votes of her opponents. A protracted appointment would therefore have entailed either our separation for most of the year or her resignation. Maybe the weather also influenced my decision. What I did was to dispatch by wire a very long message offering to come to Georgetown for a brief preview to take stock of the situation in an advisory capacity. My initial intention was to find a bright young man to do the job. Happily, my explorative gestures did not commit me irrevocably to involve anyone in what proved to be an enterprise befitting only a superannuated educational pioneer with experience of fund raising.

Before I left by plane for the Caribbean in mid-March of 1963, I had little background information about British Guiana other than the *Encyclopaedia Britannica,* some back numbers of Colonial Office reports, and a very superficial book in the Colonial Office *Corona Series*. I did not know that day-to-day happenings of a Crown Colony deemed to be worthy of little comment even in the British highbrow weeklies was front-page headline news in the New York and Washington press. With so little information at my disposal I set out alone by air on what was to be a visit of only a month.

On the drive into Georgetown, I explained to C. V. Nunes, the political parent of the University project, that I was interested in the Premier's offer only if my policy could forestall some of the shortcomings of colonial enterprise at Legon in Ghana and at Mona in Jamaica. In short, the curriculum should give priority to the requirements of a research programme tailored to the needs of the national economy.

The Portuguese papists in the Lower Chamber opposed the creation of the university as a Marxist plot to pervert the youth of the country; but I record with pleasure that the University Bill went back to the Senate for ratification of built-in safeguards of academic freedom, and that the personnel of the Board of Governors, though nominated by the Minister for Education, did not have to have a majority of Jagan's People's Progressive Party supporters. It received by proxy the Royal Assent in time to appear in the Gazette a day before I returned to Britain, after meeting my Board of Governors. All the latter were university men. Those who were Ministers were party moderates. Later, John Carter, a British graduate and Q.C. who was then on the opposition front bench, was at my suggestion invested as Pro-Chancellor. From the first I found him congenial, and my regard for him increased as I got to know him better.

Though the printed draft of the University Ordinance as presented to the Lower Chamber named me as the first Vice-Chancellor, I had committed myself in advance only to give advice with respect to policy, sources of finance and, if need be, choice of a suitable Vice-Chancellor. I had certainly not consented to take on the job myself. Perhaps the kindly welcome I received from Vernon Nunes and others dictated my decision to accept the appointment on my own terms. The Minister for Education and his colleagues in the Cabinet endorsed them without demur. In terms of policy I insisted that research units supported by the government—more especially geological survey, forestry, veterinary science and cattle breeding—should be incorporated as university institutes. I had two misgivings about the time I could commit. As mentioned, Jane now had obligations to the Denbighshire County Council, and neither of us wished to find our garden overrun with weeds or mutilated by Welsh lamb during our absence. I therefore undertook to spend at most five months of the winter each year in Georgetown and to remain in office no more than two years.

The last condition was more reasonable than might seem at first sight. British Guiana (later to become independent Guyana) was a very poor colony. Its government had embarked on a programme for higher education without a tenth of the financial resources needed to maintain even a modest university, let alone the capital sum requisite for a building programme to get it literally off the ground. Tapping the great foundations and the British government for funds with that end in view is not a task which a younger man without experience of raising money for research could undertake with a good prospect of success. The Colonial Office were at that time suspicious of the intentions of the Government in Georgetown, and Sir Ralph Grey assured me that no one could overcome their misgivings if I myself could not. What would necessarily be my main business was therefore clear. Clearly, also, I could spend seven months of the year fund-raising by personal contact in Britain more profitably than by correspondence from Georgetown.

Though I left for home on April 19 in the persuasion that it is better to travel hopefully than to survive, I did not do so without misgivings. Given adequate remuneration and security of tenure, the opportunities which an undeveloped territory offers can attract worthy young aspirants to professional fame, but such opportunities would be minimal in Georgetown until our building programme was more complete. Meanwhile, we should have to appoint incumbents of limited academic qualifications. Unless sufficiently senile to go quietly when the university was off the ground, the first contingent would block the way for promotion of younger men. There was another snag to dispose of. In a society emerging from Colonial tutelage, the indigenous and gifted young have good reason to be sick and tired of second-rate personnel fobbed off on them by Colonial Office Committees whose professorial experts are all too eager to export candidates with no further prospects of promotion at home. Like the African in a comparable situation, the Guianese demanded short term contracts for expatriates, and could rightly contend that such conditions of service suffice to attract civil engineers from more developed countries. It is difficult to convince them that a bright young man or woman in search of unique academic opportunities abroad will take no such risk, least of all if he or she contemplates undertaking research projects with no likelihood of a conclusive outcome, on a four- or five-year contract without transferable superannuation.

My preview visit had been strenuous. From my own viewpoint, it had achieved several useful results. I had gained an overall view of the Colony's known natural resources, and was therefore able to formulate provisionally the immediate priorities of a research programme geared to national needs. With the Minister for Education, I had negotiated from the Bookers group of companies the promise of a 150-acre building site with a prospect of twice as much for further development at a later date. The Chairman of its Board of Directors, Sir Jock Campbell, a delightful and erudite person, assured me this provided eventually for as much land surface as that on which lie all the colleges of his alma mater, Oxford. Of other contacts with a prospect of local financial support, I need mention only congenial relations with the top executives of the Bauxite

Corporation. I had also thoroughly inspected both Queen's College and the nearby Teacher Training College to assess adequacy of temporary accommodation for night work. Having formed my own view of the Training College, I impressed on C. V. Nunes the advantages—financial and educational—of incorporating it within the University.

If full of incident, the agreed five months I spent in Georgetown during my first year of office were not otherwise enthralling. After my preview visit, the General Strike and disorganisation of public services had virtually cut me off from British Guiana for over three months during which my deputy had carte blanche to go ahead with assembling a skeleton staff with whom I had no opportunities of personal contact in advance.[4] I had intended to withdraw unless the government agreed to delay the date of registration for a year, but I capitulated to a *cri de coeur* on behalf of the students who had already flocked to enroll. Aside from the courtesy I received from members of my Board, from others such as Ashton Chase and Jocelyn Hubbard, not to say the support of both the Governor Sir Ralph Grey and of Sir Jock Campbell, I had only one compensation for a gruelling episode: the overwhelming appreciation of an adult student body for long-deferred opportunities.

After late March 1964, I did not return to British Guiana. To persevere in my negotiations with the Ministry of Overseas Development in London, I asked for extended leave; and, when I heard from a reliable source that the Ministry had agreed to allocate at least a million and a half sterling for my building programme, I resigned. I had delivered the goods and was glad to be back in Wales, bodily intact. A new government was then in power. National Independence was assured. What had been virtually a state of civil war since I first left on the eve of the General Strike was at an end. While I was still negotiating financial backing for our building programme, emergency powers had consigned C. V. Nunes to a concentration camp in the interior. On my arrival in September 1963, I had been mildly irritated when my Board of Governors insisted on providing me with an Indian driver or, as he preferred to say, chauffeur. After a few weeks, I had come to regard him as my bodyguard, and gratefully acceded to the provision of a night watchman with a machete to stand guard over the bungalow we occupied in the College compound after Jane joined me in early November.

After I resigned as Vice-Chancellor, my life was for several years uneventful. Meanwhile, because of the steady deterioration of Jane's health and of my own strength, we became increasingly unequal to the rigours of the winters when so far from our nearest village. Eventually in 1969 we decided to sell our riverside cottage with its half an acre of rock garden, and had a bungalow built for us in the village of Llansantfraid Glyn Ceiriog. Because of the usual excuses of builders for unfulfilled undertakings, we had to reside in a local fishing inn before we entered into possession of our new home in June 1970.

It is in the centre of the main street of the village, and lies high above the surrounding houses on the slope of what was once a slate tip, now overgrown with larch and silver birch. Fern and grass provide undergrowth, above which spikes of lemon-yellow blossoms—the greater mullein—are visible in summer. Being fox-free, it is a natural bird sanctuary. Blackbirds, my favourite in the dawn chorus, are the dominant species. We named it accordingly *Lloches y Fwyalchen*, Welsh for Blackbird's Retreat.

Late in 1969, Jane was found to have a malignant breast tumour. Following mastectomy, she made a partial recovery with no indication of metastases for two years. By the beginning of 1973, however, her health deteriorated. In November she entered the nearby cottage hospital. Her physician kept her well supplied with analgesics and sedatives till she died in April 1974, very weary but fortunately with little pain.

The loss of Jane left me deprived of what had made my life after retirement so serene in the beautiful surroundings of the Ceiriog valley. I had loved her deeply, and for twelve years before her final sickness she had given me unexpected happiness.

Before I retired I resumed the study of comparative linguistics, one of many intellectual interests I shared with Jane. My book *The Mother Tongue*, 1964, had gone to press when I left Britain for Guyana, and the proofs reached me only a few days before the deadline. Consequently, I had not adequate time to correct a host of misprints. This saddened me because I never enjoyed writing any of my books more than this one.

Until we moved into the village of Glyn Ceiriog, I was fully occupied with our rock garden and with putting together notes I had made earlier for my book *The Vocabulary of Science*, 1969. Later I wrote a series of four highly illustrated books for teenagers, tracing the beginnings of science from the temple astronomers of Egypt and Mesopotamia to the death of Galileo in the same year as the birth of Newton.

In one of his stories or essays, G. K. Chesterton tells of a man who set out to find happiness by boat only to find in the end that he had landed at Brighton pier. Thus from a nonconformist childhood, I shall end my days here in the last foothold of nonconformity, in sight of the foothills of the Berwyn range. In the Ceiriog valley, twelve miles long, there are fifteen places of worship, eleven being nonconformist and four Anglican. On Sunday morning, Baptist and Calvinistic Methodist congregations pass by my bungalow in one direction, the Anglicans in the opposite. For the ladies, this is an opportunity to wear their best outdoor clothes. Striding behind them, and apart, the men garbed in funereal black and clutching their hymn books present a picture of gloom. Of late, I have never seen among them any younger than fifty. A large proportion of the male population gathers outside the door of The Royal Oak opposite my Glyn Ceiriog cottage, waiting for opening time to celebrate the Sabbath in a secular way.

One consequence of alienation of the young from chapel is that there are fewer recruits to the singing of Welsh hymns and folk songs in the pubs, which often occurred spontaneously on Saturday nights when I first came to the valley. Since all the chapels of the valley conduct their services in Welsh, the decline of their appeal to the oncoming generation also signifies that the language is noticeably losing its grip, the more so because the closure of the slate and granite quarries which formerly offered employment for the bulk of the male population of the valley has forced adolescents to seek it in towns or on building sites where English alone is acceptable.

In this milieu, and for the first time in my life, I no longer feel myself to be an alien. This would be odd were it not for the fact that Welsh nonconformity is nowadays remarkably tolerant. Happily, the Welsh people seem to lack the talent or taste for theological disputation. Though many of my neighbours are of the Calvinistic Methodist denomination, almost certainly I am (with the possible exception of the kindly and scholarly minister of that persuasion) the only resident of the Ceiriog valley to have read Calvin's atrocious *Institutes of the Christian Religion*. In Wales as a whole, it seems that only atheists like myself now derive entertainment from theology. Attendance at chapel is primarily an excuse for a good *canu*, or singsong, with spontaneous harmonising.

Without Jane, old age has few incitements to offer me and death has lost its sting. Terrified as a child by the possible second coming in the night, and of an eternity of hellfire if I missed the family bus aloft, I now regard it as a parental duty to equip children with the assurance that we reach a stage when we are too tired to play with our toys. It is then a relief when the Great Mother, who is older and wiser than all the male gods, tells us it is time to go wearily to bed and to a well-earned, long long sleep.

Epilogue

THERE was a time when one of the consolations of age was the prospect of passing on experience to an oncoming generation. The tempo of change is now such that the experience of the old is of little value to the young. For better or worse, we have forfeited the capacity for wonder in a world wherein the novelty of discovery yearly outstrips plausible speculation, wherein also the gap between incredulity and gullibility diminishes. It is a folly of youth to complain that those who are near the end had not to face the difficulties which challenge their grandchildren. It is equally the folly of the elderly to assert that life is far easier for them than it was for our own generation. To be sure, there are far greater opportunities for them than for us, but the oncoming generation is the first to grow up under the shadow cast by the imminent possibility of total annihilation of human, and indeed of all animal, life on our planet. All the good counsel elders can offer the young is the hope that they will surmount their own disabilities as we had to surmount different ones in our own youth.

Now in my eightieth year, I have lived to witness many changes and mostly, in my view, for the better. There has been a vast change in the status of women even since I myself graduated. At that time, both Cambridge and Oxford still refused to confer degrees on women students and only men had the right to vote for parliamentary candidates. In Britain, pregnancy was a permissible topic of conversation in polite society only if referred to by an evasive euphemism and birth control was unmentionable. My own generation was the first to make cohabitation without wedlock respectable. I was well over sixty when homosexuality between consenting adults ceased to be a criminal offence and capital punishment in Britain came to an end.

In my boyhood, an empire on which the sun never set was at the peak of its arrogant power. I myself can well remember the Boer

War, and I have lived to witness the creation of a police state based on apartheid as its retribution. When I was a boy, the British navy was far stronger than that of any other nation though it made little contribution to victory in successive world wars. Our air force was in its infancy when I left school. Few could then foresee the coming of civilian transport in vehicles heavier than air, still less of a return trip to the moon. Throughout my childhood electric trams and automobiles were still novelties, as were bicycles with pneumatic tyres. In the Kentish village where my paternal grandfather lived, I once watched youths riding on penny-farthings.

On the political stage, I have lived to see the House of Lords stripped of its veto, and becoming more like a Scandinavian Senate as creation of life peers increasingly curtails the influence of its hereditary personnel.

I have witnessed the emergence of a Welfare State. In my boyhood, Lloyd George made a modest beginning as a builder by the introduction of old age pensions and national health insurance. In times of unemployment, I had seen in his day hordes of hungry men sleep on the Thames Embankment, fed by mobile Salvation Army kitchens. I was in my forties when the hunger marchers from the South Wales minefields, singing their hymns as only the Welsh can do, forced Englishmen of the home counties to recognise that miners are also human. What poverty regrettably persists in Britain in 1975 is trivial compared with that in my early manhood. Two statistics are eloquent of this higher standard of living. In the quinquennium of my birth (1891–1895), mortality in England and Wales among live-born babies under one year old was 151 per thousand, and mortality among women during pregnancy and childbirth was 5 per thousand. In my seventy-fifth year, the corresponding figures were 18.1 and 0.25. During less than my lifetime, the risk of death in the first year of life has thus diminished to one eighth and of death due to childbearing to one twentieth.

Of other changes in Britain during my lifetime, the enlargement of opportunities for higher education is one of the most spectacular. The nonconformist ministry, trade union leadership or a job as compositor in a printing firm no longer offer for most males the only escape from manual work and to most spinsters a post as governess or nanny in a prosperous household the only alternative to sweated factory labour. Free higher education is now the gateway to a vast variety of remunerative and secure employment. It seems to me that some of the consequences of this ever widening choice of more attractive occupations have had too little recognition by students of our society. Henceforth, there will be fewer and fewer self-educated trade union leaders of the same intellectual calibre as Ernest Bevin or Walter Citrine in a past generation. The scholarly country parson who devotes his time largely to composing botanical memoirs will soon disappear altogether.

In several other ways, innovations during my lifetime have been less encouraging. When my book *Science for the Citizen* first appeared in 1938, atom splitting had occurred, but before the catastrophe of 1945 in Japan I had no reason to regard as imminent the release of atomic energy on a large scale. Seven years after its publication I was compelled to write a new chapter for the third edition. That we can use this new source of energy for peaceful purposes, if we sidestep the suicide of our species, is of little comfort to me. On a long view, disposal of radioactive waste material has formidable dangers to add to the prospects of pollution of our atmosphere and its degradation through denudation of forests which contribute to the maintenance of a viable balance between oxygen, carbon dioxide and water vapour. Unless we can devise some not as yet foreseeable way of disposing harmlessly of atomic waste, peaceful use of atomic power has no long-term future.

Perhaps because I figured in *Science for the Citizen* the trajectory of a rocket-launched missile to make a return journey from the vicinity of Venus, the British Interplanetary Society invited me in 1952 to deliver its annual oration. On this occasion I saw blueprints of a projected American landing on the moon. On my return to Birmingham, none of my scientific colleagues took the story seriously, and a publisher implored me to cut out from an illustrated children's book on scientific advances a simplified (circular) estimate of a likely path of a satellite in orbit around the moon. The book appeared in the month when we learned that the U.S.S.R. had accomplished the feat, and my guess of the number of hours it would take to complete a revolution was very close to the actual figure. Then, in 1969, the landing on the moon and subsequent re-entry was a *fait accompli*. Meanwhile I can as yet see nothing to justify man's costly exercises in spacemanship except the positive results of research into the storage of electricity, whence a livelier prospect for exploiting immense resources of solar, tide and wind power now inaccessible because intermittent.

Epilogue

We can foresee possible new resources to augment our inadequate food supply on a global scale. We must indeed domesticate micro-organisms to produce edible protein from our own excrement. We can already culture unicellular green algae to build up carbohydrates by utilising solar radiation, so this should not be beyond human ingenuity.

One of the less likeable foibles of old age is the disposition to lament the passing of the good old days. I need to remind myself constantly that finding rational grounds for hope calls for more intellectual ingenuity than does pessimism. In one way my present environment encourages the belief that the world is getting better. Forty years ago the closure of a quarry spelt destitution to a village community such as mine, and the workers in the neighbouring collieries of the North Wales coalfield returned from work with blackened faces. Both quarry workers and coal miners then had a low expectation of working life owing to pneumoconiosis for which the owners were exempt from responsibility for compensation. The contemporary scene is even visibly different, if only because there are now hot showers at the pit face of a socialised industry where the collier can wash before he comes home. Life in the Welsh valleys has latterly gained much in human dignity and in security.

Nonetheless, I confess that in more than one way the intellectual climate of university and professional life is now far less congenial to me than it was in my undergraduate days and when I embarked on a career of scientific research. Concentration of large-scale teamwork, financed on condition of secrecy by industrial firms and by government grants for military purposes, increasingly deprives recruits to research of opportunities for initiative and mobility. They have gained financial security and a lifelong suburban existence.

Meanwhile, because the tempo of discovery has so greatly outstripped our means of communication, the temper of instruction has become increasingly authoritarian. In our education and in our university departments of biology students learn, and research workers use, statistical devices without the slightest knowledge of their mathematical credentials. School courses on chemistry expound valency in terms of atomic models long before the learner has any clue to the evidence to justify the model itself. At one time, it was the proud boast that an authentic scientific worker took nothing for granted. As the student's store of knowledge expands today, he or she accepts more and more on the authority of the teacher.

The brilliant efflorescence of Alexandrian science during six centuries came to an end in no small measure because its tools of communication, handicapped by a grossly defective numeral system and without the aids of printing and paper, were inadequate to transmit further extensions of knowledge. As authority continues to curb the impulse to question, such may be the fate of contemporary Western science.

*Postscript**

IN June, 1970, Jane and Lancelot Hogben moved into their bungalow in the middle of Glyn Ceiriog, just across the street from The Royal Oak, where he had many friends. It had indeed become almost his club. His neighbour Lord Taylor has written about their life in the valley:

> She and Lancelot had an abiding interest in the young people of the valley, and any who showed scientific, mathematical or linguistic ability were sure of encouragement from this remarkable couple.
>
> Lancelot was the prototype of eccentric genius, the absentminded professor with his head in abstract geometry and his feet sockless in his slippers, speaking with painful deliberation as he gazed into the far distance. Strangely enough, the absence of socks was not the result of forgetfulness but of rational thought. In Glyn, socks are seldom needed climatically, and not putting them on saved a rheumatic back one added trauma.
>
> To the people of Glyn Ceiriog, Lancelot was a constant delight. In his corner seat on the settee in the private bar of the Royal Oak, he would dispense pearls of wisdom so cloaked in sesquipedalian circumlocution and subordinate clauses that most of his hearers thought he was wandering. This was not so. He was, as he said, "Labouring in the Lord's vineyard" to make straight and scientific the path of social advance of mankind.

After Jane's death in April, 1974, he was very lonely, though family or friends would sometimes come to visit him in the valley. He lived on at the bungalow with regular daily visits to the Royal Oak (though according to reliable witnesses he cut down his consumption of whisky to two doubles a day). Neighbours would go in of an evening to pass the time with him and friends across the road kept an eye on him.

---

*Excerpts from the Memoir by G. P. Wells, *Biogr. Mem. Fellows R. Soc. Lond.* Vol 24, 214–215, 1978.

One morning the bungalow seemed very still. They found him in the living room, too tired the night before to put himself to bed. He was taken to hospital where, on 22 August 1975, he died. His cremation was followed by a wake at the Royal Oak that would have delighted him, with reminiscence and singing into the small hours.

He is commemorated by a bronze plaque, with an inscription in English prose and Welsh verse, in the Ceiriog Memorial Institute. His bust, made at Cape Town by Herbert Meyerowitz, stands in a place of honour in the Medical School at Birmingham.

Notes

I Salesmanship and Salvation

1   [p. 1] The maternal grandparents (the William Prescotts) and the parents, Thomas and Margaret Hogben, lived as neighbours on the Prescott property in Stoke Newington, London, until both families moved to Southsea in 1889. The two eldest Hogben daughters, Margaret and Alice, were born in London. The younger children, Dorothy, Lancelot, Hamilton and Bernard were born in Southsea.

2   [p. 3] Miss Sarah Robinson put up, in her own words, "an iron Mission Hall, the Welcome Mission, under the care of Mr. Hogben, with whom in 1891, I had entered into a three years' engagement. Accordingly I met the expenses of the Mission until the end of 1894; since that time he and his friends have continued to carry it independently." (*Sarah Robinson: a life record.* London: Ward Lock & Co, 1898.)

3   [p. 4] The Cape Town Mission of the London Missionary Society (headquartered at Exeter Hall) worked in support of a more sympathetic native policy.

II Stoke Newington

1   [p. 7] See Margaret Hogben's *"One thing I do." Memoir of Thomas Hogben, Founder of the "One by One Band"* (Stockport: Edgeley Press, 1921).

2   [p. 8] James Usher, 1581–1656, an Irish archbishop, calculated the year 4004 B.C. by summing the 'begats' from the *Book of Genesis* to the birth of Christ. Lightfoot, a Cambridge don, refined Usher's calculation of the time to the Big Bang.

3   [p. 11] The Test Acts, which became law during the seventeenth century, excluded from public office and appointments at Oxford and Cambridge Roman Catholics and all others who refused the rites of the Church of England, including all Protestant nonconformists. While repeal of such requirements for holding public office was accomplished by 1829, religious tests remained in the English universities until passage of the university Tests Act of 1871.

III Schooldays

1   [p. 18] In 1992, Bethune Road in Stoke Newington, a part of William Prescott's "considerable estate," was a neighbourhood of large, well-preserved homes, which suggests that the circumstances of the Hogben family, after moving into one of those houses in 1907, were "relatively wealthy." Lancelot viewed life at 91 Bethune Road as more frugal than that of his classmates. His sister Dorothy, two years older, felt he was referring to the dinner table. In any event, the Hogben parents were unlikely to sanction unnecessary expenses not dedicated to the service of the Lord.

Probably none of the children were aware of the financial health of the Prescott "estate" until calamity approached about 1917. Dorothy volunteered the following in 1989, shortly before her death:

> The property was quite considerable, but bringing in little or no income. Father was too ill to take any responsibility, and Mother must have been worried out of her mind because I remember talking afterwards about near bankruptcy. From which the estate was saved by Connie, Bernard's wife who was the very capable secretary to a local estate office. She discovered that the solicitor (friend in the same brand religion) had just been sitting on everything and letting it go down the drain. It was Connie who got it moving and got it all back to what it should financially have been. I think the houses were gradually all sold off.

2   [p. 20] The following is from a draft of *Look Back with Laughter:* "In view of the veneration bestowed on this utterly evil man, a few extracts from Carlyle's article 'The Nigger Question', referring to the emancipation of the slaves in the British West Indian Colonies are worth quoting. The erratic punctuation is Carlyle's.

> Our beautiful black darlings are at last happy with little labour except to the teeth, which surely, in those excellent horse-jaws of theirs, will not fail! . . . Sitting yonder with their beautiful muzzles up to the ears in pumpkins, imbibing sweet pulps and juices; the grinder and incisor teeth ready for ever new work, and the pumpkins cheap as grass in those rich climates; while the sugar crops rot round them uncut, because labour cannot be hired, so cheap are the pumpkins. . . . . . . it may be laid down as a principle. . . . . That no Black man who will not work according to what ability the gods have given him for working has the smallest right to eat pumpkins or to any land that will grow pumpkins, however plentiful such land may be; but has an indisputable and perpetual right to be compelled, by the real proprietors of said land, to do competent work for his living. . . . "He has made us equal" would be saying a palpable falsity big with hideous ruin for all concerned in it. . . . . If Quashee will not honestly aid in bringing-out their sugars, cinnamons and nobler products of the West Indian Islands. . . . . then I say neither will the Powers permit Quashee to continue growing pumpkins there for his own lazy benefit. . . Quashee, if he will not help in bringing-out the spices, will get himself made a slave again. . . . and with *beneficent whip,* since other methods avail not, will be compelled to work.

The article, first printed in *Fraser's Magazine* December 1849 was reprinted as a separate pamphlet in 1853."

IV *On Going Up*—no references.

V *Cambridge*—no references.

VI *Marking Time*—no references.

VII *Shades of the Prison House*
1   [p. 59] See letter of Lancelot Hogben to Bertrand Russell in the *Autobiography of Bertrand Russell 1914–1944*, pages 108–109.

VIII *Marriage*
1   [p. 70] See "Introduction."

2   [p. 72] Examples of his distinctive "Pictuas" appear in his *Experiment in Autobiography*.

3   [p. 72] "So to the Club ... The poet Hogben was also there. I laid his little book on the arm of my chair ... Poor Hogben's book is worse than one might have expected—what Lytton would call 'illiterate'; under the influence of Swinburne, incredibly ungifted, & weakly rebellious." *Diary of Virginia Woolf*, vol. I. p. 127. See also pages 103 and 126.

4   [p. 73] In his autobiography, Ivor Montagu wrote:
> The principal demonstrator was Lancelot Hogben. He was slight, handsome, with an unruly quiff that kept falling over one side of his forehead. *Ariel* had just been published then, and I cannot think why he always made me think of Shelley for really he was not like him in the least. His mind was acute and brilliant, his verbal expression exceptionally lucid, his manner dry and acid, broken every now and then by a smile that had less of amiability than fleeting derision in it. ...
>
> Hogben's first wife was as dark as he was fair, and wore long, loose-fitting garments and necklaces. He insisted, disconcertingly, on pronouncing her name Enn-id, instead of Ee-nid, but he would also say Eng-land and Eng-lish as they are spelled, refusing them the usual lng. She was as brilliant as he. ... In the Cambridge of her day women were not allowed to take degrees. The two had a child, crawling about the cottage floor; they had been so young when it was born that Hogben used to say they were an example of neoteny, a zoological term for reproduction in the larval state.
>   *The Youngest Son*, pages 135–136.

IX *Edinburgh*
1   [p. 78] Richard Church wrote:
> I have a dramatic recollection of a small event which took place a quarter of

a century ago. Working with me in a dingy laboratory was a young Irishman, dour, intent, ambitious. He wanted to be a doctor, and in his apre time he was studying towards the fulfilment of this difficult ambition; difficult, because he was poor. He attached himself as an external student at London University. After he had been there about a month, attending evening lectures, I noticed an intensification of his ardour. He was a man possessed. One day he burst out of his usual taciturnity. "My boy," he said, in his rich brogue, "there's a lecturer at Birkbeck College who will bring the soul out of you! Man! he's a genius! He's younger than we are; but his knowledge, his power of mind; his vitality! It's music to listen to him. He's made zoology a new thing to me!" I listened with interest, and caught the enthusiasm. "What his name?! I said to this youth who has since become a famous orthopaedic surgeon. "Ugh!" he replied in disgust, "What's his name at all! He's bigger than his name. Nobody knows him. But I tell you, they will know him. The world will know him! His name is Lancelot Hogben."

British Authors.

X Montreal—no references.

XI Cape Town

1 [p. 98] Herrman, Louis. *A History of the Jews in South Africa from the Earliest Times to 1895.*

2 [p. 99] Obituary Notices of Fellows of the Royal Society, v.8, 1952–53, pp. 39–70.

3 [p. 101] See "Introduction."

4 [p. 102] Subject of thesis: An enquiry into metabolic changes associated with pigmentary effector activity, and the removal of the pituitary gland in *Xenopus laevis;* and a contribution to sexual differences in serum constituents of other species.

XII Dawn of Apartheid

1 [p. 105] The social life of the Hogbens has been recounted by Eddie Roux in *Rebel Pity.* Excerpts from Chapter VII, "The Happy Year," are quoted below.

> In the meantime I was making a number of new and interesting friends. The most exciting of these was Lancelot Hogben, then professor of zoology in the University of Cape Town. Hogben, at the height of his intellectual powers and in his most iconoclastic phase, was happily shocking the local philistines as well as some quite nice people in Cape Town. He had become the centre of a group of intelligent and charming people....
>
> Hogben had named his house Xenopus, after the South African clawed toad, an animal now famous among physiologists....
>
> Hogben, in spite of his flamboyant enthusiasm, I considered too much of an individualist to make a good communist. He was at the time engaged in a

controversy in the columns of the *British Labour Monthly* on the topic of dialectical materialism, his opponent being Clemens Dutt. He was objecting to the attempt, first made by Engels, to apply the concepts of dialectics to biology.... Hogben delighted in polemics, in all wordy war, in wit and subtlety. 'People will not ask the right questions,' he would say happily, 'because they're afraid of getting the left answers.'

He combined his leftist position in politics with strong opposition to religions, nationalisms and all such. He disliked flags and national anthems and did not care at all whom or how he annoyed by his gestures of iconoclasm....

Parties at Xenopus were rarely formal, almost never by invitation. What happened was that people dropped in, especially at weekends and then the most stimulating conversations would follow. As the hour grew later Hogben waxed more brilliant and outrageous. At such casual gatherings I met most of the Hogben set.

Of these Frederick Bodmer was probably the one from whom I learnt most. He was a Swiss, at that time lecturer in German at the university, also a serious student of politics. An eccentricity for which he was famous was his liking for renting some large tumble-down house, of which there were a number in the suburbs of Cape Town, and there camping in one or two of the rooms. By nature indifferent to luxury and unwilling to burden himself with possessions beyond bare necessities which included a bed and a frying pan, he led a life stripped of all trimmings, a life that was simple and even austere ... Bodmer was the ideal host, casual in his erudition, throwing off carelessly brilliant aphorisms in his oddly accented English. Here we discussed semantics as well as politics. Bodmer was already planning the book he was to write later, *The Loom of Language*, now a classic in its field.

At Xenopus, Bodmer, whose bohemianism suffered occasional lapses into an odd teutonic formalism, complained to Enid that the Hogben children did not accord him a proper respect. They addressed him as they heard the grown-ups do as 'Bodmer'. There were four children. Enid told the eldest, Sylvia, then nearly twelve, to say with exaggerated courtesy, 'Herr Doktor Bodmer, you seem to be an unassimilable alien.' ...

And at Xenopus I remember that we sang:

> It's a long way from Amphioxus
> It's a long way to us;
> It's a long way from Amphioxus
> To the meanest human cuss
>   Farewell fins and gill slits,
>   Welcome limbs and hair!
> It's a long way from Amphioxus
> But we've come from there.

2 [p. 112] However, the assertion by the Labour leaders was that they sought segregation of the blacks in 1910. (Personal communication of B. Hirson.)

3 [p. 114] Ultimately, four "native bills" were submitted to a joint session of parliament and senate in 1929.

4   [p. 115] In *Rebel Pity* Eddie Roux provides a vivid first-hand account of Enid's adventure:

> There was also in the Western Province a certain amount of illicit kafir beer drinking which was not in the interests of the wine farmers. Feelings ran high on tots and on kafir beer. Frequent beer raids by the police were resented. A protest meeting was organized for the 4th of May in Worcester. The violence that broke out was probably initiated by local whites some of whom were armed. A black man was shot and killed. At the subsequent enquiry the Congress leaders gave evidence that armed white civilians had used their guns. More violence followed when the police entered the Native location and on this occasion five Natives were killed. Now the two African leaders of the A.N.C. were already in particularly bad odour among the farmers. It was said that they were agitators who were stirring up the hitherto docile farm labourers. In the excitement that followed on the riots Ndobe and Tonjeni went into hiding in the Coloured quarter. The local whites were searching for them and it was believed that they had pickets on the station to catch the two if they should try to leave by train.
>
> We in Cape Town knew from the newspapers of the incidents of the riot but had no idea of the plight of our two comrades, till a Coloured woman approached me quietly at a meeting on the Parade. She brought a message from Ndobe and Tonjeni asking us to come and fetch them by car at eight o'clock in the evening on the following day. She supplied an address in Worcester and insisted that the car must be driven by a European since a Non-European driver would be conspicuous.
>
> I at once recalled Hogben's offer of his Nash. This was a rather conspicuous car but that could not be helped. In fact there was practically no alternative for no Party member had a car in those days. I sent him a note explaining that I needed him and his car at 7 p.m. the following evening. I got back a cryptic typed message saying 'Rhodes Memorial 7 p.m.' The famous memorial is on the lower slopes of Devil's Peak and it is a lonely place after sunset. I took Johnny Gomas with me, since he knew Worcester and I did not. When we came to the meeting place the car was there with Enid driving. 'Lancelot thought it best that I should come,' she said. 'If there is to be trouble for either of us it had better be for me. Lancelot is the breadwinner.' She did not tell us that she had only just learned to drive, having got her licence a few days before. That is discovered later.
>
> There are two ways to go from Cape Town to Worcester: a long roundabout route via Tulbagh and a shorter, rough road over the mountains via Bain's Kloof which was still about eighty miles. As it was important for us to reach Worcester at eight we went over the pass. It was a sandy loose-surfaced road, with a sheer precipice on one side. Though Enid drove extremely slowly the car skidded once or twice. It was now completely dark and long past eight o'clock. As we descended on the far side of the pass we had still quite a distance to go and we urged Enid to speed, which she did. Suddenly the car skidded and left the road. For a few moments we were travelling along on top of a fence knocking the posts down as we went. Then, by some miracle, we were back on the road. We were all shaken and Enid was trembling. We stopped and examined the car. A small side windscreen was broken; otherwise there seemed to be no damage. 'I was told

never to brake in a skid,' Enid explained. 'Had I done so we should have capsized.'

Presently we reached Worcester, then a typical country dorp with practically no lights in the streets. We saw very few people about. After some trouble we found the address and Johnny went into the house. But the two men were not there. They had moved on to another address. Eventually we found them and in this we should hardly have succeeded if I had not had the forethought to bring Johnny. We started back. There was no question of attempting the pass again and so we went the devious route by Tulbagh. It was a long road and Enid grew more and more exhausted. Occasionally she stopped and tried to sleep with her head on the steering wheel. We four big men sat there helpless. Not one of us could drive. We returned to Cape Town in the small hours of the morning.

5   [p. 118] The portrait head, executed by Meyerowitz, is now on display in the College of Medicine, University of Birmingham.

XIII London School of Economics
1   [p. 121] One aspirant was R. A. Fisher. (Box, J. F., *R. A. Fisher, The Life of a Scientist*. New York: Wiley, 1978.)

XIV *Mathematics for the Million*
1   [p. 135] "Son, not according to the flesh but according to the Spirit."

2   [p. 138] This account is correct. However, Lancelot was belatedly elected to the Royal Society in early 1936. Thus it became possible for George Allen & Unwin to publish *Mathematics for the Million* in 1936, before W. W. Norton issued it in 1937.

3   [p. 139] Solly Zuckerman describes the naming of this dining club formed in 1931 as follows:

> The question of a name was raised, but not decided until the next dinner when, after a number of conflicting suggestions, Jack Haldane remarked 'quot homines, tot sententiae'. Lancelot Hogben, who had recently returned from South Africa, then said 'the quotentots', a play on the word Hottentots, that tribe of primitive South Africans of whom he may just have encountered one or two survivors before all became extinct. And so we became, first, Quottentots, and then finally The Tots and Quots.
>
> *From Apes to Warlords*, pages 393–394.

XV *Aberdeen*
1   [p. 142] Referring to Carr Saunders earlier in *Look Back with Laughter*, Lancelot wrote:

> It used to puzzle me how any one so facelessly devoid of charm and with so mediocre intellectual equipment attained such eminence. It does so no longer. The first rung on the ladder is a place on a minor government com-

mittee. If one remains somnolently acquiescent to the pressure group in command news spreads among civil servants that one is a sound chap due to fill a vacancy on other ministerial committee, somnolently—and so on and so on.

2   [p. 147] Artificially reared immature eels (cultivated or in the laboratory) do not mature because of a failure of the pituitary to secrete gonadotropins. Appropriate endocrine treatment can induce maturation of either the *male* or female gonads. (Colombo, G. and Grandi, G., *Acta Embryol. Morphol. Exper. n.s.,* **10** (1), 67–73, 1989.) Nagahama, Y. et al. Ciba Found. Symp. 1994; 182: 255–67 & 267–70. Miura, T. et al. Proc. Natl. Acad. Sci. U.S.A. 1991 Jul 1; 88 (13): 5774–78.

3   [p. 155] The map given in *Science for the Citizen* (Fig. 306, Third edition, 1951) is that of the conjectural route of Leif Ericsson's voyage in 1000 A.D. from Matthias Thórdarson's *The Vinland Voyages,* 1930. It is now in doubt. It draws upon the *Saga of Eric the Red,* but, if accurate, his son, Leif, would have had to cross the Atlantic without reference to landmarks. The plausibility of such a route is now questioned.

Further on in his monograph, Thórdarson reconstructs from the same source a later voyage by Thorfinn Karlsefni from Bear Island, Greenland, to northeast Labrador. His map shows the route then passing L'anse aux Meadows in Newfoundland, site of a Norse settlement discovered in 1961. The southerly limit shown on the map is in the vicinity of Bar Harbor, Maine, and near the place where the "Blue Hill penny" was found (a coin confidently dated to A.D. 1065–1080). Of course, the penny could have been passed to its site of discovery from the north.

4   [p. 156] A recent account of the polarizer is given by Ramskou, T. (1967). Skalk no. 2 p. 16–17 (Copenhagen, Denmark). The following account appears in the Sagas:

> The weather was thick and it snowed heavily. The King let someone look out, and nowhere was the sky free of clouds. Then he asked Sigurd to say where the sun could be, and he said it. Then the king let the sunstone be brought forth and he held it up and saw where the rays came from the stone and concluded from it that it was as Sigurd had said.
>
> The story of the doubting King Olav who tests Sigurd's postulate and becomes convinced, was recounted earlier in an article about the Viking's methods of navigation. Unfortunately, at that time we wrote that the sagas don't state sufficiently clearly what the sunstone really was, but seemed to refer to some kind of instrument that could tell where the sun was under cloudy conditions. The author received two communications, one from flight navigator Jørgen Jensen, the other from engineer Poul Thygesen, both from SAS. Independently of each other, they both related about the

Notes, Chapters XV

same: We use that very same instrument today when we fly a DC-8 over the polar regions. Sigurd's sunstone must in principle be the same as Kollsman's sky compass, the twilight compass, which was discovered or rediscovered rather, in 1948 for use by the American Navy.

Light is a wave action; the elements in the light ray oscillate around an equilibrium and the movement is in the direction perpendicular to the direction of the propagation. Normally the oscillations take place in all directions, but under certain conditions the light becomes polarized, which means that the oscillations are all in the same direction. Polarized light does not have the same properties as ordinary light.

When the sunlight penetrates the upper atmosphere of the earth, polarized light is created and which is the basis for the twilight compass, whose important part is a piece of crystal with a peculiar characteristic—a sunstone. From the sun near the horizon the rays come in horizontally, but they are stopped by a cloudcover that does not cover the whole sky, if it does, the sunstone is of no use. The man cannot see the sun for the clouds but he can see the blue sky straight over his head. When he looks vertically upward, his eye is struck by the polarized light that sunlight causes in the atmosphere. If he holds the sunstone, the polarization filter, over his eye and turns it around a vertical axis he will experience the peculiar thing that in a certain position the stone is light and transparent while if he gives it a quarter turn it becomes darker and less transparent. The polarized light can only pass through the stone when its oscillations correspond to the direction of the molecules in the stone. The direction of the sunrays determines the direction of the oscillation of the polarized light. So the light and dark position of the stone indirectly give information as to where the sun is; one only has to understand how to interpret the signs. Practically, it was probably done by testing the stone on a cloudless day by turning the stone to where it was clearest and then marking on the stone where the sun was. That same mark could then show where the sun was even when it was hiding behind clouds. "And he saw where the rays came from the stone." Now we understand what the saga writer meant. King Olav has turned the stone to the position where it shone, that means became light and transparent. The story about the sunstone—always met with scepticism and the subject of many interpretations—suddenly becomes clear and believable. The question now is only which crystals were used by the Northmen about 1000 years ago. There are not many possibilities, because the necessary characteristics are present in very few minerals. The best known is "doubeltspat" which is found in Iceland, but for Norwegians like Sigurd and Olav there were others closer at hand: dicroit, which against polarized light is seen lighter or darker blue, and andalucit which changes from yellow to dark red. The sunstone is mentioned in another saga text, from which it appears that, even though it looks like an ordinary beach stone, it is a stone of great value. In Norway dicroit and andalucit can be found on beaches but they are rare and it takes more than ordinary luck to find those that in size and condition are suited for the purpose. It can not have been very common and the question is how much practical significance it has had.

"Nowhere was the sky free of clouds," writes the sagaman, but on this point he has exaggerated the excellence of the sunstone. If there is no blue sky straight over the head of the observer it is useless. It may surprise some that such an old, and after all rather primitive, instrument is still in use in a modern enterprise such as the polar traffic by SAS. But precisely in the area around the pole the ordinary compass becomes unreliable. That is the reason that the Viking's old tested sunstone has found honour and respect today. (Somewhat modified from a translation by Dr. Bodil Schmidt-Nielsen, Mt. Desert Island Biol. Lab., Salisbury Cove, Maine.)

5 [p. 157] "In the great waters and the waves"; "Let me feel a breeze from the hill of Calvary."

6 [p. 157] "O to remain in his love for all the days of [my] life."

XVI Scandinavia

1 [p. 166] Lancelot is, of course, referring to the putative pedigree charts used to promote eugenics. The most notorious were those of the Jukes and Kallikak families, published in 1877 and 1912, respectively (*In the Name of Eugenics,* 1985, pp. 71 and 78), but still trotted out in the thirties. Contemporary medical scientists successfully use family trees to implicate possible genes. The suspected gene in afflicted members can be sought by DNA analysis.

2 [p. 166] Lysenko was a Soviet agronomist who, perhaps with fabricated data, claimed to have proved that environmental modifications are genetically transmissible. With the support of Stalin, he promoted the discredited Lamarckism (inheritance of acquired characteristics) and purged Russian science of Mendelian geneticists. The imprisonment of Vavilov (and thus his death) at Lysenko's behest was a most shameful act. Though gifted, J. B. S. Haldane sometimes embraced positions that were anathema to Lancelot, such as Haldane's enthusiasm for military combat. His silence on Lysenko and Vavilov was more than Lancelot and others could condone.

XVII Madison, Wisconsin

1 [p. 175] About A.D. 1720 the Japanese used differentiation to arrive at a value for π correct to fifty decimal places. *Mathematics for the million,* pages 259 and 266 (Third Ed., Allen & Unwin, 1951).

2 [p. 176] Alfred (Habdanh Skarbek) Korzybski, 1879–1950, was a Polish-American linguist, engineer, educator and author. His *Science and Sanity: an introduction to non-Aristotelian systems and general semantics,* published in 1933, became the basic handbook of the general semantics movement.

3 [p. 177] Lancelot describes the rented cottage charitably. Adrian remembers this with embarrassment. It was the cheapest accommoda-

tion he could find, out in the unending prairie. He does not remember a lake. However, Lancelot and Sylvia soon settled in the splendid capital city of Madison.

4   [p. 181] Robert M. LaFollette, 1855–1925, was an American statesman who, as governor of Wisconsin, secured the enactment of a progressive legislative programme, which included a direct primary law, tax reform legislation and railroad rate control. Elected to the U.S. senate in 1905, he consistently fought for reform measures until his death. One of the founders of the Progressive Party, in 1924 he polled almost 5 million votes as its presidential candidate. Under the leadership of his sons, Robert M., Jr., and Philip F., the Progressive Party continued to dominate Wisconsin politics until 1938.

XVIII *Birmingham*

1   [p. 185] The extinction of dinosaurs continues to fascinate both scientists and laity. Because it is dramatic and simple to grasp, the hypothesis put forward by Louis W. Alvarez (*Proc. Natl. Acad. Sci.* 80: 617–42, 1983) gained wide acceptance. Based on the finding of a widely dispersed, anomalous, very thin layer of iridium and other noble metals in the appropriate geologic stratum, he suggested that a giant asteroid struck the earth, plunging it into the darkness and cold of a global false winter, which dinosaurs were unable to withstand. More recently, his assertion was bolstered by the discovery of a very large impact crater in Mexico's Yucatán peninsula. However, the Alvarez hypothesis is by no means endorsed by the scientific community. Examination of the geologic record has been inconclusive. Raup and Sepkuski (*Science* 215: 1501, 1982) found that there were peaks of extinction of marine fauna. However, Quina (*Science* 219: 1239, 1983) plotted the same data, semi-logarithmically. The peaks of extinction were no longer apparent.

In the paper Lancelot refers to (LH 1946a), he and R. L. Kirk offered a plausible explanation for the dinosaurs' extinction, with the caveat that their demise may not have had a single cause. (It is of interest that, in 1937 when Lancelot was seeing Julian Huxley frequently, Julian was a scientific advisor for an episode of Walt Disney's *Fantasia*, in which Stravinsky's *Rites of Spring* became a story of evolution. In it, the dinosaurs wither and die under a blazing sun.)

In *Why the Dinosaurs Became Extinct*, 1978, J. R. Cloudsley-Thompson examined physiologic restraints that might have favoured demise 65 million years ago. J. N. Wilford provides a very readable account in his *Riddle of the Dinosaur*, 1986.

2   [p. 186] Hogben and Crew founded a second journal, the *British Journal of Social Medicine,* published by the British Medical Associa-

tion. Lancelot was its first editor, and work conducted by his team was published in its early issues (LH 1947a–e, LH 1948a).

3   [p. 192] The United World Federalists, UWF, was founded in the U.S. after World War II by Cord Meyer, Jr. It sought to promote world government without forming a political party. It had as its presidents a U.S. Senator, Alan Cranston (D., Calif.), and later Norman Cousins, Editor of the *Saturday Review of Literature*. It became a victim of the cold war in the sixties. (The editors were active in UWF and, in 1950–51 its Danish counterpart, *Een Verden*, in Copenhagen.)

XIX Wales

1   [p. 195] The full report is lodged in the Heslop Room of University of Birmingham Library, Item A.22 of the collection of Lancelot Hogben's papers.

2   [p. 196] In *Statistical Theory* Lancelot clarifies the implications of reducing a set of data to a few statistics, and he dissects the meaning of statistical significance.

The simplest reduction of data, the mean, is so much a part of our daily lives that we hardly give it a thought. Lancelot points to *the tyranny of averages* since the mean can hide more than it reveals. He quotes from an 1865 lecture of the towering physiologist Claude Bernard:

> By destroying the biological character of phenomena, the use of *averages* in physiology and medicine usually gives only apparent accuracy to the results. . . . If for instance, we observe the number of pulsations and the degree of blood pressure by means of the oscillations of a manometer throughout one day, and if we take the average of all our figures to get the true or average blood pressure and to learn the true or average number of pulsations, we shall simply have wrong numbers.

To digress from *Statistical Theory*, the habit of drawing a line through a set of points is not a simple affair. Without attempting to be rigorous or all inconclusive, when a straight line is to be fitted to a set of points by the "method of least squares," there are usually two options. One of the two variables, e.g., height and weight, has to be designated the independent variable x and the other the dependent variable y. Consider an example where each point is determined by the weight of an egg and the corresponding weight of the chicken it produced. If weight of the egg is chosen as x and that of the chicken y, one line is obtained. Reversing the choice, x for the chicken weight and y for the egg, yields a *second*, different line. Thus the question: which comes first, the chicken or the egg? The choice of the x variable may be arbitrary, often implausible and infrequently reasonable. For two examples the choice is appropriate—when the error in one variable is less than one-hundredth of the other or if a cartographic survey is being conducted.

The dilemma is too often ignored. Generally there is a sensible and simple way to obtain a *single* straight line, the orthogonal least squares fit (Isobe et al., 1990. *Astrophys. J.* 364:104). (In so many articles, the orthogonal equation is not in its simplest form. Seek the stripped-down model.)

Lancelot dissects the meaning of statistical significance in three passages: Chapter 1, The Contemporary Crisis or the Uncertainties of Uncertain Inference; Chapter 14, Statistical Prudence and Statistical Inference; and Appendix IV, Significance as Interpreted by the School of R. A. Fisher. (These have been reprinted verbatim in *The Significance Test Controversy,* 1970.) The issues are subtle and, perhaps, poorly understood by many statisticians.

Fisherian statistics includes analysis of variance, factor analysis and maximum likelihood. Though Lancelot's critique of these methods is very important, it does not lend itself to a précis. The methods are not founded strictly on probability or derived from a stochastic model. In ordinary language they cannot be proven.

A quote from Chapter 11 might suggest Lancelot's close reasoning.

> Incorporation of the classical theory of probability in the initial postulates of factor analysis is arbitrary in more ways than one, and involves assumptions which can never be amenable to direct proof. Any classical model we press into the service of the theory may explain how certain numerical regularities *might* arise but cannot suffice to prove that they *do* so.

The gap between the preoccupation of a scientist and the sophistication of statistical theory prompted the eminent statistician E. S. Pearson to observe, as quoted by Lancelot:

> Probably there are several of us who can recall a considerable number of reports, or appendices to reports, written on both sides of the Atlantic by mathematically trained statisticians, which were hardly more than a waste of the paper on which they were written. There were cases where the results of statistical analyses were simple put on one side because the practical man, whether scientist or service technician, shrewdly sensed that the theoretical treatment was either not needed, or was actually leading to conclusions which the data could not possibly warrant. The trouble usually arose because the mathematical enthusiast has allowed his theory to run away with his common sense, or, perhaps, because he had never received an adequate training in the application of theory. It was true that biologists did extremely well in operational research; but their success often seemed due to the way in which an experimental training had taught them to handle data rather than to the fact that they mastered statistical technique quickly.

Fifty years ago the responsibilities of the scientist and the statistician were often clear. Today, this is often not the case. The concern of Egon Pearson and Lancelot Hogben is now a grave matter because of the availability of computers and software programs that seem harmless and authoritative. Statistical procedures are being used without rigorous scrutiny of their credentials, particularly when prepackaged software programs are used.

When employing statistical methods, one should not let one's reach exceed one's grasp.

3   [p. 196] Two years later Lancelot was awarded two honourary degrees: a D.Sc. by the University of Wales and an LI.D. by the University of Birmingham.

4   [p. 200] In *Look Back with Laughter,* Lancelot offered this commentary on the Guyanese political turmoil:

> In Georgetown, throughout 1964, existence was comparable to life in Londonderry ten years later; but I was still too busy with plans for the new University to acquaint myself, when there, with the background of the political situation in the colony. During the period I spent negotiating with the Ministry of Overseas Development, I had ample opportunities for doing so by contact with Ashton Chase, then President of the Senate and with Peter Simms, a congenial Cambridge graduate who resigned his university post in Georgetown and settled temporarily in London to write his admirable book *Trouble in Guyana* (1966).
>
> Peter Simms' book won him few reviews in the British Press. I can recommend it highly with only one reservation. I think he might well have devoted more attention to how much the State Department in Washington was able to harass the P.P.P. government through a daily radio campaign conducted directly or indirectly by the American Federation of Labour. The story unfolded by *Trouble in Guyana* is relevant to my decision to relinquish a post from which I could hope for little intellectual satisfaction, and therefore claims a place in my memoirs. It may also interest readers now made more ready to take stock of events in South America by recent events in Chile and disclosures about the activities of the C.I.A. divulged by recent Congressional committees set up to probe them. The C.I.A. did not need to work overtime to bring down the quasi-Marxist government of British Guiana. By sheer ineptitude, Cheddi Jagan did the job without its help.

Acknowledgments

BUT for Kathleen Lloyd, Lancelot's and our friend, it would not have been possible for us to edit this autobiography. Together with G. P. Wells, she was responsible for preserving Lancelot's papers. We have come to know her as a dedicated, kind, and thoughtful person.

In the course of ten years, we have been helped by many, and have gained new friends. We wish to thank: Robert Cawley, once a student of Lancelot's, for constructive suggestions; James and Charlene Chandler, for their skill and enthusiasm in moving the manuscript to camera-ready copy; Baruch Hirson, for sharing his knowledge of South Africa; Cynthia Hogben, Lancelot's niece, for preserving the Thomas Hogben legacy; Dorothy Hogben, Lancelot's sister (deceased); Anne Jordan for congenial computer searching; David C. Smith for valued comments; Kathrine Sorley Walker, Lancelot's literary agent, for her suggestions and her sustained support; Catherine Stoye, G. P. Wells's literary executor, for sharing G. P.'s papers; and Raymond Wrighton, closest intellectual companion during Lancelot's last two decades, for his constructive and in-depth review of successive drafts.

For graciously responding to our letters of inquiry, we extend thanks to Prof. D. C. Falconer, University of Edinburgh; Prof. Alvin R. Feinstein, Yale University School of Medicine; Prof. R. C. Lewontin, Harvard University; Prof. Kenneth W. Ludmerer, Washington University; Colin A. McLaren, University of Aberdeen Archivist; George M. Mitchell; and Keith Moore, Archivist of the Royal Society.

We were cordially received at the following libraries: The Heslop Room of the University of Birmingham; the University of Illinois; The Jackson Laboratory and Jesup Memorial Library, both of Bar Harbor, Maine; the London School of Economics; Fogler Library of the University of Maine; and the Religious Society of Friends.

Bibliography

(From *Biogr. Mem. Fellows R. Soc. Lond.* 24, 217–221. Used with permission of the Royal Society of London. Additional citations added.)

1918a *Alfred Russel Wallace: the story of a great discoverer.* London: Society for Promoting Christian Knowledge. p. 64.

  b *Exiles of the snow, and other poems.* London: A. C. Fifield.

1919a The progressive reduction of the jugal in the mammalia. *Proc. zool. Soc. London.* 1919, 71–78.

1920a On certain nuclear phenomena in the oocytes of the gall-fly *Neuroterus. J. Linn. Soc. Zool.* **34**, 327–333.

  b The problem of synapsis. *Jl R. microsc. Soc.* pp. 269–276.

  c Studies on synapsis. I. Oogenesis in the hymenoptera. *Proc. R. Soc. Lond.* B **91**, 268–293.

  d Studies on synapsis. II. Parallel conjugation and the prophase complex in *Periplaneta* with special reference to the premeiotic telophase. *Proc. R. Soc. Lond.* B **91**, 305–329.

1921a Studies on synapsis. III. The nuclear organisation of the germ cells in *Libellula depressa. Proc. R. Soc. Lond.* B **92**, 60–80.

  b A preliminary account of the spermatogenesis of *Sphenodon. Jl R. microsc. Soc.* pp. 341–352.

1922a Huxley, J. S. and Hogben, L. T. Experiments on amphibian metamorphosis and pigment responses in relation to internal secretions. *Proc. R. Soc. Lond.* B **93**, 36–53.

  b Hogben, L. T. and Winton, F. R. The pigmentary effector system. I. Reaction of frog's melanophores to pituitary extracts. Proc. R. Soc. Lond. B **93**, 318–329.

  c Hogben, L. T. and Winton, F. R. The pigmentary effector system. II. *Proc. R. Soc. Lond.* B **94**, 151–162.

  d Hogben, L. T. and Winton, F. R. Studies on the pituitary. I. The melanophore stimulant in posterior lobe extracts. *Biochem. J.* **16**, 619–630.

1923a A method of hypophysectomy in adult frogs and toads. *Q. Jl exp. Physiol.* **13**, 177–179.

  b Hogben, L. T. and Winton, F. R. The pigmentary effector system. III. Colour response in the hypophysectomised frog. *Proc. R. Soc. Lond.* B **95**, 15–31.

  c Studies on internal secretion. I. The effect of pituitary (anterior lobe) injection upon normal and thyroidectomised axolotls. *Proc. R. Soc. Lond.* B **94**, 204–215.

  d Hogben, L. T. and Crew, F. A. E. Studies on internal secretion. II. Endocrine activity in foetal and embryonic life. *Br. J. exp. Biol.* **1**, 1–13.

  e Winton, F. R. and Hogben, L. T. Studies on the pituitary. II. The influence of hypophysectomy on the rate of carbon-dioxide production in frogs. *Q. Jl exp. Physiol.* **13**, 309–322.

1924a The pigmentary effector system. IV. A further contribution to the role of pituitary secretion in amphibian colour response. *Br. J. exp. Biol.* **1**, 249–270.

  b The relation of internal secretion to reproduction and growth in the domestic fowl. II. The parenteral administration of certain endocrine extracts. *Vet. J.* **80**, no. 5, 1–8.

  c Hogben, L. T. and Hobson, A. D. Studies on internal secretion. III. The action of pituitary extract and adrenaline on contractile tissues of certain invertebrata. *Br. J. exp. Biol.* **1**, 487–500.

  d Hogben, L. T. and Schlapp, W. Studies on the pituitary. III. The vasomotor extracts throughout the vertebrate series. *Q. Jl exp. Physiol.* **14**, 229–258.

  e Hogben, L. T., Schlapp, W. and MacDonald, A. D. Studies on the pituitary. IV. Quantitative comparison of pressor activity. *Q. Jl exp. Physiol.* **14**, 301–318.

  f *The pigmentary effector system.* Edinburgh: Oliver & Boyd.

  g Hogben, L. T. and Winton, F. R. *An introduction to recent advances in comparative physiology.* London: Collins.

1925a Studies on the pituitary. V. The avine depressor response. *Q. Jl exp. Physiol.* **15**, 151–161.

  b Hogben, L. T. and de Beer, G. R. Studies on the pituitary. VI. Localisation and phyletic distribution of active materials. *Q. Jl exp. Physiol.* **15**, 163–176.

  c Studies on the comparative physiology of contractile tissues. I. The action of electrolytes on invertebrate muscle. *Q. Jl exp. Physiol.* **15**, 263–312.

  d Pantin, C. F. A. and Hogben, L. T. A colorimetric method for studying the dissociation of oxyhaemocyanin suitable for class work. *J. mar. biol. Ass. U.K.* **13**, 970–980.

1926a Hogben, L. T. and Pinhey, K. F. Viscous-elastic changes in muscular contraction. *Br. J. exp. Biol.* **4**, 196–202.

b Some observations on the dissociation of haemocyanin by the colorimetric method. *Br. J. exp. Biol.* **3**, 225–238.

c Hogben, L. T. and Pinhey, K. F. A comparison between the dissociation of the haemocyanins of *Helix* and Crustacea. *Br. J. exp. Biol.* **4**, 203–214.

d *Comparative physiology.* London: Sedgwick & Jackson; New York: MacMillan.

1927a Abel's pituitary tartrate. *Nature, Lond.* **120**, 177–179.

b A method for the study of dissociation of haemocyanin. *Trans. R. Soc. S. Afr.* **14**, 373–381.

c Hogben, L. T. and Pinhey, K. F. Some observations on the haemocyanin of *Limulus. Br. J. exp. Biol.* **5**, 55–65.

d Colorimetric determination of the oxidation of haemocyanin. *Nature, Lond.* **119**, 122–123.

e *The comparative physiology of internal secretion.* Cambridge: University Press. (Cambridge Comparative Physiology.)

f *Principles of evolutionary biology.* Cape Town and Johannesburg: Juta.

1928a Hogben, L. T. and Mirvish, L. Some observations on the production of excitement pallor in reptiles. *Trans. R. Soc. S. Afr.* **16**, 45–52.

b Hogben, L. T. and Mirvish, L. The pigmentary effector system. V. The nervous control of excitement pallor in reptiles. *Br. J. exp. Biol.* **5**, 295–305.

c Hogben, L. T. and Van Der Lingen, J. On the occurrence of haemoglobin and of erythrocytes in the perivisceral fluid of a holothurian. *Br. J. exp. Biol.* **5**, 292–294.

d Hogben, L. T. and Zoond, A. A note on the hydrogen ion concentration of surface waters around the Cape Peninsula. *S. Afr. J. Sci.* **25**, 325–328.

1929 Slome, D. and Hogben, L. T. The time factor in the chromatic responses of *Xenopus laevis. Trans. R. Soc. S. Afr.* **17**, 141–150.

1930a Some remarks on the relation of the pituitary gland to ovulation and skin secretion in *Xenopus laevis. Proc R. Soc. S. Afr.* 19 March 1930.

b Hogben, L. T. and Gordon, C. Studies on the pituitary. VII. The separate identity of the pressor and melanophore principles. *J. exp. Biol.* **7**, 286–292.

c Hogben, L. T. and Gordon, C. Studies on the comparative physiology of contractile tissues. II. The relation of electrolytes to electrical conductivity. *J. exp. Biol.* **7**, 269–285.

1930d *Principles of animal biology.* London: Christophers.

e *The nature of living matter.* London: Kegan Paul.

1931a Acromegaly in the Far North. *Nature, Lond.* **128**, 221.

b Hogben, L. T. and Slome, D. The pigmentary effector system. VI. The dual character of endocrine co-ordination in amphibian colour change. *Proc. R. Soc. Lond.* B **108**, 10–53.

c Hogben, L. T., Charles, E. and Slome, D. Studies on the pituitary. VIII. The relation of the pituitary gland to calcium metabolism and ovarian function in *Xenopus. J. exp. Biol.* **8**, 345–354.

d Jolly, W. A. and Hogben, L. T. Some observations on the retinal responses of *Xenopus laevis. Q. Jl exp. Physiol.* **21**, 37–53.

e The genetic analysis of familial traits. I. Single gene substitutions. *J. Genet.* **25**, 97–112.

f Inaugural Lecture—The foundations of social biology. With introductory remarks by H. G. Wells. *Economica,* February 1931, pp. 1–24.

g *Genetic principles in medicine and social science.* London: Williams & Norgate.

1932a The genetic analysis of familial traits. II. Double gene substitutions, with special reference to hereditary dwarfism. *J. Genet.* **25**, 211–240.

b The genetic analysis of familial traits. III. Matings involving one parent exhibiting a trait determined by a single recessive gene substitution with special reference to sex-linked conditions. *J. Genet.* **25**, 293–314.

c The factorial analysis of small families with parents of undetermined genotype. *J. Genet.* **26**, 75–79.

d Hogben, L. T., Worrall, R. L. and Zieve, I. The genetic basis of alkaptonuria. *Proc. R. Soc. Edinb.* **52**, 265–295.

e Filial and fraternal correlations in sex-linked inheritance. *Proc. R. Soc. Edinb.* **52**, 331–336.

f The correlation of relatives on the supposition of sex-linked transmission. *J. Genet.* **26**, 417–432.

g Hogben, L. T. and Charles, E. Studies on the pituitary. IX. Changes in blood calcium following injection of anterior lobe extracts and sexual excitement in female rabbits. *J. exp. Biol.* **9**, 139–148.

h (Pseud. as Kenneth Calvin Page) *A journey to Nineveh and other verses.* London: Noel Douglas.

1933a   Charles, E. and Hogben, L. T.   The serum calcium and magnesium level in the ovarian cycle of the laying hen. *Q. Jl exp. Physiol.* **23**, 343–349.

    b   Herrman, L. and Hogben, L. T.   The intellectual resemblance of twins. *Proc. R. Soc. Edinb.* **53**, 105–219.

    c   The limits of applicability of correlation technique in human genetics. *J. Genet.* **27**, 379–406.

    d   Some methodological aspects of human genetics. *Am. Nat.* **67**, 1–10.

    e   A matrix notation for Mendelian populations. *Proc. R. Soc. Edinb.* **53**, 7–25.

    f   The effect of consanguineous parentage upon metrical characters of the offspring. *Proc. R. Soc. Edinb.* **53**, 239–251.

    g   *Nature and Nurture.* London: Williams & Norgate.

1934a   The detection of linkage in human families. I. Both heterozygous genotypes indeterminate. *Proc. R. Soc. London.* B **114**, 340–352.

    b   The detection of linkage in human families. II. One heterozygous genotype indeterminate. *Proc. R. Soc. London.* B **114**, 353–363.

1935   Hogben, L. T. and Pollack, R.   A contribution to the relation of the gene loci involved in the isoagglutinin reaction, taste blindness, Friedreich's ataxia and major brachydactyly in man. *J. Genet.* **31**, 353–361.

1936a   The pigmentary effector system. VII. The chromatic function in elasmobranch fishes. *Proc. R. Soc. Lond.* B **120**, 142–158.

    b   Hogben, L. T. and Slome, D.   The pigmentary effector system. VIII. The dual receptive mechanism of the amphibian background response. *Proc. R. Soc. Lond.* B **120**, 158–173.

    c   The chromatic function in the lower vertebrates, a study in the analysis of behaviour. Moscow: State Biol. and Medical Press. **5**, 224–260 (Russian), 261–292 (English).

    d   *The retreat from reason.* (Conway Memorial Lecture.) London: Watts.

    e   *Mathematics for the million: a popular self-educator.* London: Allen & Unwin; New York: Norton 1937.

1938a   Bellerby, C. W., and Hogben, L. T.   Experimental studies on the sexual cycle of the South African clawed toad (*Xenopus laevis*). III. *J. exp. Biol.* **15**, 91–100.

    b   *Science for the citizen: a self-educator based on the social background of scientific discovery.* London: Allen & Unwin; New York: Norton.

1939a   Genetic variation and human intelligence. *Proc. Intern. Gen. Congr.* pp. 147–153.

1939b *Dangerous thoughts.* London: Allen & Unwin.

1940a Hogben, L. T. and Landgrebe, F. The pigmentary effector system. IX. The receptor fields of the teleostean visual response. *Proc. R. Soc. Lond.* B **128**, 317–343.

b *Author in transit.* New York: Norton.

1942a Croonian Lecture: Chromatic behaviour. *Proc. R. Soc. Lond.* B **131**, 111–136.

b The amphibian pituitary. *Nature, Lond.* **149**, 675.

1943a Mutation and the rhesus reaction. *Nature, Lond.* **152**, 721.

b *Interglossa.* A draft of an auxiliary for a democratic world order. Harmondsworth and New York: Penguin Books.

1944a Hogben, L. T. and Kirk, R. L. The pigmentary effector system. X. Relation of colour change to surface absorption of radiation. *Proc. R. Soc. Lond.* B **132**, 68–82.

b Hogben, L. T. and Kirk, R. L. Studies on temperature regulation. I. The pulmonata and oligochaeta. *Proc. R. Soc. Lond.* B **132**, 239–252.

1946a Kirk, R. L. and Hogben, L. T. Studies on temperature regulation. II. Amphibia and reptiles. *J. exp. Biol.* **22**, 213–220.

b Begg, M. and Hogben, L. T. Chemoreceptivity of *Drosophila melanogaster. Proc. R. Soc. Lond.* B **133**, 1–19.

c History of the Hogben test. *Br. med. J.* **2**, 554.

d *An introduction to mathematical genetics.* New York: Norton.

1947a Waterhouse, J. A. H. and Hogben, L. T. Incompatibility of mother and foetus with respect to the isoagglutinogen A and its antibody. *Br. J. Soc. Med.* **1**, 1–17.

b Truelove, S. C. and Hogben, L. T. A documentary study of jaundice, associated with syphilis treatment and blood transfusion. *Br. J. soc. Med.* **1**, 18–32.

c Hogben, L. T. and Johnstone, M. M. The relation of morbidity to age in an army population. *Br. J. soc. Med.* **1**, 149–181.

d Risk of jaundice following transfusion with pooled plasma or serum. *Br. J. soc. Med.* **1**, 209–211.

e Hogben, L. T., Johnstone, M. M. and Mullings, D. The medical ethnography of the Second World War. *Br. J. soc. Med.* **1**, 251–275.

1948a Hogben, H., Waterhouse, J. A. H. and Hogben, L. T. Studies on puberty, Part I. *Br. J. soc. Med.* **2**, 29–42.

b Hogben, L. T. and Cross, K. W. The statistical specificity of a code personnel cypher sequence. *Br. J. soc. Med.* **2**, 149.

1948c Hogben, L. T., Johnstone, M. M. and Cross, K. W. Identification of medical documents. *Br. med. J.* i, 632–645.

d Introduction, Statistical report on the health of the army, 1943–1945. London: *His Majesty's Stationery Office.*

1949a Hogben, L. T. and Kemp, K. W. Statistical models bearing on the semantics of correlation. I. The umpire bonus model. *Hum. Biol.* 21, 111–142.

b Hogben, L. T. and Waterhouse, J. A. H. Statistical models bearing on the semantics of correlation. II. The nonreplacement model. *Hum. Biol.* 21, 163–186.

c *The new authoritarianism.* (Conway Memorial Lecture.) London: Watts.

d *From Cave Painting to Comic Strip.* London: Max Parrish.

1950a Hogben, L. T. and Kemp, K. W. Statistical models bearing on the semantics of correlation. III. Expectation—accomplishment models. *Hum. Biol.* 22, 76–103.

b *Chance and choice by cardpack and chessboard, An introduction to probability in practice by visual aids,* vol. I. London: Max Parrish.

c Major Greenwood. *Biogr. Mem. R. Soc.* 7, 139–154.

1951 The formal logic of the Nature-Nurture Issue. *Acta. genet. Statist. Med.* II, 101–140.

1952a Selective limitation of sibship size. *Br. J. soc. Med.* 6, 188–189.

b Hogben, L. T. and Wrighton, R. Statistical theory of prophylactic and therapeutic trials. I. Limitations of the unique null hypothesis. *Br. J. soc. Med.* 6, 89–117.

c Hogben, L. T. and Wrighton, R. Statistical theory of prophylactic and therapeutic trials. II. Methods of operational advantage. *Br. J. Soc. Med.* 6, 205–225.

d Hogben, L. T. and Cross, K. W. Sampling from a discrete universe. *Acta. genet. Statist. Med.* 3, 305–342.

1953 Hogben, L. T. and Sim, M. The self-controlled and self-recorded clinical trial for low-grade morbidity. *Br. J. prev. soc. Med.* 7, 163–179.

1954a Hogben, L. T. and Cross, K. W. The design of records for field work. *Br. J. prev. soc. Med.* 8, 10–16.

b The assessment of remedies. *Med. Press* 232, 3–23.

1955a Figurate series and factorial notation. *Acta. genet. Statist. Med.* 5, 115–133.

b *Chance and choice by cardpack and chessboard,* vol. II. London: Max Parrish.

c *Man must measure.* London: Rathbone.

1956 Human biology and human speech. *Br. J. prev. soc. Med.* **10**, 63–74.

1957a *Statistical theory: an examination of the contemporary crisis in statistical theory from a behaviorist viewpoint.* London: Allen & Unwin.

b *Men, missiles and machines.* London: Rathbone.

1959 *Signs of civilisation.* London: Rathbone.

1960a *Mathematics in the making.* London: Macdonald.

b Hogben, L. T. and Cross, K. W. *Design of documents.* London: Macdonald.

1963a *Science in authority: Essays.* London: Allen & Unwin.

b (Assisted by Jane Hogben & Maureen Cartwright) *Essential world English.* London: Michael Joseph.

1964 *The mother tongue.* London: Secker & Warburg.

1967a *Mathematics for the million* (4th ed., extensively revised with additional material and completely re-illustrated). London: George Allen & Unwin; New York: Norton.

b *Whales for the Welsh: a tale of war and peace.* London: Repp & Carroll.

c Epistemics, axiomatics and relevance. *Int. J. Educ. Sci.* **1**, 171–178.

1968a *The wonderful world of mathematics.* London: Macdonald. (Enlarged revision of 1955c.)

b *The wonderful world of energy.* London: Macdonald. (Enlarged revision of 1957b.)

1969a *The wonderful world of communication.* London: Macdonald. (Enlarged revision of 1959.)

b (Assisted by Maureen Cartwright) *The vocabulary of science.* London: Heinemann.

c A university in a changing society. *Int. J. Educ. Sci.* **3**, 5–14.

d Some agenda for reform of mathematical symbolism. *Int. J. Educ. Sci.* **3**, 15–18.

1970 *Beginnings and blunders, or before science began.* London: Heinemann. (The beginnings of science, 1.)

1972 *Astronomer, priest and ancient mariner.* London: Heinemann. (The beginnings of science, 2.)

1973a Modern civilization and scientific knowledge. *Philosophy Forums*, **12**, 245–271.

b *Maps, mirrors and mechanics.* London: Heinemann. (The beginnings of science, 3.)

1974a Francis Albert Eley Crew. *Biogr. Mem. Fellows R. Soc. Lond.* **20**, 135–153.
    b *Columbus, the cannon ball and the common pump.* London: Heinemann.
    c The origins of the Society. Reprinted in *The Society for Experimental Biology, origins and history 1923–1973.* Cambridge: Company of Biologists.

Note: 24 essays and addresses in the period 1935–1961 are reprinted in *Dangerous Thoughts*, 1939b, and *Science in Authority*, 1963a.

Supplemental Bibliography

Ashby, W. and Clark, R. *Central Glosa.* Surrey: Glosa. 1993.

Bentham, G. and Hooker, J. D. *Handbook of the British flora.* Ashford, Kent: Reeve & Co. Ltd. 1930.

Bodmer, F. *The loom of language—a guide to foreign languages for the home student* (edited and arranged by Lancelot Hogben). Primers for the Age of Plenty no. 3. London: Allen and Unwin. 1944. New York: Norton.

British Association for the Advancement of Science. Report of the 97th Meeting—South Africa. 1929.

Charles, E. *The twilight of parenthood.* New York: Norton. 1934.

Church, R. *British authors—a twentieth century gallery.* British Council. London: Longmans, Green & Co. 1943.

Cloudsley-Thompson, J. R. *Why the dinosaurs became extinct.* Durham: Meadowfield Press. 1978.

Clow, A. and N. L. *The chemical revolution. A contribution to social technology.* London: Botchworth Press. 1952.

Crew, F. A. E. Biological pregnancy diagnosis tests—a comparison of the rabbit, the mouse and the 'clawed toad' (*Xenopus laevis*) as the experimental animal. *Brit. Med. J.* 15 April 1939, p. 766.

Dahlberg, G. *Race, reason and rubbish. An examination of biological essentials of the Nazi creed.* Translated from the Swedish by Lancelot Hogben. London: Allen & Unwin. 1942.

Darwin, C. R. and Wallace, A. R. *On the origin of species by means of natural selection, or the preservation of favoured races in the struggle for life.* J. Linn. Soc. (Zool.) 1859.

Hamilton, H. *History of the homeland. The story of the British background* (ed. Lancelot Hogben). Primers for the Age of Plenty no. 4. London: Allen & Unwin. 1947. New York: Norton.

Herrman, L. *A history of the Jews in South Africa from the earliest times to 1895.* London: Gollancz. 1930.

Hogben, M. *"One thing I do." Memoir of Thomas Hogben, founder of the "One by One Band."* Stockport: Edgeley Press. 1921.

Hogben, T. *God's plan for soul winning.* London: Ward Lock & Co. 1906.

Hogben, T. *My witnesses.* London: "One by One Band." 1909.

Huxley, J. S. *Memories.* New York: Harper & Row. 1970

Kevles, D. J. *In the name of eugenics: genetics and the uses of human heredity.* New York: Knopf. 1985.

Landgrebe, F. W. The maintenance of reproductive activity in *Xenopus laevis* for pregnancy diagnosis. *J. exp. Biol.* 16. 89–95. 1939.

Meredith, G. P. *Algebra by visual aids.* Under the Editorship of Lancelot Hogben. 4 vols. London: Allen & Unwin. 1948.

Montagu, Ivor. *The youngest son.* London: Lawrence & Wishart. 1970.

Morgan, T. H. *The physical basis of heredity.* Philadelphia: Lippincott. 1919.

Morrison, D. E. and Henkel, R. E. *The significance test controversy.* Chicago: Aldine Publishing Co. 1970.

Neurath, M. *How the first men lived.* (Ed. Lancelot Hogben.) New York: Chanticleer Press. 1950.

Neurath, O. and M. and Lauwerys, J. A. *Visual history of mankind.* (Honorary Ed. Lancelot Hogben.) London: Adprint. 1948.

Ogden, C. K. *Basic English, a general introduction with rules and grammar.* London: Kegan Paul. 1932.

Political arithmetic, a symposium of population studies (ed. Lancelot Hogben.) London: Allen & Unwin. 1938.

Primers for the Age of Plenty (ed. by Lancelot Hogben.) London: Allen & Unwin. 1937.

Remskou, T. *Skalk* no. 2 pp. 16–17. Copenhagen. 1967. (Translation courtesy of Bodil Schmidt-Nielsen.)

Roux, E. & W. *Rebel pity.* London: Rex Collings. 1970.

Russell, B. The autobiography of Bertrand Russell 1914–1944. London: Allen & Unwin. 1968.

Simms, P. *Trouble in Guyana.* London: Allen & Unwin. 1966.

Taylor, Lord Professor Lancelot Hogben. The Border Counties Advertiser. 17 September 1975.

Thórdarson, M. *The Vinland voyages.* New York: American Geographical Society. 1930.

Unwin, S. *The truth about a publisher.* London: Allen & Unwin. 1960.

Wallace, A. R. *My life, a record of events and opinions,* vol. I. London: Chapman & Hall. 1905.

Waring, H. *Colour change mechanisms of cold-blooded vertebrates.* New York and London: Academic Press. 1963.

Webb, S. & B. *Soviet communism: A new civilisation?* London: Longmans, Green & Co. Ltd. 1935.

Wells, G. P. *Father and sons.* 1981 Unpublished. In the Hogben collection in the Heslop Room, University of Birmingham Library.

Wells, G. P. Lancelot Thomas Hogben, 1895–1975. *Biogr. Mem. Fellows R. Soc. Lond.* **24**, 183–221.

Wells, H. G. *Experiment in autobiography.* New York: Macmillan. 1934.

Wells, H. G. *Outline of history.* New York: Macmillan. 1920.

Wheatcroft, G. *The randlords.* New York: Atheneum. 1986.

Wilford, J. N. *The riddle of the dinosaur.* New York: Knopf. 1986.

Woolf, V. *The diary of Virginia Woolf.* (Ed. Anne Olivier Bell.) vol. I. New York: Harcourt. 1977.

Zuckerman, S. *From apes to warlords.* New York and London: Harper & Row. 1978.

Zuckerman, S. *Monkeys, men and missiles.* London: Collins. 1988.

Index

Illustrations are indicated in bold.

Aberdeen University   xv, 88, 125, 129, 133, 136, 140, 143–144, 146, 148–154, 157, 159, 161, 165, 175–177, 181–184, 187, 190–191; Marischal College **11B**
Adler, A.   187
Adrian, E. D. (later Lord)   31
Afrikaans   104, 105, 112, 115
Alexander, Ruth   41, 63, 99, 114
Alice, Princess   116–117
Allen, Clifford   57
antibiotics   186
apartheid   42, 104, 109, 121, 127, 136, 205
Asquith, H.   43, 58, 59
Athenaeum, The   64
Athlone, Earl of   116
Attlee, Clement   66

Babbage, C.   155
Bacon, Sir Francis   133
Baker, Philip Noel   48
Barcroft, Sir Joseph   40, 51, 58, 80, 188
Barnato, Barney   110
Barnes, E. W.   31, 36–37
Basic English   33, 136, 153, 155, 172
Beard, Charles   179
Beard, Mary   179
Beard, William   179
Bellerby, C. W.   *xiii*, 101
Bender, Rabbi   98, 114

Bentham and Hooker   16, 21, 125
Berkeley, California   176
Bernal, J. D.   139
Bevan, Aneurin   81
Beveridge, William (Lord)   *xiii, xiv,* 119–122, 127, 131–134, 136, 142, 144, 158, 191, **12B**
Bevin, Ernest   159, 188, 206
Bidder, G. P.   80
Bing, Geoffrey   183, 195
Birkbeck College   *xi,* 21, 24, 64, 65, 69, 78, 80, 96, 98
Birrell, Frances   49
Black, Dora   136–137
Blackett, P. M. S.   139, 159
Bodmer, Frederick   *xv,* 105, 116, 155, 158, 175, 184, **9A**
Boers   4, 104, 110, 111, 113
Boer War   4, 17, 41–42, 104, 108, 111, 135, 204
Bondfield, Margaret   65
Brailsford, H. N.   42
British Association   112, 115, 156
British Flora   16
British Guiana   197, 198, 200
British Socialist Party   15, 61
British South Africa Act of 1909   5
British South Africa Act of 1910   99, 109, 114
Brockway, Fenner   57, 127
Broom, Robert L.   99–100
Bukharin, Nikolai Ivanovich   129
Burbidge, P. W.   28
Burns, John   44, 145
Butler, Montagu   22–23, 25, 38, 162

Calder, Ritchie   139–140, 143–144, 153, 159, 188
Cambridge University   *xi,* 17, 22, 27–42, 45–48, 51–54, 58, 65, 71, 75, 77, 79–80, 82, 85, 98, 102, 104, 112, 129, 133, 135–136, 154, 156, 184, 188, 204
Cambridge, Lady May   116
Campbell, Sir Jock   9, 57, 199–200
Carlyle, Thomas   20, 212

Carroll, Sir Antony   147

Carter, John   198

Celtic language   5, 67, 152

Chamberlain, Joseph   4, 110–111, 159

Chaplin, Charlie   38

Charles, Enid   x–xv; forebears 65–66; Lancelot's friend in Cambridge Society 51; arrival in London 65; feminism and socialism 65; marriage 66; birth of Sylvia 68; visit to Easton Glebe 71; receipt of Cambridge M.A. degree 77; freedom to pursue biology 77; at Plymouth 82; at Woods Hole 87; long-standing interest in and aptitude for biology 102; Ph.D. from University of Cape Town 102; opposition to apartheid 104; intense scientific activity 105; heroic rescue of two natives 114–115, 215–217; research on ovarian function   xiii, xiv, 122; research fellowship 131; international reputation as a demographer 131; partnership with Kuczynski in study of differential fertility by new statistical techniques 132; travel to Canada with Clare and David for research position with the Dominion Bureau of Statistics 160, 176; return to England 190; acceptance of statistical directorship for World Health Organisation in Southeast Asia 193; divorce 193; **15A**

Charles, Thomas   65

Chase, Ashton   200

Chesterton, G. K.   10, 58, 202

Childe, Gordon   51, 125

Christie, Agatha   125

chromatic   77, 95, 146, 184, 185

chromosome   xi, 3–4, 69–70, 101

Citrine, Walter   206

Clark, G. N. (Sir George)   129

Clow, Archie   148

cockroach   70, 189

Codex Argenteus   165

Cole, G. D. H.   33, 51–53, 71

Cole, Margaret   52, 71

colonialism   25, 42, 52–53, 73, 99, 103, 110, 116, 118, 126, 130, 158, 195–199

colour change   xii, xiii, 76, 100, 101, 147, **5C**

communism, communist   22, 51, 90, 112, 128–129, 133, 139

compulsory military service   56–57

conscience clause   56–57

conscientious objector, objection   17, 56–57, 59–61, 64, 68, 184

Index

conscription *x*, 44, 48, 50, 56–57, 59
Cooper, Clive Foster 31–32
Court martial 57
Creswell, Col. 111–112
Crew, F. A. E. *xi*, *xvi*, 69, 76–77, 79–81, 102, 127, 140, 142, 159, 185, **12A**
Croonian lecture 77, 147, 185
Cross, K. W. 50, 73, 121
Crowther, J. G. 139
cytology, cytological *xi*, 69, 70, 72, 73, 76

Dahlberg, Gunnar *xiii*, 153–154, 160, 164–167
Darwin, Charles 11, 82
de Beer, Gavin R. 78–79
Devon *xiii*, 40–41, 43, 124, 129, 134, 136, 145, 191–192
Dickinson, H. W. 128
Dickinson, Lowes 53
Dingwall, E. J. 54–55
Doncaster, Leonard 24, 40, 69
Douglas, Edgar (Lord) Adrian 60
Dunnico, Herbert 63–64
Dutt, Clements 52
Dutt, R. Palme 52, 196

Easton Glebe 72
Eddington, Sir Arthur 40
Edwards, Dorothy 51
Einstein, Albert 192
Elliott, Walter 140, 143, 153
endocrine, endocrinology *xi*, *xii*, 72, 76–78, 106, 131
Engels, F. 128, 215
eugenics *x*, 74, 121, 142, 166
Exeter Hall tradition 4

Fabian Society 22, 33, 40, 42, 44–47, 51–53, 57, 61, 67, 119–120, 125, 132, 140, 188
Farmer and Moore 70
Farrington, Benjamin 105
Federal Union 158, 159

feminism, feminist xi, 44, 54, 65, 99
Fisher, R. A. xiii, 124, 217, 223
FitzGerald, Edward 23
Fletcher, Sir Walter 131
Florence, Philip Sargant 184
Foges, W. 196
Fox, H. M. 123
Freud, Sigmund 55, 108, 187–188
Friends Ambulance Unit 48, 49, 186
Fyfe, Hamilton (later Sir William) 144, 148

Gaelic language 152
Gaitskell, Hugh 52, 136
gall wasp 147
Gandhi, Mohandas K. (Mahatma) 99
Garnett, David 49
Gates, Ruggles 80
Georgetown 197–200
Ghana 183, 194–197
Gissing, A. C. 50–51
Glyn Ceiriog xiv, 201–202, 209, **16B**
Gold Coast 16, 118, 194
Gollancz, Victor 138
gonorrhoea 186
Gordon, Cecil 101, 107, 147
Great Pyramid of Khufu 186
Grey, Sir Ralph 198, 200
Guyana 198, 201

haemocyanin xii, 83, 86, 87, 102
Haldane, J. B. S. x–xi, xiii, 79–80, 122–124, 139, 147, 166, **10B**
Hamilton, Henry 43, 144, 148, 186
Hardy, Keir 47
Harvey, T. E. 48, 63
Henderson, Arthur 67
Heretics 33, 53, 54
Herrman, Louis 98, 104, 132

Index

Hertzog, J. B. M.   109, 117, 135–136
Hessen, Boris   129
Hill, A. V.   15, 86, 137, 146
Hitler, A.   20, 107, 127, 128, 133, 161
Hobson, A. D.   33
Hofmeyr, Jan Hendrik (Onze Jan)   109, 114
Hofmeyr, J. H.   114
Hogben, Adrian (son)   74, 125–126, 159, 176–177, 182, 215, 221
Hogben, Alice (sister)   1, 5, 211
Hogben, Bernard (youngest brother)   1, 5, 13–14, 211–212
Hogben, Clare (daughter)   xv, 84, 125–126, 160, 165, 179, 215, **13A**
Hogben, Connie (Bernard's wife)   212
Hogben, David (son)   xv, 124, 126, 160, 165, 179, 191, 215
Hogben, Dorothy (sister)   1, 5, 14, 211–212
Hogben family portrait   **3A**
Hogben, George (grandfather)   2, 205
Hogben, Hamilton (brother)   1, 5, 14, 43, 148, 186, 211
Hogben, Jane   194, 196, 198, 200–201, 203, 209
Hogben, Lancelot
  Aberdeen University: return from U.S.A. unexpected   181–182, 184
  Ambulance Corps   **3C**
  Birmingham University: Honorary Ll.D.   224
  birth and forebears   1–3
  British Association, Cape Town meeting of   139, 143
  bust   **1**
  Cambridge University: Cambridge Society 51; Fabian Society 33, 40, 42, 51; friendships 47, 51–52; graduation with M.A. degree 51; Heretics 33, 53–54; Moral Sciences (Moral Stinks) Club 33; Oxford contemporaries 51–53; Union Debating Society 33
  cartoon, "New Statesman"   **10A**
  colonialism, opposition to   30, 44, 52–53, 126
  conscientious objection, personally ridiculed for   73
  court martial for military service refused   61
  coworkers—*see C. W. Bellerby; F. A. E. Crew; K. W. Cross; Gavin R. de Beer; Cecil Gordon; R. L. Kirk; F. Landgrebe; H. Waring; F. Winton; R. Wrighton*
  Croonian Lecture (Royal Society)   147, 185
  Dahlberg, Gunnar, stay with as host during World War II   164–167
  education, early: Dr. Cody's elementary school in Portsmouth 18–19;

Middlesex County Secondary School in Tottenham 18; Stoke–Newington Library 19–21; self-teaching 19,22; London County Council Hackney Polytechnic 21; Birkbeck College night course in zoology 21, 24

Enid—*see also Enid Charles;* arrival in London 65; marriage 66; wartime residence in Canada 176, 179, 182; return to England 190; position with World Health Organisation in S. E. Asia 193; divorce 193

eugenics, opposition to   x, 74, 89, 121, 128, 162, 166

family portrait   **3A**

founding of Journal of Social Medicine   221

founding of Society for Experimental Biology and its journal   79–80

Freud and psychoanalysis, assessment of   187–188

Friends' Ambulance Unit   48–49

Ghana, official mission and survey   194–196, 222

Guyana, University of: preview visit 197–198; acceptance of appointment 198; first year of office 199–200; fund-raising for building programme 200; resignation 200

history of science: efflorescence of Lunar Circle, Edinburgh Royal Society, Manchester Philosophical Society 88; International Congress on 129; interrelations between Birmingham industry and Scottish science during latter half of eighteenth century   148

hospitalisations   137, 185, 193

Iceland, visit to   155–157

imprisonment in World War I   61–63

Interglossa   86, 158, 184, 189

Jane—*see also Jane Hogben;* friendship 194; Gold Coast trip 194; marriage 196; illness 201; last years 201, 209

journalism: at *Peace Society* 63; *The Daily Herald* 64; *The Athenaeum* 64; *Kentish Times* 64

Keith Gold Medal and Prize (Edinburgh Royal Society)   123

Labour Party, support for   80, 82

linguistics   1, 5, 10–11, 86, 88, 105, 136, 152–158, 175, 184, 201

London University B.Sc.   45

London University D.Sc.   70

Loom of Language, The   xv, 105, 158, 175, 184

love of nature and lure of biology   2, 13, 15–17, 19, 21–22, 24, 40, 78, 93

Mackinnon Studentship (Royal Society)   77

Marine Biological Laboratory, Plymouth   40–41, 81–84, 101, 125

Marine Biological Laboratory, Woods Hole   86–87

Mathematics for the Million   xv, 137–138

Nazis, escape from   162–164

noncombatant service, World War I 48–51

Norse navigation 155–156

pacifism 17, 25, 44, 47, 50, 56–57, 59–60, 63–64, 68, 184

Penybont, Wales **15B**

political activity: Stepney Herald League 65; political secretary of Stepney Trades Council 66; political organising for Labour Party in Aldgate, Stepney and Limehouse, Dec. 1918 election 66; withdrawal from politics 69

parenthood, enjoyment of 153

professional career: Birkbeck College: Lecturer, zoology 64; Imperial College of Science: Junior Lecturer 69; Senior Lecturer 70; Edinburgh University: Deputy Director, Animal Breeding Research Laboratory 76; Senior Lecturer, Dept. of Physiology 77; McGill University: Assistant Professor of Medical Zoology 84; Cape Town, University of: Professor and Head, Dept. of Zoology 90; London School of Economics, Professor of Social Biology 122; Aberdeen University: Regius Professor of Natural History 142; Wisconsin, University of: Visiting Professor 177; Birmingham University: Mason Professor of Zoology 184; War Office: Deputy Director of Biological Research, Acting Director of Medical Statistics 185–187; Birmingham University: Professor and Chairman, Dept. of Medical Statistics 190; Guyana, University of: Vice-Chancellor 197

racism, opposition to 20, 42, 99, 103, 105, 112–113, 122, 126–127, 134, 162, 167, 205

Ray Lankester Investigatorship of Marine Biological Association 81

religious beliefs: evangelical Christian upbringing 1, 3–5, 7–10, 12–13; baptism 14–15; doubts 14–16, 22–23, 44, 46; freeing himself from fundamentalism 20; leaving Methodist Church 39; joining Society of Friends 40; rejection of theism 69

residences: Bethune Road **3B**; Gray's Inn Road, London 66; Stepney 66; Amersham in the Chilterns 70; St. Anne de Bellevue, Montreal 85; Xenopus, Cape Town 114; Putney Common 124; Mortonhampstead in Devon 124, **9B**; Inverdon in Aberdeen 144, **11A**; Penybont, Denbighshire 192; granite cottage, Denbighshire 194; *Lloches y Fwalchen* (Blackbird's Retreat), Glyn Ceiriog 201, **16A**

Science for the Citizen xiv, 124, 133, 136, 138, 155, 183

scientific work: colour change—*see pituitary;* colorimetry and work on haemocyanins 83, 86–87, 102; cytology: antennaless *Drosophila* 147–148; parasynapsis xi, 69–70; parthenogenetic hymenoptera 69–70; genetics, experimental—*see cytology;* genetics, human or medical: William Withering Lectures 123; *Nature and Nurture* 123; genetics, mathematical 122–126, 166; mathematical statistics: challenge 189–190; *Chance and Choice* 190; *Statistical Theory* 123–124, 196, 223; medical statistics: venereal disease discoveries 186–187; therapeutic trials 187; devising of self-coding documents 189; pituitary, anterior lobe: effect on ovarian function and reproduction 101, 121–123; relation to metamorphosis 73, 77; pituitary, posterior lobe: chromatic function 76–77, 101, 146; lemanin dispersing hormone *xi*, 101; oxytocin *xii*; thyroid 77; vibrating spring gauge 86

self–education 19, 22, 47, 70, 85, 92

social biology 119–121, 131–132

teaching: in an elementary school 48, 63; college level 73, 78–79, 81, 85, 97, 147, 213

Trinity College: Major Entrance Scholarship 25; residence in Whewell's Court 28–29; domestic routine 29–30, 35–36; intellectual atmosphere 30–31, 35; mentors 31–32; Trinity Scholars Club 33; social blunders 33, 36–39; Senior Scholarship 46; Frank Smart Prize 47–48, 56

Wales: weekending 192–193; retirement there 196; design and building of Blackbird's Retreat 201; last years 201–203, 209–210

Wales, University of: Honorary D.Sc. 224

Webb, Beatrice and Sydney 33, 119–120, 134–136

Wells, H. G. and Catherine, visit to 71–72

Woods Hole, Massachusetts **6A**

Hogben, Margaret (eldest sister) 1, 5, 7, 8, 211

Hogben, Margaret Prescott (mother) 1–8, 10, 12–14, 16, 18, 24, 27, 36, 64, 75, 84, 86, 211–212, 215

Hogben, Sylvia (daughter) *xv*, 68, 124, 126, 159–160, 162–164, 171, 175–178, 182, 215

Hogben, Thomas (father) 1–5, 7–9, 13–18, 27, 41, 43, 47, 64, 75, 211–212

Horrabin, Frank *xiv*, 71, 127, 138

Hougham 1–2

Hubbard, Jocelyn 200

human genetics 122, 123, 131, 189

Huxley, Aldous 73

Huxley, Julian *x*, *xi*, 45, 72–73, 79, 92, 134, 139, 142, 153, 183, **4B**

Huxley, Thomas Henry 71, 96, 135

hypophysectomy 77

Iceland 150, 155, 156, 219

Iceland spar 156

Imperial College of Science *xi*, 49, 69–71, 73, 74, 76, 100, 123, 126

Independent Labour Party 47, 51, 57, 67

Interglossa 86, 158, 184, 189

International Congress of Genetics 159

Jagan, Cheddi   197–198
Jameson, Starr   105, 110–111
Jameson Raid   105, 110, 111
Japan   136, 170–176, 180, 189, 206
Jones, Ernest   187
Jones, Garro (later Lord Trefgarne)   184
Jonsson, Snaebjørn   155–157
Journal of Experimental Biology   102
Journal of the Peace Society   63, 64
Jung   187

Keith Gold Medal   *xiii*, 123, **9c**
Kentish Times   64
King Edward VIII   143
Kinsey, A. C.   192
Kirk, R. L.   151, 184
Kobe   171, 173–175
Korzybski, Count   176
Krogh, August   77
Kuczynski, R. R.   131–132
Kyoto   174, 175

Labour Party, labour   *xv*, 33, 42, 47, 48, 51–53, 57, 63, 65–68, 81, 109, 111, 128, 133, 135, 136, 139, 158, 184, 188, 189
Lanchester, Elsa   72
Landgrebe, F.   *xiii*, 78, 145–146
Lansbury, George   64–65, 67
Laski, Harold   *xiv*, 121, 127, 130, 134, 188, 196
LCC Hackney Polytechnic   21, 29
Lee, Jennie   81
Left Book Club   138
Leibniz, G. W.   175
Leonard, William Ellery   180
Levy, Hyman   70, 126–128
Lewis, Sinclair   180
Lightfoot's chronology   8

Linklater, Eric 149
Lloyd George, David 56, 67, 68, 136, 205
London School of Economics (L.S.E.) *xiii, xiv,* 107, 113, 119, 121, 123, 127, 129, 131–133, 136, 150, 179
Loom of Language, The xv, 105, 158, 175, 184
Lucas, Keith 31
Lunar Society 88
Lunt, Storer 177
Lysenko 166

MacBride, E. W. 74
MacDonald, Ramsay 51, 67, 136
Malinowski, Branislaw 130
Malleson, Miles 72
Mallowan, Michael 125
Manchester Philosophical Society 88
Mann, Tom 134
Marine Biological Association 81
Marine Biological Laboratory at Woods Hole *xii,* 86, 87, 178
Marshall, John 28, 37
Martin, Kingsley 128, 186
Marx, Karl 15, 82, 105, 128, 133
Marxism 44, 66, 99, 103, 129, 196, 197, 224
mathematical genetics *xi–xiii*
Mathematics for the Million xiv, 137–138, 145, 159
Matthews, Clare—*see Clare Hogben*
McCarthy, McCarthyism 179
McCrory, Sylvia—*see Sylvia Hogben*
McGill University *xii,* 84–86, 88–89, 97, 113, 179
McTaggart, John 31
medical statistics *xvi,* 185–187, 189–192
meiosis 70
melanophore 77, 101, 146, **5D**
Methodist 1–2, 9–10, 12, 14, 17, 20, 39, 46, 150, 202
Meyer, F. B. 15, 60
Meyerowitz 99, 105, 114, 118, 210; bust created by **1**
Middlesex County Secondary School 18, 22, 24, 29, 38

Missionary   1, 3–4, 6–7, 12–13, 18, 23, 41, 46, 90, 92, 98, 109, 137, 175, 195
Mohr, Lois   160, 162, 163
Mohr, Otto   160, 162
Montague, Ivor   73–74, 121, 128
Moody and Sankey   8
Moore, Gilbert   33, 59, 66
Moral Sciences Club   33
Morel, E. D.   42, 54
Morgan, T. H.   *xi*, 69–70, **5A**
Morley, John   44
Morrell, Lady Otteline   73
Morrell, Phillip   60
Morrison, Herbert   *xvi*, 68
Moscow   167–168, 170, 172
Mosley's Black Shirts   133
MSH   *xii*
Muller, H. J.   *xi*, 167, 192, **5B**
Müller, Max   11, 154
Murray, Gilbert   59, 66

National Health Service   *xiii*, 189
Nature of Living Matter, The   113
Natural Selection, Theory of   **2**
Nazi   *xv*, 45, 128, 131, 154, 155, 158, 161–163, 186
Needham, Joseph   139
Neill, R. M.   146–147
Nevinson, Henry   45
New Deal   178
New York City   13, 176, 177, 182, 192, 197
Newton, Sir Isaac   129, 175, 202
1917 Club   72, 116
Nkrumah   183, 195–196
No-Conscription Fellowship   57, 63
Norse navigation   155, 156
Norton, Warder   62, 137–138, 176–178
Nunes, C. Vernon   197–198

Ogden, C. K.   33, 53, 136, 153–154

Olivier, Lord   127

Omar Khayyam   23

One by One Band   7

Origin of Species   11, 154, **2**

Orr, John Boyd (Lord)   *xv,* 139–140, 143, 149–151, 153, 157–159, **12c**

Orwell, George   4

Oslo   *xv,* 153–154, 160, 162–165, 171, 183

Oxford University   11, 14, 21, 22, 33, 51–53, 58, 72, 73, 82, 111, 129, 135, 142, 144, 148, 199, 204, 211

oxytocin   *xii*

pacifism, pacifist   *x,* 25, 31, 44, 51, 53

Padmore, George   196

Pankhurst, Sylvia   66, 68, 137

Pantin, C. F. A.   *xii,* 80, 83, **6B**

parasynapsis   *xi*

Parsons, Sir Leonard   189

Passfield Corner   34, 120, 134, 135

Payne-Townshend, Charlotte   120

Pease, Edward   119

Peet, Hubert   60

Penrose, Lionel   *xiii, xv,* **13A**

Petty, Sir William   132

Phillips, Morgan   189

Pinhey, K. H.   86

pituitary   *xii, xiii,* 73, 76, 77, 82, 86, 100, 101, 106, 121, 146, 183

Plant, Arnold   113

Plymouth Brother, Brethren   14, 41, 92

Plymouth Marine Biological Laboratory   *xii,* 101, 125

politician, political activity   *xvi,* 25, 33, 42, 45, 50, 52–53, 65–69, 71–72, 90, 99, 104–105, 112–113, 119–121, 127, 129, 132–133, 135, 150–151, 158–159, 171, 179, 192, 197, 205

Portsmouth   3, 4, 18, 42, 98

Postan, M.   129, 150

posterior lobe extract   *xii,* 77, 101

Postgate, Raymond   51

Power, Eileen   *xiv,* 129, 133–134, 136

pregnancy test   *xiii,* 101

Prescott, Margaret (grandmother) 2–3, 5, 211
Prescott, William (grandfather) 1–3, 5, 211
pressor activity 77, 78, 101
Priestley, Adam 51, 57–58, 61, 180

Quaker Adult School 40
Quiller-Couch 31

racism 4, 20, 74, 121, 126, 154
Reaney 1
Rhodes, Cecil 4, 110–111, 117
Richardson, Maurice 20, 82
Riga 167
Robbins, Lionel 130
Rockefeller Foundation 119, 131, 146
Roux, Eddie 112, 214, 216
Royal Oak, The 202, 209–210
Royal Society 31, 69, 76, 79, 84, 88, 130, 138, 139, 142, 149, 156, 159, 184, 185, 189, 214, 217
Royal Society of Edinburgh *xiii*, 123
Royal Society of South Africa 86, 102, 120
Russell, Bertrand 33, 53, 59, 136–137

San Francisco 175–176
Sang, James 147
Sansom, Sir George 175
Saunders, Carr 142, 217
Schäfer, E. S. (Sir Edward Sharpey-Schafer) 76–78, 81, 84
Schreiner, Olive 99, 109
Schreiner, W. P. 99, 109
Science Advisory Committee of the Labour Party 159, 188–189
Science for the Citizen *xiv*, 124, 133, 136, 138, 140, 148, 155, 159, 183, 206
Shaw, G. B. 45, 82, 120, 188
Siberia 169–170, 178
Simpson, Mrs. Wallis Warfield 143
Slome, D. *xiii*
Smith, Sir Henry Abel 116

Smuts, Jan Christian   99, 109, 112–114, 127
Snow, C. P. (later Lord Snow)   133, 180
Snowden, Philip   51
social biology   *xiii, xiv,* 119–121, 131–132
socialism, socialist   *xi, xvi,* 4–5, 15, 31, 42, 44–46, 51–53, 57, 61, 65–66, 68, 72, 74, 81, 100, 119, 157–158, 196, 207
Society for Experimental Biology   79, 147
Society of Friends   40, 46, 48, 50, 58, 63
Science of Language, The   11, 154
Southsea   3–6, 18
Stalin, Josef   90, 107, 129, 133, 169, 175, 220
Statistical Theory   *xvi,* 123–124, 196
Stepney Herald   65, 66
Stockholm   154, 163, 165, 167–168, 171, 190
Strachey, Lytton   72
sulphonamides   *xvi,* 186
Summerskill, Dr. Edith   117
Sweden   *xiii, xv,* 154, 163, 165, 167–168, 178, 182
Swinburne, A.   66, 69, 213
synapsis   *xi,* 69–70

Taylor, Lord   209
Tennessee Valley Authority   179
Test Acts   11, 150–151
therapeutic effect   186–187
To Any Child   8
Tokyo   171, 174–176, 180
Tots and Quots   139, 217
trade unionism   *xi,* 12, 33, 57, 65, 111, 159, 188, 205, 206
Trades Union Congress   188
Trevelyan, G. M.   31
Trinity College   22, 24, 25, 27–31, 33, 38, 40, 46, 47, 51; "backs"   **4A**
Tsuruga   168, 171–172
Turnbull   123

University of Birmingham   *xiii, xv, xvi,* 31, 56, 88, 111, 115, 123, 128, 133, 148, 158, 178, 180–181, 184–185, 187, 189–190, 192–193, 196, 206, 210; Chamberlain Tower **14A** ; College of Medicine **14B**

University of California   176
University of Cape Town   4, 84, 86, 90, 96–98; Zoological Building   **7B**
University of Edinburgh   xi, xii, xv, 51, 72, 75–80, 88–89, 100–102, 105–106, 111, 123, 125, 128, 142–143, 149, 151, 160
University of Wisconsin   xiii, xv, 126, 159, 177–178, 180, **13B**
Unwin, Stanley   138
Uppsala   153–154, 164–165
Usher, James   211

Vavilov, N. I.   166, 220
Vemmestad, Dagny   154
Vice-chancellor   197, 198, 200
Vladivostok   168–171, 175
von Hayek, Frederick   130
Voortrekkers   109

Waley, Arthur   136, 175
Walker, Eric   104–105, 113, 149, 156
Wallace, A. R.   x, 11, **2**
Wallace, Henry   179–180, 182
Wallas, Graham   22, 132
Wallis, John   175
Walvis Bay   117
War Office   xvi, 59, 185–187
Waring, H.   78, 146
War Victims Contingent   48
Webb, Beatrice   33, 120, 134–136
Webb, Sidney   33, 119, 134–136
Wedgwood, Helen   37, 51, 127
Welcome Mission   3, 4, 6, 7, 18, 41, 211
Wells, Catherine   71
Wells, Frank   71, 79
Wells, G. P.   125, **4B**
Wells, H. G.   xi, xiv, 19, 24, 45, 79, 108, **4B**
Wesleyan Hymn Book   8
Wesleyan Methodist church   10, 39
Willey, Dean   180
William Withering lectures   xiii, 123–124

Winton, F. R.   54, 77, 79, 127
witch-hunting   9, 90, 179
Wolf, Abraham   64, 129–130, 136
women's suffrage, suffragette   26, 42, 65
Woolf, Virginia   213
Wootton, Barbara   128, 158
Wormwood, Scrubs   61, 63
Wrighton, R.   225

Xenopus   *xii*, *xiii*, 101, 121, **7A**

Yokohama   175–176

zoology   *xv*, 19, 21–22, 24, 40, 47–48, 64, 68, 76, 78, 80, 82, 84, 90, 93, 117, 123, 139, 142–143, 149, 184
Zuckerman, S.   139, 217